D0322702

99

THE LOST WOMEN OF
ROCK MUSIC

781.66 RED

GOWER COLLEGE SWANSEA
LEARNING RESOURCE CENTRE
LLWYN-Y-BRYN
77 WALTER ROAD
SWANSEA SA1 4QF

Studies in Popular Music

Series Editors: Alyn Shipton, journalist, broadcaster and former lecturer in music at Oxford Brookes University, and Christopher Partridge, Professor of Religious Studies, Department of Politics, Philosophy and Religion at Lancaster University

From jazz to reggae, bhangra to heavy metal, electronica to qawwali, and from production to consumption, Studies in Popular Music is a multi-disciplinary series which aims to contribute to a comprehensive understanding of popular music. It will provide analyses of theoretical perspectives, a broad range of case studies, and discussion of key issues.

Published

Open Up the Doors: Music in the Modern Church
Mark Evans

Technomad: Global Raving Countercultures
Graham St. John

Dub in Babylon: Understanding the Evolution and Significance of Dub Reggae in Jamaica and Britain from King Tubby to Post-Punk
Christopher Partridge

Send in the Clones: A Cultural Study of the Tribute Band
Georgina Gregory

Forthcoming

Global Tribe: Technology, Spirituality and Psytrance
Graham St. John

Heavy Metal: Controversies and Countercultures
Edited by Titus Hjelm, Keith Kahn-Harris and Mark LeVine

GOWER COLLEGE SWANSEA
LEARNING RESOURCE CENTRE
GORSEINON
TYCOCH ROAD
SWANSEA SA2 9EB

THE LOST WOMEN OF
ROCK MUSIC

FEMALE MUSICIANS OF THE PUNK ERA

SECOND EDITION

HELEN REDDINGTON

In memory of Ari Up (1962–2010) and Poly Styrene (1953–2011),
two beautiful women with an immeasurable ability to both entertain
and inspire

Published by Equinox Publishing Ltd.

UK: Kelham House, 3 Lancaster Street, Sheffield, S3 8AF
USA: ISD, 70 Enterprise Drive, Bristol, CT 06010

www.equinoxpub.com

First edition published in hardback by Ashgate Publishing in 2007.

© Helen Reddington 2012

All rights reserved. No part of this publication may be reproduced or transmitted in any form or by any means, electronic or mechanical, including photocopying, recording or any information storage or retrieval system, without prior permission in writing from the publishers.

British Library Cataloguing-in-Publication Data
A catalogue record for this book is available from the British Library.

Library of Congress Cataloging-in-Publication Data
Reddington, Helen.
  The lost women of rock music : female musicians of the punk era /
Helen Reddington. -- 2nd ed.
     p. cm. -- (Studies in popular music)
  Includes bibliographical references and index.
  ISBN 978-1-84553-957-3 (pb)
  1. Punk rock music--History and criticism. 2. Rock musicians. 3.
Women rock musicians. I. Title.
  ML3534.R3855 2012
  781.66082'0941--dc22
                          2011012088

ISBN 978-1-84553-957-3 (paperback)

Typeset by CA Typesetting Ltd, www.publisherservices.co.uk
Printed and bound in Great Britain by Lightning Source UK Ltd., Milton Keynes and Lightning Source Inc., La Vergne, TN

Contents

Acknowledgements

I should like to thank the following for participating in the realization of this book:

Zillah Ashworth, Steve Bassam, Mavis Bayton, Steve Beresford, Mufti Berridge, Stevie Bezencenet, Gina Birch, Gaye Black, Julie Blair, Rick Blair, Carrie Booth, Rachel Bor, Sue Bradley, Brunel University, Phil Byford, Patrick Campbell, Sara Cohen, Caroline Coon, Rhoda Dakar, Heather De Lyon, Barb Dwyer, Nick Dwyer, Sally Feldman, Sara Furse, Martin Greaves, Rachel Groom, Kate Hayes, Kienda Hoji, Suzy Home, Joby Jackson, Dave Laing, Andrew Linehan, Lora Logic, Paloma McLardy, Wendy Malem, Diana Mavroleon, June Miles-Kingston, Stuart Morgan, David Muggleton, Liz Naylor, Keith Negus, Nora Normal, Lucy O'Brien, Alex Ogg, Nadya Ostroff, Sarah-Jane Owen, Dave Peacock, the late John Peel, Tessa Pollitt, Annie Randall, Sheila Ravenscroft, Penny Rimbaud, Mel Ritter, Christine Robertson, Rockin' Rina, Jean Seaton, Clive Selwood, Hester Smith, Ros Smith, Alison Sorrell, Attila the Stockbroker, Poly Styrene, Vi Subversa, Penelope Tobin, Geoff Travis, the University of Westminster, the University of Wolverhampton, Ari Up, Enid Williams, Jane Woodgate, Adrian York, my family, all those who answered the original questionnaires in 2001,[1] and my students for their interest and feedback.

For the second edition I would also like to thank:

Viv Albertine, Shanne Bradley, Stella Clifford, Daniel Coston, Jane Munro, Pauline Murray, Bethan Peters, Kate Stephenson, Martin Stephenson, Poly Styrene, Lucy ('Toothpaste') Whitman, Lesley Woods, and the University of East London.

Particular thanks go to Caroline Coon for her photograph of Tessa Pollitt, bass-player of The Slits, used on the cover. Caroline explains:

> I took the photo on 15 June 1977 at Sussex University, Brighton. It is early evening, still light outside, as The Slits are on first as support for The Clash, whose urban landscape backdrop can just be seen propped up behind Tessa against the student hall windows. Tessa joined The Slits two weeks before their first gig in March 1977 – so when I took this photo she had only been performing for three months.

General Editor's Preface

The upheaval that occurred in musicology during the last two decades of the twentieth century has created a new urgency for the study of popular music alongside the development of new critical and theoretical models. A relativistic outlook has replaced the universal perspective of modernism (the international ambitions of the 12-note style); the grand narrative of the evolution and dissolution of tonality has been challenged, and emphasis has shifted to cultural context, reception and subject position. Together, these have conspired to eat away at the status of canonical composers and categories of high and low in music. A need has arisen, also, to recognize and address the emergence of crossovers, mixed and new genres, to engage in debates concerning the vexed problem of what constitutes authenticity in music and to offer a critique of musical practice as the product of free, individual expression.

Popular musicology is now a vital and exciting area of scholarship, and the *Ashgate Popular and Folk Music Series* aims to present the best research in the field. Authors will be concerned with locating musical practices, values and meanings in cultural context, and may draw upon methodologies and theories developed in cultural studies, semiotics, poststructuralism, psychology and sociology. The series will focus on popular musics of the twentieth and twenty-first centuries. It is designed to embrace the world's popular musics from Acid Jazz to Zydeco, whether high tech or low tech, commercial or non-commercial, contemporary or traditional.

Professor Derek B. Scott
University of Leeds, UK

Introduction

The location was the Music and Power Conference at Brunel University in 2001. I had just presented a paper relating to this study, and I was taking questions. A male member of the audience asked the following question: "I have a friend who plays in an all-girl band. On their posters they have a photograph of the band. Why should they resort to a gimmick like this if they want to be taken seriously?"

The fact that, twenty-six years after the Sex Discrimination Act, an all-girl band should still be regarded as a gimmick, and that their use of a photograph on their posters (as many male bands do) should be regarded as an attempt to cash in on this gimmick did not strike him as remarkable at all.

Rationale

The original study that preceded this book was undertaken because, as one of the participants in what I had thought was going to be a revolution in rock music, I became more and more frustrated at the lack of documentation about what actually happened at the time from the point of view of its *female* protagonists.[1] Histories of punk are often personal and metrocentric, from Jon Savage's *England's Dreaming*[2] to Malcolm McLaren's many versions of events (in particular his film *The Great Rock'n'Roll Swindle*[3]) in which he is the star and everyone else supporting players. One of British punk's myths *is* the London-focused span of some histories: the enduring version of punk as described by some sources started in 1976 and ended in 1978 with the demise of The Sex Pistols. I contend that punk, by its anarchic nature, existed in many forms long before and long after this; it existed and continues to exist as a self-definition by certain people regardless of location. In the period covered here, it was a sort of voluntary therapy invented and undertaken by an "unwanted" generation. This work is a social and cultural study that relies heavily, in places, on my personal memories and involvement, and on oral sources; there are therefore tensions between my own involvement in the history and its narrative and the other sources that are drawn upon. These tensions are acknowledged and assessed where appropriate.

My main intention has been to bust the stereotype of young punk women in fishnet stockings with panda-eyes, stilettos and spiky blonde hair. There *were* some punk women like this, but for many the ideology counted for more than, or as much as, the fashion. I felt indignant that the image of punk that had been set in stone was not what I had experienced firsthand; I felt that if I did not undertake this work, the experiences of a whole generation of women instrumentalists might disappear from history. A comment by writer Caroline Coon in the interview she gave to me made a controversial point: "It would be possible to write the whole history of punk music without mentioning any male bands at all – and I think a lot of them would find that very surprising."[4] I describe here a very clear world-within-a-world of women performers, aware of what each other had achieved at the time and with strong opinions about music made by other bands with female personnel, and indeed other punk bands in general.

As many of those involved in punk and punk rock music reach their forties and fifties, nostalgia for their youth inevitably leads them to explore the relevance to their current status of the experiences that they had at that time, and to start to recall those aspects of punk that have left them with some sort of legacy, whether musical, political, moral or entrepreneurial in nature. It is at this point, where there is a convergence of autobiographical material not only in the media but also in academic and public services environments, that given histories of the moment start to be questioned and revised, and the opportunity has arisen to rectify the omission made by so many social histories. The heart of this work is, therefore, an analysis of the role of female instrumentalists in punk and rock bands during the socio-political changes that happened in Great Britain throughout the period from 1976 (the last throes of "old" Labour government) to 1984 (the consolidation of Thatcherism as a political force with the aftermath of the Falklands conflict). It examines their relationship to the punk subculture, and has been prompted by my own perception of the many revisionist versions of events during that time. This led to further questioning: why did this influx of women rock instrumentalists apparently come to a halt and not lead to a revolution in rock band personnel, with mixed-gender rock bands becoming the norm in Britain as opposed to the exception? Why has rock music been the slowest of all recent cultural phenomena to incorporate the female creative producer?[5]

Women and Research: A Brief Discussion

Sociologist Ann Oakley produced one of the first purely female-oriented sociological research documents in 1974 and identified a major problem:

> Male orientation may so colour the organization of sociology as a dis-
> cipline that the invisibility of women is a structural weakness, rather
> than simply a superficial flaw. The male focus, incorporated into the
> definition of subject-areas, reduces women to a side-issue from the
> start.[6]

Nearly twenty years later, Jenny Garber found a similar gap in her research on girls and youth culture:

> Very little seems to have been written about the role of girls in youth
> cultural groupings. They are absent from the classic subcultural eth-
> nographic studies, the pop histories, the personal accounts and the
> journalistic surveys of the field... The objective and popular image of
> a subculture is likely to be one which emphasises male membership,
> male focal concerns and masculine values.[7]

It is hardly surprising that girls are seen as consumers of pop whereas boys are seen as connoisseurs of rock, for as Garber remarks when talking about images of motorbike girls used in soft porn and advertising, "girls and women have always been located nearer to the point of consumerism than to the 'ritual of resistance'";[8] and as Barbara Hudson observes, there is no perception in the male world of girls being adolescent anyway: "adolescence is a 'mas-culine' construct."[9] Male adolescence and deviance are often perceived to go hand-in-hand, whereas young women perhaps fail to conform to a stereotype of deviance. Christine Griffin remarks that there is no such thing as a typically deviant young woman:

> It was not always possible to identify a particular group of girls
> as "deviants" or troublemakers who were also opposed to school
> and academic work, *and* destined for factory jobs. It was equally
> difficult to find "good girls" who were pro-school *and* hoped to go
> on to college or office jobs. The situation was far more complex
> than analyses of male counter-school cultures might lead one to
> expect.[10]

As a young girl in the north-east of England in the 1960s, I was not aware of young male Mods, but I was aware of the many women in their late teens with towering platinum-blonde or jet-black beehives or buns, wearing chif-fon headscarves, three-quarter-length leather jackets, miniskirts and kitten-heeled sandals, even in midwinter. Perhaps all they were doing was waiting for men to notice them, as Frith would have us believe: "all this female activ-ity, whatever its fun and style and art as a collective occupation, is done, in the end, individually, for the boys' sake. It is the male gaze that gives the girls' beauty work its meaning."[11] Frith demonstrates a typical "male-writer's assess-ment" of the relationship of young women to a subculture he recognizes as male. John Berger articulated this attitude more starkly in 1972 in the book *Ways of Seeing.* Although the book's main focus is on the visual arts, there is a section that discusses specifically the objectification of women. Although Berger begins, "According to usage and conventions which are at last being questioned but have by no means been overcome...," the concluding para-graph appears to be written very much more in Berger's voice than that of the "conventions" he mentions:

> Men act and women appear. Men look at women. Women watch themselves being looked at. This determines not only most relations between men and women but also the relation of women to them-selves. The surveyor of woman in herself is male: the surveyed female. Thus she turns herself into an object – and most particularly an object of vision: a sight.[12]

In the world of film, Laura Mulvey asserts that this attitude is inherent to maleness: "Woman...stands in patriarchal culture as signifier for the male other...bound to her place as a bearer of meaning, not a maker of mean-ing,"[13] which is why (as will be explored in greater depth later) when women use creative technology, they are regarded as non-feminine; as Lucy Green writes:

> Women's instrumental performance threatens to break out of patri-archal definitions and offer a femininity which controls, a femininity which alienates itself in an object and impinges on the world.[14]

Stereotyping of genders offers a form of control over both men and women, and channels each gender into a set way of behaviour which is regarded as innate. Judith Butler's influential essay of 1985 articulates the deeply ingrained rationale behind the differences in gender that society creates; for Butler,

> Gender is in no way a stable identity or locus of agency from which various acts proceed; rather, it is an identity tenuously constituted in time – an identity instituted through a *stylised repetition of acts.*[15]

This would imply that masculinity is as constructed as much as femininity, and neither has anything to do with a person's sex.[16] But, as Bourdieu says, the status quo appears "natural" and any challenge to it "unnatural,"[17] and the responsibility of challenging the status quo is fraught with difficulties. Mean-while, Margaret Marshment reminds us of an age-old dilemma:

> Should we aim to appropriate the definitions and qualities assigned
> to men, in an attempt to prove women's ability to participate equally
> at all levels of society? Or should we concentrate on presenting a re-
> evaluation of existing definitions of femininity? Either strategy lays
> us open to reappropriation through stereotyping, or to validation of
> masculine values.[18]

Later, we shall see how this translates into a practical difficulty for female musicians in the world of rock music. Women simply cannot win, even in the field of research: the "natural" male researcher may come across as untrustworthy due to his social class or possibly his age, but for women there is an additional problem. Christine Griffin discovered that she herself unwittingly became an obstacle in her own research:

> I was assumed to be a feminist on several occasions before people
> had even seen me, because of the predominantly "female" nature of
> the research. This assumption had positive connotations for women
> and negative ones for men... The main point here is not whether my
> approach was biased, political or subjective, but that I was *seen* as
> biased regardless of my appearance or political perspective, whilst far
> larger and predominantly male studies are presented as objective and
> value-free.[19]

Thus the male memory of the punk moment is no more "true" than the female memory; historically, it is the latter that is likely to be forgotten. Malcolm McLaren's assertions have already been debunked by writers such as Jon Savage, but Savage has not explored the female aspects of the subculture, and his study is also very much metrocentric. Punk bands created a new "pathway"[20] at odds with that of previous rock forms and there was constant soul-searching about the degree of involvement they should have with traditional music-business discourses and, by definition, the attitudes they had towards female artists.[21] As Johnny Rotten said at the time, "During the Pistols era, women were out there playing with the men, taking us on in equal terms... It wasn't combative, but compatible."[22] This remark will be returned to later.

Finally in this section, I would like to include a quotation from Jean Genet, noted by Dick Hebdige, which I believe summarizes the position of any woman who makes artefacts in the "male domain"; it has an additional irony given Hebdige's exclusion of punk women from his study:

> It is perhaps a new source of anguish for the black man to realise that
> if he writes a masterpiece, it is his enemy's language, his enemy's
> treasury, which is enriched by the additional jewel he has so furiously
> and lovingly carved.[23]

Time and Place Parameters

Britain in the late 1970s was in a state of crisis. The British economy had to be bolstered in 1976 with a loan from the International Monetary Fund, conditional on huge cuts in public funding; in mid-1977, unemployment levels reached more than one-and-a-half million people. There was a general feeling of collapse and despondency, almost as though the energy and vitality of the 1960s had finally fizzled out, leaving a country with run-down industries, a fragmenting empire, a redundant social system and an employment environment dominated by panicking unions and aggressive industrial relations. There had been crises in the fuel industry that led to a three-day week, with power cuts and disrupted schooling, and by 1978 there was a constant stream of strikes in vital services – refuse collection, ambulances and even gravediggers. The so-called "winter of discontent" in 1978/79 led to the then Labour government being brought down.[24] A country in crisis looks to its youth for optimism and hope; but instead of this, the abrupt fall in employment opportunities led to an atmosphere of lethargy and depression among this generation. Some way for the young people to energize themselves and voice their feelings was needed, and this is where punk found its foothold.

The London-based Sex Pistols, formed by entrepreneur and political activist Malcolm McLaren, were the primary catalyst for the punk movement in Britain, and this is why the time parameters of the study have been set according to the first "overground" appearance of the band in 1976 and the onset of the Falklands War in 1982. It would be naïve to suggest that history is naturally divisible into neat chunks,[25] but during this period there was a concentration of media interest not only on punk itself but also on the sudden appearance of girl instrumentalists in the new bands in Britain. There was also an increase in interest in local music-making (in 1982 *Melody Maker* visited a series of towns around Britain to investigate their music scenes) that was probably due to the rise in small-label activity that followed the DIY ethic espoused by punk. A selection of music papers (*New Musical Express, Sounds, Melody Maker*) have been examined for their attitudes to female instrumentalists, and the debate on their pages is compared with that of *Spare Rib*, whose feminist agenda reflects another facet of the subject.

The aim of this book is to explore *British* punk and *British* musicians, as punk manifested itself differently in other countries at this time,[26] with an acknowledgement that certain US acts (in particular, The Velvet Underground, Talking Heads, Blondie and Patti Smith) had a powerful influence in Britain, not only because their strong woman performers were role models for women who could now aspire to be player-participants in music-making, but also because they "prepared the ground" for the young male rock audiences to appreciate woman guitarists, bass-players and so on. Rather than basing the study on London's Chelsea, which for the tabloid press was the epicentre of punk, I have drawn interviewees from the East London scene (Canning Town), the West London scene (Notting Hill), Manchester, Leeds, Birmingham, Oxford and other parts of the UK, in addition to the case study of the punk scene in Brighton.

Another respect in which punk was very different from earlier subcultures (or at least those examined by the Birmingham CCCS[27]) was its full-time nature. Although writers have focused on the styles, the music and the politics of punk, it had significance among some of its protagonists as a sort of "life-concept." Many were unemployed, and the idea of "buying in" to a lifestyle via its discs, clothing and club entrance fees was beyond their financial capability. It therefore supplied an alternative validation for some of those rejected by the system, and this is when the customization process – where the phenomenon devolved to the provinces and was tailored to the needs and desires of local participants – evolved from the original burst of energy from Chelsea in London into a sometimes more politicized, and often more diverse, version of punk. Michael Bracewell noted the importance of the portability of the punk ethic for those (young men) ready for change in the late 1970s: "it was the regional experience of punk – as opposed to its metropolitan base in media, arts and fashion – which really galvanized the search for the young soul rebels."[28] Punk had a uniquely therapeutic nature as a subculture for a generation of unemployed people: it provided them with a reason to get up in the morning.[29]

The third chapter of this book will demonstrate how a particular community of people in Brighton, who formed what I refer to in places as a "micro-subculture," customized punk in 1977 to create a musical and political interpretation of the punk *idea* which embraced a wide variety of people of both genders and varying ages. Within this community, a platform was created for women to pick up traditionally male rock instruments (in particular electric bass and guitar) and to learn how to play them while performing on stage. The case study of Brighton is written in such a way as to try to reconstruct a dynamic scene from the interviewees' recollections, fanzines and so on. There were several distinct groups of music-makers in Brighton at the time, some of which overlapped musically, politically or accidentally; there was also a very active women-only live music scene. Mavis Bayton[30] has explored the nature of women-only music-making in more detail than is possible here, although I have included interviews with women whose musical activities overlapped those of the punk bands. The distinctions I have made here are subjective and necessary in order to relate those musicians I have spoken to in Brighton to those who played in bands with similar attitudes elsewhere.[31] As with the general political overview discussed above, information will be included that provides a context for the primary material.

Methodology

In order to contact women who had been in bands but had not achieved fame or notoriety in the national press, whether musical or otherwise, letters were written to more than 250 local newspapers around the UK requesting women who had played in bands to contact me.[32] The letters were sometimes adapted into editorials, unfortunately with misleading headlines which rendered them useless; however, there was one very useful result, in that a journalist from *The Independent* newspaper made contact and wrote an article based very closely on our discussion, which led to further information and interviewees as well as enquiries from two documentary film production companies. Unfortunately, further journalistic enquiries resulted in the reduction of this research to tabloid caricature and misrepresentation, and I decided not to speak to or contact mainstream press again.[33]

I prepared a questionnaire to send to anyone who responded to my letters. I received fifteen requests for questionnaires, in addition to various letters offering to share memories or expressing support, and also one piece of anonymous hate-mail.

The press interest led to some women contacting me via the University of Westminster, where I worked at the time; some of these women's careers were of great interest and I interviewed them directly. As the research progressed, I realized the value of "word of mouth" as a means of finding women to interview and I have now spoken to more than 25 women instrumentalists about their involvement in punk music, after being given the opportunity to revise this book (see the Appendix for a detailed list of women musicians interviewed). The bands represented here in interview form are The Mistakes, Gay Animals, Girlschool, X-Ray Spex, The Raincoats, The Slits, Dolly Mixture, The Bodysnatchers, The Belle Stars, The Mo-dettes, The Gymslips, The Adverts, The Bright Girls, The Catholic Girls, The Reward System, The Objeks, Essential Logic, The Mockingbirds, Rubella Ballet, The Au Pairs, Delta 5, The Nips and Poison Girls. In addition to this, and in order to help to provide a context, I interviewed male and female band members who had been in bands with female players; Caroline Coon, who worked as a journalist at *Melody Maker* during part of the time in question; the music business "gatekeepers" John Peel and Geoff Travis; Paul Cook from The Sex Pistols, as he was cited as an enabler by two of the women I spoke to; and some men who were prominent in the Brighton punk scene. Some musicians responded by email from the US, including Sarah-Jane from The Belle Stars, Melissa Ritter from The Mo-dettes and Paloma McLardy (Palmolive) from The Slits. There are many people I did not have the opportunity to speak to – for instance, The Marine Girls, Chrissie Hynde, The Passions, The Sadista Sisters, The Elgin Marbles and The Accelerators, to name but a few. I have in some cases discussed these women with reference to their press coverage, for instance, but I am fully aware that there are omissions in this work. It seemed better to focus on the experiences of fewer women in greater depth, but this does not mean that others are disrespected by the author in any way.

It was important to examine the way women instrumentalists were portrayed by the music press; their shifting and different attitudes would have had an effect on the way their readers perceived this phenomenon, in spite of the fact that there was an increasing use of fanzines produced from within the subculture, as sources of information and "attitude." Research has therefore been undertaken into these publications as well as, when available, fanzines published at the time, including an interview with Lucy Toothpaste, who started the women-focused fanzine *Jolt*.

The enduring tabloid version of the female punk consists of the aforementioned young woman in fishnet tights with spiky hair and extreme black eye make-up. Laing[34] discusses the difference context makes to the viewing of photographs, with particular reference to female punks; I have chosen in this instance to avoid lengthy analysis of the tabloid attitude to punk women in bands because my focus here is on the music world, not the punk style. Here, I explore the "entry level" of women into the mediated rock discourse, as for many of the women discussed or interviewed this was as far as they got. The feminist press (represented here by *Spare Rib*) is introduced to give a more rounded, if necessarily sparse, perspective. The reason for the integration of primary research with secondary research, which includes academic sources, general music histories, music periodicals and fanzines, is in order to reassess the period as completely as possible. Conflicting accounts are acknowledged where they arise, and are included to show the subjectivity inherent in all such studies.

There is now a reasonably large body of work dedicated to women in rock and pop music that asserts women's right to appear in histories of rock music,[35] many of which have been very useful. However, while consulting them I became aware of the unfortunate fact that the male nature of rock fandom means that, as such histories deal exclusively with women artists, they might well be regarded as irrelevant to the rock discourse and be left on the shelves by men. As comments made by Caroline Coon will confirm, male gatekeepers are mainly interested in disseminating ideas about a particularly

Cover of *Jolt* number 2. Illustration © Ros Past-It, reproduced with her kind permission

limited range of stereotypical female forms, especially if they are tragic.[36] The two types of work exist as though in different worlds. There is also a marked difference in the type of experience performers have in the two other main English-speaking rock music-producing countries, the US and the UK. Australia makes continual inroads into rock music production (and benefited from the same opening in markets as the bands and musicians I write about here), but rock music is "old" in Britain and the US; Sir Paul McCartney is of pensionable age and rock has developed enough over a lifetime for British and American writers to be able to draw some conclusions.

Although most of the studies on women in rock have been undertaken by biographers such as Lucy O'Brien,[37] Gillian Gaar[38] and Barbara O'Dair,[39] academics such as Lucy Green and Mavis Bayton (*Music, Gender, Education* and *Frock Rock* respectively) have also contributed valuable work to the genre. Additionally, writers who normally specialize in exploring classical music, such as Susan McClary,[40] Carol Neuls-Bates,[41] Jill Halstead[42] and Marcia Citron,[43] have valuable insights into women's cultural position as producers of rock and pop music. I should also like to acknowledge briefly the ongoing debate regarding Madonna – is she a disgrace to the female gender or the first truly liberated woman? Writers from Camille Paglia[44] to tabloid journalists find her a constant source of inspiration, and there are many studies that either affirm or deny stereotyping in the music industry. Other publications concerning women and rock music have often taken the form of series of interviews, such as Amy Raphael's,[45] or collections of essays, such as Sarah Cooper's,[46] and these are particularly interesting for their portrayal of their subjects as real people, as well as talented musicians. However, this work rescues some less famous women's stories from obscurity, underlining the fact that punk was just as much about individual empowerment as making music, and one of the forms this empowerment took was taking to the stage and playing music (or making noise) just for the experience of it.

Problems

There were several obstacles that hindered or altered the progress of this research. The most frustrating problem was the difficulty of contacting women punk musicians active at the time. Sometimes it was possible to locate them, but they were unwilling to participate in the research or the trail "ran dry." There is undoubtedly suspicion surrounding academic research (one interviewee "accused" me of being a sociologist), but also, I believe, an unwillingness to consolidate personal memories for analysis and transcription by another person. Jeanette Lee, for instance, has decided not to talk about her experiences with Johnny Rotten's post-punk group PIL at all, and other women felt that they had spoken enough about their past and wanted to concentrate on "now."

This has affected the outcome of the research and I have sometimes been working against the denial of some interviewees that there was anything different about the moment at all. This is probably a by-product of the very diverse and inclusive nature of regional punk, which defied stereotype; it is probably also a manifestation of Buckingham's[47] "cynical chic." Related to this, some of the information given to me is confidential, or disputed. This causes a moral dilemma especially when it has a strong bearing on my hypothesis. This information has been included only when deemed essential, and using anonymity.

Other problems are the previously mentioned lack of feminist writing about females in subcultures and female rock instrumentalists, and a corresponding lack of writing by men about females in subcultures and female instrumentalists. Joanne Hollows notes the dilemmas faced by feminists writing about popular music as they sometimes find themselves drawn towards forbidden areas, pop being seen as fluffy and girly whereas rock being perceived as macho and exclusive:

> Like girls who invest in "subcultural capital," feminist critics are not immune to the desire for the feelings of cultural distinction which comes from being "one of the boys"... For women working in the field, producing feminist work may be hard enough, without having the added burden of being seen to take "girly music" seriously.[48]

Many participants in punk left no material evidence of their existence anyway: for instance, although there was a well-documented increase in independent record label activity at the time, not all of the bands made records, and when they did they may not have been reviewed. This reflects Bradley's comments about an earlier period in the history of rock'n'roll:

> I would argue very strongly that the view which sees the period 1955–63 in Britain as a mere "background," to Beat and other later styles, is heavily distorted by an almost fetishistic attention to the charts (i.e. the successes of The Beatles, etc.) and that, sales of records notwithstanding, the development of a "youth culture" in Britain, and of a music of that youth culture, can only be understood by reversing that process. In a very real sense, there is an element of *myth* in the way rock histories skip from one commercial peak to another, or from one "great artist" to another, ignoring almost totally the social roots of both the music making and the listening, which ought to be among their objects of study.[49]

Again, this was an example of "entry-level" restriction; in another example of this, Sanjek[50] discusses the way in which female rockabilly singers in the US were forgotten due to the lack or destruction of vinyl evidence, and I feel this makes the primary research here all the more valuable.

An unanticipated problem was that of my own anger, brought on gradually as the tapes of the interviews were transcribed. It is tempting to blame the self-deprecation of some of the subjects for their lack of success, but the environment further afield than the punk world in which their music developed will be shown to have caused this. Attitudes of the music press and the record business, while scornful of male bands often as a matter of course, veered from the patronizing to the outright abusive in the case of female musicians. It became difficult not to interfere in the replies of the interview subjects, and this was a downside of having been involved in the scene myself; this, though, was counterbalanced by the fact that I shared a common past experience with many of the women I interviewed.

Finally, when deconstructing a stereotype, the resulting conclusions should not be expected to be tidy (not only as a result of the inevitable problem of contextualizing this work: is it a feminist analysis, a subcultural analysis, or a rock music analysis?); the two main stimuli for the phenomenon I am exploring appeared to be the Sex Discrimination Act and the atmosphere it generated for young women, and the enabling environment of the punk subculture. The reasons for its demise were far more complex and varied, and reflected the mixture of personalities, backgrounds and ages of the women I interviewed. This study is not intended to be a definitive work; ideally, it will stimulate further discussion and debate, which in turn will achieve my intended outcome – to reinstate a lost part of women's social history.

What is presented here is a chapter exploring access to a new facility in playing music via the punk subculture; an examination of the cultural intermediaries who brokered punk and post-punk music; a case study of my own punk environment in Brighton; a chapter that explores noisemaking and aggression in rock music; a discussion of the reasons for the fading-out of the phenomenon of female instrumentalists in the punk and post-punk scenes given the changing commercial and political context; and an academic context. I end with an analytical conclusion.

1 A Ladder Through the Glass Ceiling?

> These success stories had ambiguous implications. As with every other "youth revolution" (e.g. the beat boom, the mod explosion and the Swinging Sixties) the relative success of a few individuals created the impression of energy, expansion and limitless upward mobility.[1]

Hebdige, above, utters words of caution as the music press rejoices in punk bands getting record deals, bank clerks metamorphosing into fanzine editors (Mark Perry of Sniffin' Glue) and then into music journalists and so on; subcultures become focused on "a handful of brilliant nonconformists," he claims. By presenting the experiences of a group of contemporaries I interviewed, who were in bands in East and West London, Cambridge, Brighton, Oxford, Southampton, Birmingham, Leeds, Newcastle and Manchester,[2] we will see how their experiences empowered them, and how the punk community supported them. What these women have in common is that they started playing instruments in bands around 1976–77, during the moment that punk first became a major youth subculture; their mass-cultural reference points are therefore very similar, although at the time their ages would have varied from sixteen to forty-five. Some of these women (for example, Lora Logic) made recordings and were quite prominent musicians at the time, with reviews and interviews in the music press. Others made no recordings and gave no interviews, but were just as deeply involved in the production of music and living in the punk subculture.

Pinning down the energy and excitement of a movement, or a moment, like British punk is impossible to do in words, and boxing in the resulting captive within academia might seem like a crime. For a writer like myself, punk came first and academic education followed years behind it; analysis is necessary to consolidate the experiences of my generation, but should not distract the reader from the uniqueness of the punk experience for its community. The abrasive sound of the music matched our desperation; for us, it blew away the polished and smug sounds of progressive rock, epitomized by Rick Wakeman's progressive rock musical on ice that featured the by-then familiar expensive lighting rigs and sound systems plus a massive cast including horses; not only did this way of presenting music have no relationship to young people's life experiences, but it made music-making seem like a millionaire's activity – how could the average person in the street afford banks of keyboards, stacks of amplifiers, and exotic stage dressing and costumes? At the other end of the spectrum, the undoubted genius of Kate Bush filled a very large gap in popular music. In 1978, her hot-housed talent was advertised on hoardings, buses, the music press: the woman-to-end-all-women was not only a prodigy musically, but was marketed very much in terms of her sexuality, photographed in a tight T-shirt that left little to the imagination. She was obviously a very high-main-tenance prospect in terms of music; even the average listener could discern that a huge financial investment had been made not only in her studio record-ings but also in the presentation of her oeuvre. The world of music and its potential as either a career or a method of communication therefore seemed impossible to penetrate until punk came and changed all the rules by force. It bypassed the tastes of the traditional gatekeepers; we were creating an atmos-phere, a homemade expression of anger and dissatisfaction, redistributing power, and it cost us next to nothing; this was often read by the establishment as a celebration of amateurism and shambolic organization. Sometimes it was admired, in the way that those who analyse extreme activities seem secretly to admire their subjects, and sometimes attempts were made to co-opt the energy of the moment and divert it to other ends. Capitalism is so woven into the developed world that rejecting it as a starting-point for creative activity seems incomprehensible, unless one is in a position where capitalism makes no sense whatsoever.

This was a temporary subcultural and musical revolution stirred up by the concurrent activities of a group of very different but equally creative women who were active in different locations at the same time, and it is necessary to sail through what might seem like a sea of sociology in order to put this into a political and social context. History is not complete without attempts to fill in the missing parts, and this book is my attempt to right the misconceptions about what punk could mean to women (or, at the time, often girl) instrumentalists who were involved at its revolutionary core. To some of its protagonists, punk *was* a social revolution; for a while, it cer-tainly introduced some revolutionary behaviour into the "frame." It was also a musical revolution, and the female punk bands had a particular sort of influence on British pop music that is also frequently underplayed, especially in their incorporation of reggae into the musical discourse. Arguably, if *male* bands had developed the sort of innovations in music that The Slits and The Raincoats, for instance, made, they would have become household names.[3] Later, we will see that a sort of closed shop mentality was in operation in the written histories of subcultures in general, let alone those that had music at their core. I will place punk in the context of other youth subcultures both before and since; mostly, those involved in writing "serious" histories of youth subcultures have concerned themselves only with the young men involved. The tensions between music-makers and the recording industry have a profound effect on gender perceptions among music fans of all ages, and I will show how frequently writers in the academic field subscribe unwittingly to gender-hegemonic assumptions and values. All too often, new eras for women in rock music are discovered[4] but the inroads made by women into this genre of music are temporary, and always on male terms. As US journalist Toby Goldstein remarked in 1975:

> Every women's band has been called a sign of some dawning era. So far that includes Birtha, Fanny, April Lawton's Ramatam, Suzi Quatro and perhaps, if they had ever been reviewed at the time, Goldie and the Gingerbreads way back in 1964 too. Women's bands proliferate in today's media, to be sure. But women playing music are still badly underreviewed and consequently underestimated. The "times" have been giving signs of things to come for as long as rock has been reviewed. When women are no longer asked why are you, you? [sic] we'll know the millennium has arrived.[5]

Carson, Lewis and Shaw report that, post-2000, Goldstein's millennium has still not arrived; they quote an interview in *Cleveland Scene* with Bikini Kill's guitarist Kathleen Hanna in which she challenges the reporter for asking her about feminism rather than music, and he acknowledges that three-quarters of the way through the interview he has yet to ask her about the music.[6] There are constant attempts to isolate women's achievements in the fields of art and music, with a resulting detachment of experience that makes it very difficult to assess and value even one's own work, as articulated by the lead singer of The Slits, Ari:

> It's really hard to relate to people after you've been through a revolution, because it's like talking to a Vietnam veteran, you know when the Vietnam people went though a war like that and they seem really normal and okay, and they come to this point when they can't talk about things 'cos they've got no one to relate to, so that's like with me, I keep that point quiet then suddenly I go into this memory. Right now I'm like a Vietnam veteran, feeling all these emotions, all these things, all these good explosions that we had, expressions of freedom that we were able to make [remembering], at the same time this completely tormented, constant sabotage that we were getting.[7]

Various different elements enabled the women players to begin their career (or sometimes, hobby) as rock and pop instrumentalists. Bayton[8] has already identified many of these factors; there is no doubt that the moment of punk rock resulted in a much higher visibility of female instrumentalists in bands and an acknowledgement (sometimes grudging and misogynistic in tone) by the music papers normally targeted at a young male rock audience that some women were becoming present in more "male" roles in bands on the entry-level circuit of pubs, clubs and student venues. The punk moment, and its attraction for the unemployed, provided a unique context for changes in music-making.

Extended Childhood and Creative Opportunity

Virginia Caputo's study of the "transformation, through various processes, of the child into a competent member of adult culture" describes childhood itself being regarded as inconsequential by adults; it is merely a stage during which the child makes up for what they "lack" in order to grow up: "This conceptualisation depicts children as 'partially cultural'."[9] This is useful in discussing what could be described as the permanent childhood state of punks which was a feature of the subculture, as they were unable or unwilling to undertake the rite of passage provided by employment. As Glyptis writes:

> One of the main confirmations that adulthood had been reached was the attainment of full-time employment, which signalled the beginning of "real" adult life, in an adult world and on adult terms, with concomitant financial independence.[10]

Caputo provides another useful insight in her essay, commenting:

> With regard to the issue of time, this element is significant for both youth and children. While one could argue that, for children at least, it appears that there is a connection between the loss of control over their time and a decrease in the production of culture, it cannot be substantiated.[11]

There is a logical link between "control over their time" and the fact that by nature of being unemployed and therefore infantilized, the punks, both male and female, developed a productive subculture to continue and replace that of their childhood in a reversal of what happens to a child as school absorbs more and more of their time. This productive involvement, whether musical, political or otherwise, in the creation of their subculture would have been psychologically rewarding. Stephen Harding's study, "Values and the Nature of Psychological Well-being," investigates what people do when they have nothing (compulsory) to occupy themselves with – for instance, in the case of those who are retired, or unemployed. People can achieve worth through activity, and he concludes that active engagement – whether socially useful or personally fulfilling (for instance, sports) – makes people happier than inactivity:

> The evidence...points to the role of social interaction and voluntary activity as a means of enhancing personal well-being...whilst the eradication of dissatisfying social conditions may not be achieved overnight, and may be to an extent beyond the individual's direct ability to control, the finding that affective experience is related to voluntary social activity suggests that, at least as far as this component of the model is concerned, an individual's well-being may well be in his own hands.[12]

The fact that the labour market could not absorb large numbers of young people in the late 1970s was potentially disastrous for British society; what the punk subculture did for many of young people was to valorize them and their activities, whatever their gender. As Glyptis says:

> The "gains" of unemployment are tempered by circumstance. Free time will be a gain for those who are able to use it in ways that are personally satisfying. Freedom from obligations will be a gain for those who can thrive without external demands. But even in these circumstances, neither is likely to be a gain unless those affected by it are cushioned financially, *or have access to something equivalent to the financial and social rewards of work.*[13]

She discusses people's need for daily structure, and their need to be needed, in the context of youth unemployment at this time: "The unemployed do not only feel different and useless. They often feel deviant and stigmatized."[14] Punks *needed* each other, and used these feelings of deviance and stigmatization to create their own equivalent to the "financial and social rewards of work," creating their own voluntary social activity, or self-administered occupational therapy, to enhance their personal well-being. Within a relatively short period of time, the boundaries of leisure and work time had been blurred. Pre-recession, those involved in the counterculture had *chosen* to opt out of the mainstream; their working occupations were often closely interwoven with their "own" time and interests. They had had the choice of redefining the organization of their time:

> The counter culture's rejection of work involved a rejection of the division between work and leisure, as well as a rejection of the concept of leisure as something earned by the worker in compensation for the loss of freedom caused by work.[15]

In some respects, this provided a blueprint for what was to follow. Although punks detested hippies, each group's rejection of mainstream culture and attempts to create an "outside" existence was a common factor.

The Bohemian Lifestyle and Punk

Control over time was one of the things the hippy subculture had in common with punk and, of course, with the state of childhood; and with time comes a consolidation of the beliefs and identity of the subculture itself. Therefore, according to Paul Willis:

> If we can supply the premises, dynamics, logical relations of responses which look quite untheoretical and lived out "merely" as cultures, we will uncover a cultural politics – although, of course, disjointing what is most characteristic about it: its detailed incorporation and synthesis with a life-style and concrete forms of symbolic and artistic production.[16]

And Frith, during a discussion on Marx's views of the leisure time permitted to the worker as part of the capitalist ethos, remarked:

> [B]ohemians articulate a leisure critique of the work ethic. They are cultural radicals not just as the source of the formalist avant-garde, but also in institutional terms – they don't work (and thus outraged bourgeois moralists have always denounced successful bohemians who, it seems, make their money out of play).[17]

Bohemia tended to cast women as the muse, rather than the protagonist; but in spite of this, Elizabeth Wilson, when discussing the rejection of male definition by feminists in the 1970s, observes:

> Women as bohemians were outside the remit of this feminist re-evaluation of art history. This was ironic, given that the women's movements of the Western world came with all the trappings of bohemian lifestyle... The connection between "lifestyle politics" and an earlier bohemianism was never made.[18]

It is hardly surprising that there was a bohemian element in the customized punk rock that found its way into the lifestyles of unemployed youth in

Britain. Enforced leisure makes the temptation of cultural radicalism more appealing than its alternative, giving in to feelings of rejection.[19] It was a busy subculture. One can be defined as "unemployed" or, euphemistically, "looking for work"; punks "worked at" the subculture twenty-four hours a day, creating a space for themselves that was outside the definition of mainstream society, whether official (according to the then Department of Health and Social Security) or mediated (by, principally, the tabloid press). I believe that the extension of the childhood state brought about by unemployment provided an opportunity for young women to avoid "growing up" and to reassess their future with a degree of equality that had not been present during times of full employment. Walkerdine describes the ways "through which the modern order, patriarchal and capitalist as it is, produces the positions for subjects to enter,"[20] citing Foucault's views of "technologies of the social":

> Scientific knowledges...constantly define girls and women as patholog-
> ical, deviating from the norm and lacking, but they also define them as
> necessary to the procreation and rearing of democratic citizens.[21]

Playing in a band provided a wonderful opportunity for the rejection of this definition and for fighting against the natural order. Several of my interviewees described their *need* for an alternative destiny. For instance, musician/writer Liz Naylor said:

> I had a really strong sense of not being in the straight world. I was
> listening to some punk record the other day and I was thinking [that]
> I really identified [it] as "us" in some way. When I was on my own in
> my bedroom, I knew what I was against: my cousins, and the girls at
> my school. I went to an all-girls school, and they were so square I just
> thought they were awful. I had this real sense of the other world. I
> thought there'd be some kind of revolution in some way. I wanted to
> destroy it, I really wanted to destroy it.

She continues, "My mum would say things like, 'Why don't you go to secretarial college – shorthand is always useful.' And I thought, 'I want to be Janis Joplin, I don't want to go to fucking secretarial college'."[22] Similarly, Mavis Bayton of The Mistakes told me: "they kept dragging us round factories saying, 'This is your future,' and I was getting quite upset because I hadn't envisaged my future working in a factory. I didn't know what my future was, but it wasn't working in a factory."[23] Gina Birch adds:

> I never felt that I was going to be a "lady"... I probably always had a fear
> of growing up, and getting old, and I still do. I don't have a handbag... I

don't have the accoutrements of being a woman, and I am completely
label-phobic about being "Mrs," or a "woman" – not woman, but what
"woman" represents...[24]

There was a frustration with the idea of growing up to be a "lady" with all
the implications associated with such a destiny. Sheila Rowbotham had observed in 1973 that her "own sense of self as a person directly conflicted with
the kind of girl who was sung about in pop songs."[25] Although Walkerdine has
claimed that "Middle-class girls...do not need to fantasize being somebody,
they are told clearly at every turn that they are: it is simply not a battle to be
entered into,"[26] it is evident that, across class boundaries at this time, there
was a redefinition of femaleness by certain women drawn to deviant behaviour through lack of future employment prospects.[27] I interviewed women
from many different backgrounds, and all of them were quite clear about the
opportunities to engage in a different world provided by the upheavals in the
late 1970s: Walkerdine's theory does not hold true, according to the women
involved in musical activity at this time.[28]

The fantasies many of the women might have had as girls about making music were now on a par with the fantasy jobs created by the government during this recession in an attempt to stimulate the economy: rather
than competing with men for "men's jobs," they could create "employment"
(though often unpaid) for themselves. The rite of passage into adulthood provided by entry into the labour market was no longer relevant: "Special meas-
ures for training and work experience do not fill this role. They tend to be seen
as second best. In a sense they are make-believe";[29] unemployment was as
much a reality for middle-class graduates as it was for the school-leaver who
had previously gone straight into the labour market. The introduction of the
government's Enterprise Allowance Scheme in 1983 encouraged "accidental
musicians" to opt in to the scheme (business plans, guaranteed income of
£40 per week plus rent, and no DHSS hassles for a year) or remain external
and excluded; this led to a degree of soul-searching regarding the oppositional
nature of music-making later in their "careers."

The apparent gender-levelling effect of mass unemployment and the do-
it-yourself nature of the punk ethos would prove to be both an advantage and
a disadvantage to the girl instrumentalists; what was regarded as an advantage for male musicians was often a disadvantage for women, just because
of assumptions based on their gender. For instance, Cohen describes how a
certain degree of musical incompetence in the male bands she studied was
seen to be almost endearing,[30] yet in a conversation I had with bass-player
Suzi Quatro, she cited the incompetence of female instrumentalists in punk
bands as being one of the major reasons why their profile in the rock world

was not sustained,[31] although in reality many of the women became skilled on their instruments but were never reassessed by the media.

Not being a musical genius was not seen to be an obstacle. The Velvet Underground, a band with a female drummer, Mo Tucker, was cited by many of the women who wrote to me as a strong influence.[32] As John Cale remarked at the time of the band's performing life:

> We had so much trouble with drummers but Mo was good at being basic so she was brought in. Actually, Lou was always saying, "Sterling can't play guitar and Mo can't play." He kept saying, "But man, she can't play." My idea was to keep the sound simple, but by overlaying the instruments' simplistic patterns the accumulative effect of the sound would be incredibly powerful.[33]

This respect for the "can't play" musician was definitely a factor that encouraged young women to play in bands; it is interesting to note that in response to Quatro's comments, Geoff Travis articulated the ethos of the moment thus:

> I just see it as a really interesting moment in time that certainly empowered a lot of people to make music who probably would not have made music, if Suzi Quatro's definition of who should be allowed to play music was the overriding rule. She probably prides herself in making her way in a men's game and beating the men at it. Whereas those rules went out the window really during the punk era, because it wasn't really a competition to see who could be the biggest and best, or the fastest. It was just, who could do something interesting.[34]

Some of the musicians I interviewed did indeed fall into the category of "one chord wonders," but others had been trained at school or at home to a high degree of musicianship, as Bayton also discovered in her research. Often, those who had started off knowing little about their instrument became relatively competent relatively quickly. It is also hard to decipher from the reportage of live performances how much of the incompetence was assumed and expected and how much of it was genuine. There is one fact that is incontrovertible: almost all of the young women that I interviewed felt that their involvement in making punk music was facilitated by the anarchic ideals of the subculture, and although there had been no specific mention of girls and young women in any of punk's "manifestos," this and the atmosphere of enablement in the mid-1970s that was formally created for women by the Sex Discrimination Act provided an additional force to their feeling that they were entitled to their position on stage alongside young men of their generation. Christine Robertson (manager of The Slits) told me:

> When punk happened it broke down gender roles, not because women had the feeling, "Oh we must do it for our sisters," but [because] women were emerging as strong individuals; they'd been through an education system and a culture that was telling them that they were now equal – the Equal Opportunities Act [sic] had been passed, and your work could now earn the same as a man. A lot of stereotypes for roles had been broken down. And punk just exploded onto the scene. The reason so many women were involved was that it liberated them from predefined roles that society might have in mind for them... It also broke the rules of how things should be done. Previously if you were a band you had to be virtuoso, you had to do years and years of touring, gigging, being ripped off by record companies to get exposure. But then suddenly, punk's on the scene and anybody can get exposure.[35]

The chains of empowerment – one band helps another band, who in turn helps another band, and so on – will later be seen to apply to many of the women I spoke to, or who responded to the questionnaires that I sent out.

Fantasies and Reality: Motivation and Role Models

Walkerdine[36] describes household and playground scenes that are familiar to many girls and women: the fantasy pop band, singing current chart hits and imagining themselves to be on stage, performing to an audience. Singing and dancing are part of childhood's rites of passage, as documented by Iona and Peter Opie;[37] Virginia Caputo also notes the importance of song-making to children as a method of defining and controlling the adult world:

> Themes of songs dealing explicitly with issues such as female fear, females as property, physical abuse, control of the State, and traditional female and male roles, abound in the children's repertoire. Songs that carry these messages are repeated over and over again by children in predominantly "chant" form. The chants indicate that they are not merely reflective of the surrounding adult world, but that children are actively engaged in the process of shaping their worlds.[38]

It is interesting to compare this with Attali's remarks about the correlation between music and violence:

> This channelization of childhood through music is a politically essential substitute for violence, which no longer finds ritual enactment. The youth see it as the expression of their revolts, the mouthpiece of their dreams and needs, when it is in fact a channelization of the imaginary, a pedagogy of the general confinement of social relations in the commodity.[39]

It is not unusual for girls to express themselves in song; making the transition into bands is therefore a cultural issue rather than one of ability. I found that the idea of forming a band was not problematic; what had been difficult was the identification, mostly by men, of playing in a rock band as adolescent male territory. Previously (if Attali's theory is correct and applied to the male-gendered rock discourse), only young men had the right to express revolt through the consumption and creation of music.

The following letter to *Sounds*, written in 1976 before punk had really taken off nationally, expresses the frustration of a woman instrumentalist, and possibly predicts the influx of girls into rock bands:

> ...I'm a bass guitarist who would like to play good, heavy rock (i.e. Sabs, Fairies), but because I'm a girl, no one's interested... You see I just want to stand on stage and play bass and that is (at the moment) unacceptable because I know (from experience) that men don't like the idea that girls can play as well, if not better, than them (I'm no women's libber – I'm talking about musical ability). I don't believe I'm the only person who feels this way, but if I am, surely I've not been devoting my life to an ambition which is doomed to failure just because I'm "the wrong sex" for a bassist? Maybe the answer lies in mixed bands... (Joy [the ferret], Carpenders Park, Watford, Herts).[40]

The coming-into-existence of the punk ethos made it easier for women like Joy to form bands; there was a cultural shift away from the idea that "only a special (usually male) person can be in a band," and this directly affected the way some young women perceived themselves. Previous to this period, women's contact with the rock world was often to take on the role of groupie, providing sex for rock stars after the show.[41] Chrissie Hynde articulates the frustration that she felt at the time, according to Amy Raphael, who mentions that Chrissie Hynde gave Johnny Rotten guitar lessons, and later tried rock journalism as a career, but:

> ...Hynde had an epiphany: she had no desire to live her life through others. She was more concerned with her own experience than writing about others' and intent upon not being regarded as a Pistols' groupie;[42] she later said of the period, "Everyone had a band except me and it used to make me cry."[43]

There was a sharp transition from the activities of the younger adolescent females at the time. McRobbie and Garber, writing on teenybopper culture, say:

There seems little doubt that the fantasy relationships which characterise this resistance depend for their very existence on the subordinate, adoring female in awe of the male on a pedestal... The small, structured and highly manufactured space that is available for ten to fifteen year old girls to create a personal and autonomous area seems to be offered only on the understanding that these strategies also symbolise a future general subordination – as well as a present one.[44]

Deciding to Form a Band

Some of the women I spoke to had had fantasies of being in bands (similar to those described by Walkerdine) with siblings or friends,[45] and later made what must have seemed a natural transition into the real thing, pushing aside the "fantasy relationships" of their earlier years and claiming the pedestal for themselves. This early and easy transition from fantasy to practice was common to several of them; Zillah Ashworth of Rubella Ballet, for instance, told me:

> My dad had been drafted into the army. He pretended he could play trombone. They did ask us if we wanted to have music lessons. We [would have] had to have free lessons, [but] they didn't do free lessons. Playing instruments was seen as a middle-class thing to do. It was still seen as a posh thing to do. I did want to be in a band from the beginning. I used to watch *Top of the Pops* and dress up as Pan's People with my sisters.[46]

As a child, Hester Smith of Dolly Mixture had played at being in a band anyway:

> Me and Debsey already had a pretend band of our own...it sounds so childish...so obviously it was exciting to be in a real band, even if we were just backing-singers. Then we decided to form our own... You know what it was, it was *Rock Follies*.[47] That was really exciting! We used to watch it every week and found it really thrilling. It would look so tacky probably now, but at the time, yeah![48]

Jane Munro of The Au Pairs had made props to use in her fantasy band:

> Oh yes, I was an instrumentalist! I played guitar. We used to make cardboard guitar things... it was me and a little boy; there were only two of us. It was very driven by me, perhaps because he was a bit younger. I was an only child and I was inventive. I used to play all sorts of things. I was quite imaginative. We used to play along to records and we used to make a little stage on a low table. We were whoever we were playing along to.[49]

Jane Munro, The Au Pairs. Unknown photographer

Poly Styrene (of X-ray Spex)'s early ambitions were focused on more traditional performance:

> I wanted to be an actress, I wanted to be in musicals and we lived quite near the Granada TV studios on Kennington Road. I remember when I was really little we used to walk past there and I would start singing and dancing and hoping that someone would discover me.
>
> My thing was singing like maybe The Supremes, so I always thought of being in a musical, that kind of thing, rather than being in a band. I used to do singing and dancing at school to entertain the other children.[50]

This feeling of 'playing at' something was not unique to British bands; Tina Weymouth, bass-player with new-wave US band Talking Heads, described a similar feeling among all of the band-members, male and female: "There was a time...when we felt like people pretending to be a band. Then all of a sudden we were a band."[51] Other women needed a catalyst – and seeing other women play live made performing seem easy enough to try, sometimes as a transition from political activity with a group of peers. This is what happened to Lucy O'Brien, who formed The Catholic Girls in Southampton:

> We first formed the band in about 1978. We were all at school and we were very bored. There was four of us who were really good friends in the sixth form. We got into punk; we'd been on demonstrations together, we'd got involved in things like hunt saboteurs, with the Anti-Nazi League, and we'd just got very fired up by seeing Gang of Four and The Delta 5 on the back of a lorry at a pro-Abortion march in London. We just thought they were having so much fun, and punk is about do it yourself, and why don't we just go out and get some instruments and form a band? So that's how it started.[52]

Both Gina Birch and June Miles-Kingston cited seeing The Slits live as their personal catalysts; Rhoda Dakar saw The Mo-dettes and was inspired to look for a band to join. Away from the larger urban centres like Cambridge or Southampton, it was more difficult to join or start a band: Sue Bradley had to wait until she had left home to attend Brighton Polytechnic before she could play with other musicians:

> At school I always knew I wanted to play in bands. I came from a very small village. The boys tended to get together and play guitars but there wasn't anything for the girls at all. The girls just didn't do that. The girls just spent most of their time getting themselves ready to go out with boys; they didn't have group activities like that.[53]

For others, living in a musical household, with equipment lying around waiting to be played, was enough to get them started, as will be shown later in the Brighton chapter, when the drum kit that was permanently set up in a shared house encouraged a young woman to start drumming. Jane Woodgate, who formed The Mo-dettes, describes an almost accidental series of events that led to the band getting together:

> A great friend of mine had a satellite band called The Tesco Bombers; he would change the line-up for each song. I was to sing two songs... Gina Birch of The Raincoats played bass on a few of the numbers as well. The only constant in the band was to be the friend himself. At

> the beginning of 1979 there was to be a gig at the Acklam Hall [in West London] and I thought it would be a cheeky idea if we had a line-up that didn't include him by having only girls, so I asked Ramona to sing and looked about me for a guitarist and drummer. I happened on Kate Korus in the Lisson Grove dole queue, she and June had been looking for a bassist and singer, it was a done deal.[54]

Interestingly, the ability or desire to play an instrument did not always lead to a role as an instrumentalist. Penetration's Pauline Murray started at the age of fourteen as a folk singer/guitarist playing covers of songs like Peter Paul and Mary's *Leaving on a Jetplane*, gravitating at the age of fifteen to a band that played covers of songs by David Bowie and Cockney Rebel, before taking on the role of vocalist in the band. She was quite happy with this role, until later when she joined The Invisible Girls in 1980, and she took up guitar (and keyboards) again in the studio.

Choice of Instrument and Learning to Play

I found a variety of attitudes and abilities here. Some women (for instance, Enid Williams, Lora Logic, Nora Normal) were dedicated from their early teens to a particular instrument and were therefore "raring to go" when the opportunity arose to join or form a band. Their reasons for becoming involved in bands were positive, and they were ambitious to have careers in music. Rachel Bor of Dolly Mixture, on the other hand, was actively against the idea of being a musician:

> It was accidental. I didn't want anything to do with music. That was the one thing I said I'd never do, because my parents were both musicians. I thought I'd go to art college, that was the only thing I had in mind. It was only because Debsey and Hester had to get this band together for a party that I got involved.[55]

For others, in particular Liz Naylor, it was a way out of a claustrophobic upbringing, as her previous comments have shown (see above). Palmolive, drummer with The Slits, originally wanted to be a mime artist or street clown. She had been living with Joe Strummer (later of The Clash) and dancing at gigs by the 101'ers before deciding to try something on her own:

> I met these people...they said, "Yeah, you can join us, but we only need someone to play drums when someone does something difficult." I didn't get on with the guy, I didn't like him, so I had a fight with him and left. But I had already kind of played the drums, and I thought, Ahhh! That's not hard! I can do this! So I started going "mm-cha, mm-

mm-cha." It went from there. And I really wanted to change, really wanted to do something different.[56]

Whatever the skills or motivation of the women I interviewed, they often displayed an extremely self-effacing attitude to their abilities as musicians. Gina Birch, bass-player and guitarist with The Raincoats, articulates feelings that describe the combined insecurity and excitement of the pioneer:

> In spite of my feeling [that] things were not difficult, I had a certain sense of modesty and I thought that one note was easier than chords... so I started to play... I actually put a lot into it, but I always thought that I was terrible. And when people said they thought what I did was interesting and good I didn't really believe them. And yet part of me did and part of me didn't.[57]

Sometimes, the choice of instrument was imposed, but suited the personality of the player. Tessa Pollitt was asked to join The Slits as a bass-player even though she had originally intended otherwise:

> I originally was planning to play the guitar, but it's only because I was asked to play the bass – it wasn't a decision coming from me; I think it's the best thing that ever happened. The bass is the perfect instrument for my character – it's just the deep tones – I've never really analysed it, but I feel much more comfortable with the bass than the guitar. It's a much more earthy character – the bass and the drums are the backbone. It's a much safer place for my character to be. I'm just not a guitarist – not that you should play just one instrument, but I think each person has an instrument that suits their character. I was just so quiet, it was just more me.[58]

The retrospective attitude of some women was that the "package" of skills they had was worth more than their mastery of one particular instrument. Enid Williams of Girlschool told me:

> I listened to some records and tried to copy them. I had a few music lessons from some guy, but not very much. The thing is that we were never "musician" musicians, we were always performers. The musicality was of a reasonable standard, but we weren't musos. We were always band-members, so we were entertainers, songwriters, musicians, all rolled into one. It was always, "Yeah, let's give that a go, let's see how it works, pick up a bit here, pick up a bit there," it was never a case of, "Let's study an instrument."[59]

Some women were almost reluctantly propelled towards playing and had to be guided towards their destiny, as Mavis Bayton explains:

> When I came into Oxford, I was a bit depressed and alienated from the city and looking for something to do. And a friend said to me, "You've always wanted to play guitar, why don't you have some lessons?" And I found somebody in the scene, who I think gave me six lessons. I think I learned how to do a bar chord – I think it was the F shape. After six weeks of me, he just said, Look, there's this ad in the *Backstreet Bugle*. And it said that they wanted women to get together to be in a band and he said, "Why don't you go along?," and I said, obviously, "I can't play the guitar"; his response was, "Well, they won't be able to play either." I think he wanted to get rid of me![60]

Choice of instrument was often dictated by the limitations of other band-members; Rachel from Dolly Mixture was the only member of her fantasy band who could actually play anything at the outset:

> My parents were both musicians and we'd always played instruments. I played piano and cello and taught myself guitar. I started learning chords and things when I was about twelve... Debsey and Hester had been in a band together. We just picked our instruments and I was the only one who could play anything so I played the guitar.[61]

And sometimes, choice of instrument was by default, as Hester, drummer with the band, explains:

> It was one of those flukes; it wasn't one of those things I'd thought of doing, ever, although I'd seen Karen Carpenter play on TV and I remember thinking, that looks fun. A load of people just seemed to be in bands – not girls though, only blokes. A friend of ours was a singer and she and a couple of friends had formed this band. She asked me and Debsey to do backing vocals. There was me, Debsey and Rachel... Rachel could play a bit of guitar, Debsey wanted to play bass and my hands were quite small so they said, "You can play drums." This was a big thing... Rachel said, "You can use my brother's drums." Rachel's brother was in Cambridge's only punk band and Rachel said, "and he'll teach you." Really I should never have been a drummer, I never got on with it that well, but that's how it happened. I fell into it.[62]

Punk violin-player Sue Bradley, of Brighton band The Reward System, appeared to have no choice but to find a band that would include her skills after discovering that her environment was not supportive of girls who wanted to play rock instruments; her rural upbringing meant that at first she had no contact with the DIY ethos and its application to music-making:

> I decided that I really wanted to learn the guitar. The only way that I could think to do this was to have guitar lessons. And of course the only lessons that were offered at school were classical guitar, and classical guitars have got a very wide neck. And I've got very small hands and so I just didn't get on with it at all[63] so I gave up on that. Which is a real shame because in retrospect, I think I'd have liked to play the bass, if I'd known any other girls that were doing it... It just didn't occur to me, oh yeah, buy a bass and just copy it off other bands, listen and play by ear. No one had introduced me to that and if they had, I'd have been off![64]

For Karen ("Nora Normal"), drummer with The Gymslips, encouragement came from her family, who refused to subscribe to the gender conventions of "the outside world." Karen's father is a musician, and was more than happy to encourage his daughter in her choice of instrument:

> I never had any training, I never had any lessons. I just taught myself by playing along with records and things like that, although my family are musical. But I never learned any other sort of instrument. My dad is a folk musician, English folk music. I can't say that I was given any confidence generally, but on the other hand it was helpful. It's quite unusual that girls would play drums, and part of it, any kid who says, "Oh mum, I wanna play drums," their parents would say, "No, because they're so noisy," and if you're a girl you'd get laughed at. At school I got laughed at by teachers, but at home it was different. My dad did encourage me. My dad helped me when I was sixteen to buy a second-hand drum kit. So in that way it was very helpful.[65]

The contrasting abilities of three keyboard-players show how difficult it is to stereotype the women I spoke to. First, Lucy O'Brien described how she transferred the piano-playing skills she already had to synthesizer:

> I had learned the piano, I was up to about Grade 4 on the piano, I'd had lessons since I was about thirteen so I was already quite au fait with that and also with music theory. So it wasn't too hard to transpose and to actually play the keyboards. What I loved was all the extra bits, playing around with all these sort of psychedelic sounds, with these different knobs. I don't think I used the synthesizer to its full capacity at all, but it was really nice to have a piano with all these effects.[66]

Julie Blair, from The Mockingbirds, practised her parts on the piano at home before playing a borrowed Vox organ at rehearsals:

> I had a Vox organ, and Rick [her partner] just showed me a few chords, literally. We've always had a piano at home, so I used to practise a few chords on the piano, then just fiddled around; it was very simple, what we did. I think I added to that and learned how to play a 12-bar blues on the piano, and learned how to play reggae sort of rhythms, but they were never really kosher.[67]

The Gay Animals' keyboard-player, Liz Naylor, fits in more with the idea of the stereotypical punk player. She had no familiarity with playing an instrument, but she was carried away with the idea of being in a band and went ahead and joined one anyway:

> [Previous to this time] it just seemed you could never do that, it was something boys did, and I had no musical ability, I wasn't at all gifted in any way in music, and didn't own any instruments. I didn't own an instrument and I just answered this advert which is a great indication of how great punk was. I thought, Well I'll just form a band, and I played keyboards... Really I can't play, all the keys had stickers on, like C, A, D, and all my keys had C, C, C.[68]

From the above, it can be seen that there was a considerable determination to participate in bands regardless of skill, instrument played, or expectation. These young women were energetic and resourceful and had put the inherent political message of punk into practice: participation and action, rather than watching and absorbing. As Ari says here, within the London community there was also a lot of encouragement from men:

> The only reason we really got in is because the boys were supportive – we were up against the world, all of us were. The boys were up against the world, so of course the girls were even more up against the world. If you put one and one [sic] ...and it was no problem for us, we were fully supported.[69]

The Slits were particularly aided in the studio by Keith Levene when they started recording. Levene also taught Viv Albertine to play guitar, when he was fourteen and she was seventeen:

> Keith took me seriously as a musician even though I'd never played in my life and it was just the hugest gift actually, to have him. He was younger than me; it may be that the dynamic of that was quite good; that he looked up to me in other ways. Maybe he fancied me! I didn't

feel threatened by him. I'd be so depressed, I'd play day after day, and I didn't get a bit better. You could talk to him about the most minute feelings you had, you could say, "Oh God I'm so depressed, I've spent two weeks now not getting any better. I've reached a plateau."

[He'd say] "That's called guitar depression, that's perfectly normal."

He would have words and understanding for whatever minute little mood you were going through, and make sense of it.[70]

Encouragement came for at least two bands from Paul Cook of The Sex Pistols, first for June Miles-Kingston:

> Paul Cook came in one day to the office and said, "I need some money," and I said, "Well, I can't just give you some money," and he said, "I've got an old drum kit, do you know anyone who wants to buy it?," and I bought this drum kit for forty quid, set it up in the squat in the basement and just messed about. Paul showed me how to put it together. Kate played guitar anyway, 'cos she'd previously been in The Slits, way back. So we were just jamming along, Joe [Strummer, from the Clash] used to join in, Steve [Jones, from the Sex Pistols] used to join in, and I thought, I can do this.[71]

Paul told me:

> Because it was good to see we helped the band out, giving loads of encouragement. [Punk] was an outpouring of talent that broke a lot of barriers. We didn't know what the future was going to be, we didn't know how long it was going to last at the time, but we knew there was a change in the air.[72]

Cook also helped out with The Bodysnatchers, according to Rhoda Dakar:

> Who helped? SJ's boyfriend, people's boyfriends. SJ's boyfriend was in a band; I guess he must have helped her with the guitar. It was all done outside. The only person who ever came into rehearsals was Cooky, to help June with her drumming. She hadn't quite got it, and I'd asked him to come in and show her.[73]

Siouxsie and the Banshees were helped by Johnny Thunders and the Heartbreakers: the band lent them equipment, money and rehearsal space, which meant they could carry on uncompromisingly until a record label would accept them regardless of their controversial image. The Damned invited The Adverts to tour the UK with them. Rubella Ballet shared a large house with Poison Girls, who encouraged them. There was a spirit of camaraderie between bands that was encouraged by the fact that they felt part of a community of outcasts, right from the start. I also found that the breaking-down of the divisions between audience and performer could be so complete that joining a band could be as easy and direct as an invitation from the stage, as in the case of The Thompson Twins:

> At Thompson Twins' gigs people are nearly always invited up on stage to participate, to bang or blow something and contribute to the music... It was by clambering on stage that two new members, Joe Leeway (congas and percussion) and Jane Shorter (sax and keyboards), came to join recently.[74]

Brighton band The Mockingbirds described a similar convention:

> We had this brilliant song called "I Like Boys" that just lent itself to a reggae rhythm, and it left lots of space. We had all these percussion instruments, so we used to get people to come up and sort of bang lots of different percussion things to fill all this space that we, as inadequate musicians, couldn't fill. *Like a collaboration with the audience?* Yes.[75]

Perhaps the oddest source of encouragement I was told about was the nuns at Lucy O'Brien's school:

> It surprised us hugely, because we went to quite a strict convent school and we assumed that they'd be really anti what we were doing. The interesting thing about nuns is that, thinking about it with hindsight, there's a sort of feminist subtext to being a nun (albeit a bit screwed up!). Basically in our school I remember them really admiring girls who went into careers and did really well educationally, who did well for themselves. There was no problem about women being independent. It was just felt that yes, marriage was an option and if you went into that, you had to do the whole thing and have children and be submissive to your husband; but I just felt that there was a message coming through as well about being independent educated women and doing stuff for yourself. So actually I felt they were secretly admiring of our chutzpah, of our ability to get something together like that.[76]

However, "the boys" were not always encouraging, as this experience by Sue from Prag Vec reveals – a normal rite of passage for boys was ridiculed when practised by a girl:

> I had a guitar when I was about fifteen. I had a copy of *Highway 61 Revisited*, and I learned to play "Tambourine Man." I remember sitting in my bedroom playing and I could hear my brother and his friend outside the window. They were laughing at me.[77]

Other members of the family could also be disparaging: Lesley Woods of The Au Pairs describes her mother telling her that she had a voice "like a foghorn," and Stella Clifford of Brighton's Objeks said:

> When I was fifteen I had a guitar for my birthday and I learned to play *American Pie*; one day I was playing it and my brother ran into the room and started singing it with me. I remember thinking this is the most fun I've ever, ever had. And my mum used to shout upstairs "Go down the garden if you're going to make all that noise." So I didn't have any encouragement at home.[78]

Acquiring the First Instrument

Recycling discarded musical instruments was very much part of the ethos. While old music styles (and often, consequently, lifestyles) are discarded by the record business in order to pave the way for new styles for new generations of young consumers, Willis notes:

> Commodities can be taken out of context, claimed in a particular way, developed and repossessed to express something deeply and thereby to change somewhat the very feelings which are their product. And this can happen under the very nose of the dominant class – and with their products ... it is sometimes the dispossessed who are best placed to exploit the revolutionary double edge of unexplored things around us.[79]

Although Willis is referring to black jazz musicians using discarded white people's instruments to make music, this is exactly what happened during punk, which started and continued to exist often with little or no capital investment by either the artists or external business; instruments were often borrowed, stolen at gigs from bands who were perceived to have "made it," or bought second-hand.[80]

Possessing an instrument imposed a commitment on the aspiring musician to learn to play the instrument, and in this particular environment to perform live with it, straight away. The nature of the punk scene was that bands were often performing their first gigs within weeks, or even days, of forming; often there was little rehearsal. For some, like June (above), an opportune moment could lead to the acquisition of an instrument. Borrowing was also very common, particularly for the first few gigs, and this was one of the elements of informal mentoring that enabled women to join bands. Rachel's first guitar was borrowed:

> I borrowed it off somebody and it was a Woolworth's guitar. It had a great name...it was a Thunder something or other. Every rehearsal I had to solder it back together again. This little wire inside it was getting shorter and shorter. We learned quite a lot as we went along.[81]

Julie Blair also borrowed her first instrument:

> It was James's keyboard from The Parrots. I think everyone borrowed instruments, as far as I can remember.[82]

However, the spectacle of punk gigs and the energy of the moment meant that a band could become busy very quickly however inexperienced they were, and this could cause problems with conflicting gig engagements: a shared guitar could not be in two venues at the same time. It would become necessary to buy an instrument of one's own.[83] Because most of these bands (even Girlschool, a heavy-metal band) were actively, as Enid says, against "musos," the quality of the instrument did not matter. Cheapness was essential, unless a parent could be persuaded to pay for the instrument – more likely in the case of instruments perceived to be jazz or classical in nature, less likely if the instrument was designed for rock. Karen's father's empathy with his daughter's musical ambitions led him to help her to purchase her first drum kit:

> I got my first kit from a drum shop in Stratford. It was a very old jazz kit. I only had £100. The bloke in the shop was really helpful in trying to get something together for little money... When I was sixteen I had an endowment – they [her parents] had been putting a bit of money away for me every year. Also, I was working in Sainsburys on a Saturday.[84]

Lora Logic's parents were keen at first to support their daughter's musical ambitions and bought a saxophone for her when she was fourteen; when asked what instrument she'd like to play, she asked for one, "half thinking they'd never buy me a saxophone because it was so big and so expensive, but they did."[85] Liz Naylor had had a difficult relationship with her mother, but still managed to persuade her that she should buy her first keyboard for her:

> I actually did make my mum buy it; I must have guilt-tripped her; it was from A1 Music in Oxford Street in Manchester...it sounded like Una Baines's from The Fall and it [was] kind of some plinky piano thing and it was about a hundred quid...and then I came across a second-hand Vox Jaguar. I signed on during this time [so] God knows how I got the money![86]

Although some of the younger instrumentalists could persuade their parents to buy their instruments, this was not a possibility for older girls. Some of the younger ones also had to buy their own equipment and could be naïve about what to expect as they did not necessarily socialize in a music environment. As Enid says,

> I bought it [bass guitar] second-hand out of my paper round, it was thirteen pounds, I was very shocked that it only had four strings, 'cos I thought that all guitars had six.[87]

Gina Birch's first purchase was spontaneous:

> I bought my first bass guitar in the beginning of 1977. I had no musical education...there were very few female bands around but a band called The Slits had started to play and I was so amazed and so wanted to do this when I saw them. I was at an Art and Politics conference at the Acme Gallery and it was just near Charing Cross Road where all the guitar shops are. So at lunchtime I went for a couple of drinks and when I came out of the pub I just walked straight into a guitar shop and bought a really cheap nasty brown bass guitar, took it home, and sprayed it with some sparkly car spray paint.[88]

There was a considerable degree of determination and initiative present in Southampton's sixth-form band The Catholic Girls, as Lucy O'Brien explains:

> My keyboards were actually assembled from a kit that was made by the keyboard-player from another punk band (who had a bit of a crush on me at the time). I'd saved up, I had a Saturday job and I'd saved up for this new synthesizer, and it was really exciting because synthesizers were just coming into play then, synthesizers were the new big thing... One of the big instruments was the drum kit. 'Cos we were all in the sixth form we didn't have a lot of money between us so we used to make cakes and earrings and things at school and sell them and with the money from that we got a drum kit on hire purchase and paid I think it was about nine pounds a week, or maybe it was less. So we gradually assembled our instruments.[89]

Bands whose members had jobs had more money to spend on musical equipment; some felt embarrassed by this, due to the poverty ethos of punk, and would go to great lengths to disguise their relative wealth, as Mavis Bayton reveals:

> Within a few weeks we said, "Let's get equipment." We looked at the ads in the paper. We bought a whole band's equipment – it was

> really rubbish – for a hundred pounds. Mic stands, harmonicas, eve-
> rything, it was really rubbish. Me and the mandolin-player shared an
> amp together, it was an old valve amp. It was really difficult sharing.
> Then after six months we thought, "Let's get our own gear then." I
> remember I went from this really crap guitar to a Les Paul. I was kind
> of embarrassed to have a Les Paul, and that was 'cos I had a job, I was
> teaching and I had the money to do it. I had the definite impression
> that a Les Paul just wasn't very punk. So I put elastoplast all over the
> Les Paul and sort of stuck stickers on it so it looked a bit nasty 'cos I
> thought it looked too posh.[90]

More unusually perhaps, Lesley Woods of The Au Pairs persuaded her father to buy her a guitar at the age of seventeen when she joined a club band:

> I first got an electric guitar because after I got into writing songs with
> an acoustic guitar I actually joined a group, a social club outfit who
> would go round social clubs, like labour clubs, singing (sings) "Hey
> hey Paul, I've been waiting for you; Hey, hey Paul I want to marry you
> too..." that sort of really corny thing! That's when I got my first elec-
> tric guitar, 'cos I played with them. My dad bought it for me – a very,
> very bad, bad, bad, cheap, nasty electric guitar! (*Wasn't this unusual
> at the time?*) Yeah, but they insisted. I was the only girl. All I remember
> is that my Dad went and bought me an electric guitar. Maybe I was
> lying when I said they told me that they needed me to play the electric
> guitar![91]

I found that everybody who responded to my questionnaires had displayed considerable determination in order to acquire their instruments; the following replies show the variety of sources that supplied instruments for women players. For example it could be a gift from a friend, as, for instance, in the case of female drummer S.B., from Autonomy, north of England: "Mostly the drum kit was given by a friend – a very old, knackered Salvation Army drum kit. I bought a few bits for it from local musicians, classifieds, etcetera." An instrument might also be bought through the diversion of savings intended for another purpose, as for bass-player Suzanne Long, in Gateshead: "We were planning to get married and we had saved £100 and he insisted I bought a bass with the money as there was one in a sale for £112. It was an Ibanez Blazer bass." Factory work at unsocial hours could accrue enough money to pay for a bass. M.H. from The Passage, Manchester, wrote: "I bought my first bass guitar by working nights in a factory, chosen with Gus Gangrene of The Drones (ugh!)." Instruments might also be bought second-hand or borrowed: M.H.'s sister L.H., who was a synth-player in the same band, writes, "Bought the Vox (amplifier) and borrowed the synth from Dick Witts." Poor-quality equipment could be bought cheaply – E.T., of The Syphletix in Hounslow, played a bass that was "Bought for £5!" – or bought in instalments: Sian Treherne, of the band Scream and Scream Again, in Gloucester, bought her bass guitar from "a catalogue! Needless to say it was not a 'name make' but I could pay weekly!" Finally, one woman eventually had a guitar made by an enthusiastic friend: Vi Subversa, guitarist with Poison Girls, told me, "I bought one second-hand in Brighton. I don't recall it particularly – I remember it was too heavy for me and I eventually found a guitar comfortable for me. Richard [Famous] *made* me a superb one which accommodated my curves."[92]

Trading also could enable a musician to acquire a large and expensive piece of "kit":

> I had a car, a Renault 10, and the water pump broke, and I thought the car was finished. My brother, who never missed an opportunity to make money, knew that I wanted a guitar amp and he said, "If you give me the car I'll buy you a guitar amp." And he bought me this great combo H&H which I thought was fantastic.[93]

The First Gigs

Like musical amateurism, finding gigs was an issue that held both advantage and disadvantage for girls in bands. Girls playing instruments in bands have continually been seen as a novelty by promoters, and indeed by almost all facets of the music industry, and within punk there was a dual ethic of promoting bands with women members, first, because they would draw crowds (men perhaps to gawp, women perhaps to admire) and, second, because of the ideological clout one would acquire. The supportive nature of local scenes, whether through Women's Centres (Mavis Bayton), sibling encouragement (Rachel Bor), mentoring (Vi Subversa and various other women), or just being "on the punk scene" (Liz Naylor, June Miles-Kingston, Rhoda Dakar) meant that the first step to live performance often bypassed a more normal way of getting a live gig – sending a demo tape. The atmosphere of facilitation was quite different from the competitive situation that exists when venues are scarce and audiences for live music are dwindling. An important potential hurdle, that of getting past the entry-level live gatekeeper, was thus avoided. Much has been made of Siouxsie and the Banshees' first gig, in which they performed an extended version of 'The Lord's Prayer' – it is tempting in retrospect to regard this as part of punk mythology, but the examples below show how frequently the rules of access were broken or pushed aside; as punk poet Attila the Stockbroker told me, it was expected that a band would ask to perform at another band's gig, and to refuse was to seem unreasonable. Hester Smith's comments about Dolly Mixture bear this out:

> We didn't really need a lot of help [to get gigs], we found it quite easy... We used to go to gigs and then just go up to the bands and say, "Can we support you?," and they usually said yes – I think they were just intrigued. Or we would go to colleges if we heard of any students who had bands, we'd go and visit them and say, "Can we play with you?" We were quite, you know, forward in that way. Just anyone, we'd ask if we could play.[94]

The audience was usually prepared to accept whatever was on offer: Stuart Home has commented that he was often unaware of the line-up of bands before he went to a gig; he just went along for the experience.[95] This attitude was typical of people attending gigs at this time, and was displayed by the promoters I spoke to. For instance, Christine Robertson, who started promoting punk gigs at various venues in Reading when she was at university there, describes the nature of gigs in Reading at this time:

> The reason I was promoting concerts was because there were no good concerts being put on in our locality, it was just stuck in a time warp, and this was a way of addressing my need for good music.
> *How did you find bands?*
> I used to come to London a lot. It was more something that was in the air – there were a lot of people thinking along similar lines somehow; and it didn't matter whether it was a successful punk band or something that was unknown. It was whether a band was available for the gig and if they were someone you'd vaguely heard of in that scene – so it was very much events based.[96]

Attila organized gigs at the University of Kent, and describes the young promoters' willingness to gamble at the time:

> The scene in Canterbury was mainly based at the University because we had the venues. I'd go to London and see bands and it would be their first gig and I'd ask them to play, and I booked them. [Once] the Gay Society asked me to organize something. I booked this band for fifty quid to play one of the venues. By the time the gig arrived they were on the front page of the *Melody Maker* and *NME*. The Gay Society were really chuffed with it, they made loads of money.[97]

Christine Robertson continues:

> I can't remember a lot of the bands that I saw. You always remember
> the key ones that went on to be famous. I saw *loads* of bands, *loads*
> of bands; some of the support acts we had were really, really good
> and perhaps never got the audience they deserved... There was a real
> proliferation.[98]

It can be surmised from these comments that there was no preconception
about what a band would sound like or look like, as long as they could provide an experience for the audience. Musical competence, gender, style and
content were arbitrary; the audience was expected to be open-minded. This
was very much a feature of early punk (the so-called "first wave") and allowed
unusual bands to take to the stage.[99] Sometimes, a party would provide the
setting for the first gig, and this would not only lead to other bookings, but
also provide the vitally important factor for any successful band at the time –
a local following. This is what started the performing careers of Dolly Mixture,
and The Mistakes:

> It was at a party in a hall. I don't know if it was like this when you
> were growing up, but there just seemed to be parties every weekend.
> Somebody would hire a hall, you wouldn't necessarily have to know
> them but everybody went. It was one of those. When this woman
> heard that we were going to form a band she said, "Oh, you can play
> at my party." So we had two or three weeks to get ready to play our
> first gig. Just this hall in Cambridge, a church hall.[100]
>
> The first gig we did was the party of a friend and we thought that
> would be a safe environment to come out as a band in. We had a
> following from day one; there were just so many people...what was
> important was the following. We were a breath of fresh air: within
> eight weeks of forming we played outdoors to one-and-a-half thou-
> sand people in the open air festival, the annual Mayfly, down by the
> river, and the organizer of that had heard about us, so we were cata-
> pulted onto that, really.[101]

Frequently, planning the first gig provided the stimulus for formally writing the first songs, taking the band from being just an idea to the reality of live
performance. For The Catholic Girls,

> The first gig was sort of by accident as often happens with punk things.
> We'd just about scraped together all the instruments between us. I
> think Judith had just bought her bass guitar from Woolworth's really
> cheap. There were some male friends of ours who had heard that

"there's this all-girl band, we'll get them to support us," 'cos they had a gig at a place called The Joiners Arms (which actually I've noticed is still on the circuit). So they just rang us and said, "We've got a gig for you," and we thought, "Oh shit, we'd better write some songs!," so we just got about three songs together in as many days and just got up on stage and it was the most frightening experience of my life – but I was hooked from then on.[102]

The Catholic Girls, used by kind permission of Mark Baker

Bands would do gigs further afield from their local area en masse, sharing transport, equipment and moral support. Lucy continues:

There were about four or five local bands in Southampton and we all would do gigs together and support each other, and gigs around the south coast and maybe a few in London; it was quite a tight-knit little scene really.[103]

There was an advantage to shared gigs for the beginner bands – three songs are not enough for a full band set, as bass-player G.S. acknowledges:

We shared some equipment, like PA systems, with other local bands, and did joint gigs, which helps when you don't have much material![104]

The smallness (and sometimes the oppositional nature) of the scene, even in a large city like Manchester, often meant that bands clumped together and encouraged each other almost as a show of strength. Liz Naylor says:

> Manchester at that time was really small; it was a tiny musical community and if you say to people, "Of course I knew Joy Division," it's nothing – they were just blokes you sat with. So we supported The Fall on lots of dates, it didn't mean anything to us. In a way we took it seriously because we thought we were great – I mean, we were appalling, but we didn't think of it as a career, it was just an experience, and we were there. Me and Cath [Carroll, later to become a journalist] thought we were kind of somebody in this tiny Manchester scene and our band was just the thing we did.[105]

In Leeds, there was a loose community of musicians that included The Gang of Four, The Mekons and The Delta 5 and who were connected by friendship and a common interest in music. The most successful of these bands, The Gang of Four, facilitated the activities of the others; Bethan Peters describes the way this worked:

> I was at the Polytechnic doing art stuff, Ros [second bass-player] was doing Fine Art at the University and the guys were doing other stuff. Jools [vocalist] was just a friend. The Gang of Four had a rehearsal space and we just went in and used the space; they'd finish rehearsing in the evening and we'd pick the stuff up! We borrowed Dave Allen, bass-player from The Gang of Four, as our first drummer, John Langford from The Mekons as our guitarist and we just sort of did five or six songs...our first gig was supporting Gang of Four...
>
> Then Gang of Four signed with EMI so we tended to get studio time; their manager Rob Ewer was the one who got us into studios. After they had finished recording in the Old Kent Road we went in there 'cos EMI didn't want to sign us...it all sort of happened quite effortlessly though I don't know where my head was at the time. It was like a gang really.[106]

For Girlschool, their recognizably heavy-metal style meant that a gig circuit already existed, and this gave them a great advantage over punk or new-wave bands whose music may have challenged the ears of promoters. Enid adds:

> It was a big help being female in the sense of getting gigs – because it was like, great! women on stage, or girls on stage as they would see it, we'll pull the punters in, you know, it was a little bit of a novelty; it made us stand out. It was definitely a help in terms of getting

> work and in terms of getting publicity in the music press. But it was
> a hindrance in terms of being taken seriously. We got an agent in '78
> who got us lots and lots of gigs. So he was helpful in the sense of we
> wouldn't have been working if he hadn't been getting us gigs...but it
> was just business; he wasn't pro female bands or anything like that. It
> was just that he thought we were sellable[107] and he could get us work.
> I don't think that was any different to a male band that would have an
> angle or something.[108]

The above shows that promoters were keen on the "sellable" (gimmicky)
aspect of all-female bands. For some bands, early exposure to the music press
accelerated their progress from a local to national profile within a matter of
weeks. Dolly Mixture progressed rapidly:

> Our fourth gig was at the Cambridge Corn Exchange.[109] I think it was
> The Fall and Kevin Rowland's band and The Nips. Somehow we got
> on the bill and the *NME* were there and they gave us a really, really
> good review and after that it was really, really easy – there were a
> lot of people interested in us in Cambridge, interested in managing
> us. There just seemed to be a lot of interest in what we were doing,
> everywhere. We were very, very lucky; it was easy.[110]

Penetration benefited for a while from being the only punk band in the north-
east, and were invited to support the more nationally well-known bands as
they toured and played the larger venues in Newcastle upon Tyne:

> We used to get all the supports up here because there were no other
> bands like us. So we supported The Stranglers very early on, we did
> three nights at the Marquee with The Vibrators, we just played with
> lots of the bands that were coming up here.[111]

In London, the bands had progressed in a similar way. Tessa describes the ease
with which The Slits started touring:

> The Pistols helped us, The Clash helped us on the White Riot Tour.
> They offered to take us on board with them. I think Don Letts had to
> pay Bernie Rhodes to take us, 'cos he just saw it as trouble. The coach
> driver had to be bribed to have us on the coach, but the actual groups
> themselves were very supportive, partly because Mick [Jones, of The
> Clash] had a relationship with Viv, and likewise Joe [Strummer] with
> Palmolive, so they were all close friends anyway.[112]

The Modettes also found themselves touring very soon after getting together
as a group:

> Kate said, "Well, I know some other people, that we could get to-
> gether," and we started to get together with Jane and she had met
> Ramona, the singer, and she brought Ramona down, and within
> about three months we were off, touring! Joe gave us a spot, Mad-
> ness gave us a spot, Siouxsie gave us a spot, just supporting all these
> people at this great time... And then we just started playing gigs off
> our own back.[113]

For The Bodysnatchers, it was almost as if the space already existed for them to play; they were the only all-female band who could fit into the Two Tone category, starting with punk characteristics and idealism, but falling much more into the category of early Two Tone:

> It was mad: the second gig we did, Jerry [Dammers] turned up and
> offered us the second Two Tone Tour pretty much right there. We
> kind of got into it straight away.[114]

They were fortuitous in their choice of boyfriends, as guitarist Sarah-Jane explains:

> Both Stella and I had boyfriends that were gigging the London circuit.
> It was Stella's boyfriend who leaked our debut gig at the Windsor Cas-
> tle to the press... The word was out that an all-girl ska band was going
> to play, so we were all surprised when most if not all of The Selecter
> and The Specials showed up, led by Jerry Dammers who wanted to
> sign us up for a major tour supporting his bands.[115]

Others were propelled even further afield: after a few gigs playing local pubs "treading where the 101'ers[116] had played before," The Raincoats played a pub in West London called the Chippenham:

> There was this guy over from Warsaw who was organizing this inter-
> national performance art festival...they liked us so much they invited
> us to go to Poland...so off we go...the fourth, fifth, sixth and seventh
> gig I ever did were in Warsaw.[117]

The Influence of Seeing The Sex Pistols

There is no doubt that Malcolm McLaren's project succeeded in galvanis-ing young people into making music, and in the group of women that I interviewed for the second edition of this book; Shanne Bradley had been brought up in St Albans and saw the group at the art school there in 1975:

That's how I got drawn into the whole thing. It wasn't called Punk. We were wearing the same sort of thing; I had short spiky hair after a peroxide accident with henna, and a lot of piercings, and holsters and ripped-up fishnets and ice-skating boots and stuff from Oxfam shops.

And McLaren was there and they were just like yeah, you gotta come to the shop and [they] just started inviting me to everything, it was synchronicity or something. It was November 75, just after Halloween. They had played at St Martins the week before and it was their second gig, they just came along and gate-crashed. They had some plan to play all the art schools. And we just laughed at them because we thought they were piss-taking, a sort of 60s band. I got into them more when I saw them after that.[118]

The attitude of the band proved infectious for Viv Albertine:

I think I'd seen the Pistols once, and having seen the Pistols, I *knew*; I immediately got it. It wasn't about how well you play; it was about you've got something to say that no-one else is saying. And I utterly got that: otherwise I'd never have thought in a million years of buying a guitar because I couldn't play, and I'd never played, and I didn't consider myself a musician. But it was just so liberating seeing the Pistols because I thought "Oh, you don't have to be a musician, you just have something you desperately want to say and the bollocks to get up and say it."[119]

Pauline Murray had seen one of the earliest gigs in Yorkshire:

The first time it was in Northallerton and it was in a night club, it was just full of ordinary Saturday night punters and they came on and it was just hilarious, it was just funny. It was the attitude, you know, we're just doing it and we don't care what you think, I mean that's a really liberating attitude because people are frightened to do things because they are worried about what will other people think and that's quite restricting. We really don't care what you think, we're gonna have a go anyway, we've got some good ideas and we're young.[120]

Therefore it can be seen that a combination of circumstances – inspiration from barrier-breaking role models, the "time being right," easy access to equipment and gigs, help from boyfriends, and a continued interest in, and support for, new bands from an eager and tolerant audience – elevated these women to an unprecedented level of self-expression in musical performance. It is interesting to note how few of the women I spoke to had *no* musical skill: some of them, such as Lucy O'Brien, transferred existing skills to a similar instrument. Others had picked up skills, or at least enabling ideas, from the school system or home musical environments. Some of the bands, like Dolly Mixture and, later, The Marine Girls, were "user-friendly" and almost gentle and child-like in their style; others' music, for instance that of The Slits, was sometimes downright aggressive, but just as inspirational to the women (and men) who came to see them. The attitude of the press, in particular the music press – the "inkies"[121] – was to play an important part in the way bands with women players were received. As the punk bands moved from subcultural to mainstream consciousness, from local to national audiences, they began a real engagement with national media institutions.

2 Media Gatekeepers and Cultural Intermediaries

New Musical Express, 29 June 1978, p. 3, "News Desk," features separate photographs of three female bass-players: Gaye Black from The Adverts, Tina Weymouth [from Talking Heads] and Gislaine of The Killjoys, whom it says has split up; all are playing bass guitars. These are the only photos on this page.

Some male commentators regarded the influx of high-profile women into their rock world of gigs, radio, print and recording with bafflement, for these women did not seek out male approval for their activities. Such approval was seen as a necessary evil in order to pass through the various stages that led to a platform for expression of musical and political ideas, for in order to be consumed, disseminated and publicized, or in any way to communicate, youth music must pass through a filter; this may take the form of a media or record company gatekeeper, in which case aesthetic decisions are involved, or a potentially less judgemental intermediary. This chapter will examine the unusual engagement at this time of these gatekeepers and intermediaries, with the musicians, with reference to the weekly music press, small record labels and the *John Peel Show*. The industrial hazards experienced by women musicians in the music industry are also explored at the end of this chapter, as there is more to gatekeeping than simple aesthetic judgement in print and other media: sexual availability is an implicit concern in the promotion of female artists. Later in the book, the idea of "appearance" will be investigated further.

The Rock Press

The authenticity granted to punk musicians by the audience's perception of them as "learning on stage" and "just like me" (and, in some cases, their "refusal of expertise"[1]) could help female instrumentalists greatly, although this was often misinterpreted by rock journalists. For instance, during my research I found that both Tina Weymouth (from US band Talking Heads) and Gaye Black (from UK band The Adverts) were alternately patronized and scolded for the simplicity of their playing by rock newspapers such as *Sounds, Melody Maker* and the *New Musical Express*.

However, gradually, over a series of gigs by each of the bands, journalists began to realize that not only were the simple bass lines intentional, but they were an integral part of the music that the band was playing and that the reviewer was enjoying.[2] It is also interesting to follow the reassessment of musical skills according to the gender of the reviewer (although sometimes female reviewers were tougher than males). For instance, consider the patronizing male reviewer, writing about Talking Heads' bass-player, Tina Weymouth:

> Tina has short blonde hair and black jeans and looks sexy like a girl on a tennis court...it's only Tina who fills out the sound with her strong bass line. She has a nice new red and white bass and jerks her head with every beat, worriedly checking first her fingering and then making sure she is playing the correct string. Sometimes she glances anxiously over to David to make sure everything's okay... When Tina left the stage her blouse was sticking to her back – a sign of something.[3]

The "we can tolerate incompetence if the woman is sexy" style of review was very common and was often applied to Gaye Black.[4] Her photograph would frequently appear next to small news items or gig dates (often without her bass guitar, thus rendering her a less threatening pin-up punk). For instance, there are marked similarities between the above review and this one about Gaye:

> Gaye Advert [sic] – a far more appealing punkette than any of The Slits – provides point of visual attention (A). Oh to be gazed upon by those sultry, tempting eyes which Gaye fixes on the audience at least two or three times during every number. No more than two or three times mind you, because Gaye likes to look at her bass very hard because she doesn't know how to play it very well yet, and so it helps if she watches where she puts her fingers. Her playing is just about okay.[5]

Compare this with the more thoughtful female reviewer, who has reassessed Gaye's playing abilities:

> ...which brings me to my biggest realisation of the gig – that Gaye's bass playing is far from the hilarious joke one has been led to believe, since she's graduated from her initially fearful and delicate finger placement to an adequately ballsy attack.[6]

In order to retaliate, the female reviewer has had to pull Gaye into the male arena: rather than discuss her musicianship, by describing her playing style as "ballsy" and using the word "attack" she is praising the fact that Gaye has transcended her gender to achieve, through aggression, the status of an honorary man! Lucy Green has noted the advantages that the punks' "disdain for musical technicalities" had for female instrumentalists;[7] however, Gaye Black was expected by many reviewers to be technically better at playing bass than a male player in the same context, since she had the audacity to appear on stage alongside male musicians to whom they thought punk rock belonged.[8] June Miles-Kingston told me that bands like The Mo-dettes were in a relatively much stronger position because:

> It's almost like a jungle thing – having four women together they are quite strong. But if you're one woman, in a male domain, you're weaker. We came across as like The Slits, sort of strong, you don't mess with us, 'cos we're a gang all together and we've got you sussed. Whereas one woman in a predominantly male band probably looked as though they were out on a limb a bit, and it's like picking the weaker thing off.[9]

Gaye Black and Tim Smith, The Adverts. Photographer Ian Dickson

Gaye is described as a "punkette" by the male reviewer in order to reinforce the impression that she is trespassing on male territory. I asked her how she felt about being the press focus as the only female member of the band, and she replied:

I didn't like it at all, and it caused friction in the band, because the drummer resented it. I really didn't want that because what I liked about bands was the songs, not what sex they were. I didn't particularly want to be "a female in a band," but it's just that I hadn't got any choice really! People drawing attention to it all the time was a bit annoying. I never had the urge to dress in pretty frocks and things and make the most of it – I just liked to keep my head down and get on with it. Constantly having pictures taken while the others could go off and do other things, [I'd think] oh no, not again! When the first single came out it just had a picture of me on the cover. I was so annoyed that for the second single I refused to be on it and so they had the rest of the band – and my bass! I was more of a sitting target when I was doing gigs. I could run away the rest of the time.[10]

She was not the only female instrumentalist to be singled out and denigrated with this label; a gig by Manchester band The Passage at Goldsmiths College was reviewed in this way by journalist Geoff Hill:

As for the punkette on keyboards – she looks a bit of a goner. Poker face, poring over a musical score on the dashboard; limp-wristed, decidedly non-percussive perusal of the ivories... It gives the whole sound an erie [sic] quality however which presumably matches up to their intentions.[11]

Zillah Ashworth, who still performs with punk band Rubella Ballet, articulates her feelings about the way the press stereotyped male and female roles in the punk scene:

They changed the word "punk rocker" to "punkette" for girls. None of us were "punkettes." They tried to devalue the whole thing by trying to split it into punk girls and punk men, whereas everybody was just in the same scene... when I was becoming a punk in '75, [there was] a sort of universal mind.[12]

Dale Spender has noted the way that "ette" is added to the description of a person's occupation if they are female, and explains why:

Masculinity is the unmarked form: the assumption is that the world is male unless proven otherwise... [a woman] must signify that the norm, the positive, does not apply and so she becomes a lady doctor, a female surgeon, a woman lawyer, or else, in less prestigious occupations, a waitress, a stewardess, a majorette.[13]

Whatever encouragement was happening "on the street," thus defined, the bands were coming up against mostly male gatekeepers in the form of music press journalists,[14] or sometimes even female gatekeepers who wrote in malespeak. An example of this is the following review of Lesser Known Tunisians at Dingwalls in London by Sue Denom: "This is a band that attempts to shock shock shock – their girl lead guitarist has even grown a moustache";[15] she carries on to review the band Babylon, playing on the same bill, as follows:

> Babylon used to be The Sadista Sisters. Lady bass player, lady vocalist/ front woman. Male guitarist, male keyboards, and I couldn't see the drummer... If you want to see The Little Ladies[16] live go to see Babylon. Tough little woman, you're almost a man. I'm getting sick of female musicians trying to play like men... – good musicians though.[17]

A strong element in the rock newspapers (*NME, Sounds* and *Melody Maker*) felt that female instrumentalists were just a gimmick.[18] This was part of a continuous debate in the music press during the early months of punk, in which both male and female reviewers adopted challenging stances regarding the "girls in bands" issue. For instance, Julie Burchill (*NME*) was against whereas Vivien Goldman (*Sounds*) was for; Phil McNeill (*NME*) was for whereas Garry Bushell (*Sounds*) was against.

After 1979, the whole punk scene fragmented into a "second wave" of proto-skinhead punk (dubbed "Oi" by its champion Garry Bushell): art-punk bands such as The Raincoats, Gang of Four and Scritti Politti; overtly feminist bands such as Jam Today; and the more mainstream "new wave" bands such as Elvis Costello and the Attractions and Squeeze. This fragmentation of subcultures had happened before – Hebdige documents the breakdown of the Mod subculture into smaller scenes with different taste characteristics.[19] In the case of punk, the separation of the different elements later allowed the "rock" part to be reclaimed by adolescent males.[20]

In each paper a debate was being held at editorial meetings about the worth of punk rock itself. Caroline Coon describes the difficulties she had in persuading her colleagues at *Melody Maker* that something new was happening in music:

> ...not only I was a woman (and therefore they weren't taking me seriously), but I was telling them there was something quite threatening occurring. I thought this was going to be the new defining counterculture, which was coming after hippies; it was the cultural dialectic, the reaction against the perceived failure of hippiedom.[21]

Within this debate, which essentially reflected the hippy generation's realization that they had now become the establishment, there was therefore an added discomfort about the influx of women into punk and new wave. In an attempt to put women in their place, editors would sometimes go to extreme lengths to "undo" the appreciation a female artist had earned; for instance, the *NME* included a couscous recipe by respected rock poet Patti Smith (it had never published a recipe before), and finished the feature with the following: "Joe Stevens, our man in New York, pronounced the couscous delicious and added that Patti could roast his raisins anytime."[22] She therefore exists as defined by male journalists and editors for the consumption of the male reader, who can rest assured that she possesses culinary skills as well as revolutionary ones. As Sally Potter observes:

> "Femininity" demands the appearance of lack of skill and emphasises nurturance and appreciation of the skills of men... success for women often means gaining the precarious position of token achiever in a male-dominated profession. This position is circumscribed in such a way that as more women achieve in a given area they are forced to compete with each other for the same space rather than the space itself expanding.[23]

The "lack of skill" of these punk instrumentalists did not always go hand-in-hand with femininity, however. (And the competition for "space" caused problems which will be discussed shortly.) Many of these women did not care about being sexually alluring. Caroline took The Slits' album (on the cover of which they were photographed naked from the waist up, and covered in mud) to Richard Williams, her editor at *Melody Maker*, because she wanted to write about it; his response was to declare, "Take it away from me. How can they do that? They look so revolting and so fat."[24] However, there was also a strong groundswell of written opinion that criticized the macho attitudes of rock that were being carried forward into punk music. The Stranglers in particular were singled out for criticism; they were slightly older than many of the other punk bands and used the standardized rock rebellion of misogynistic lyrics to make their statement.[25]

It is interesting to note that, at the other end of the scale, Lucy Toothpaste was having trouble convincing her colleagues at *Spare Rib* that punk could provide a platform for young women as well as young men to express themselves:

> In 1977, feminist music was still very much dominated by American, acoustic, folky duos; though when I got involved with *Spare Rib* we did review all sorts of kinds of music, but there was this whole thing at the

beginning of punk [that] most feminists found very threatening and unpleasant, and just assumed it was just as macho as all the rest of rock music and so were very hostile to it. I was one of the first people to challenge the *Spare Rib* collective with the idea that punk wasn't all the same as the rest of rock music and it had a lot of positive elements, notwithstanding some of its more negative elements, but there was definitely hostility and suspicion. I don't mean hostility to me, there was hostility to the idea of it. [26]

However, regardless of how male reviewers felt, the foregrounding of women musicians in the music press provided instant role models for girls who had had none beforehand; in the case of Girlschool, who played "male" music in a recognizable and less aurally challenging style than some of the bands at the time, reviewers were aware that they were writing about a band who played a discernible genre of music very competently. Enid Williams thought the writers must have enjoyed being part of the band experience:

We had quite a few journalists who gave us some great reviews. They liked the band and hopefully wrote what they thought. One of the reasons that people liked us was that we were very friendly with journalists, it wasn't some kind of political manoeuvre or anything, it's just that we were young, outgoing...it was like a big family thing, like let's have a laugh, everyone can join in; journalists would just jump in the back of the van with us, have a few drinks and let's have a party. Robbi Millar liked the band and wrote good things about us and there were other male journalists, although with her it was slightly different 'cos she did have a female perspective on it. We did have other male journalists, perhaps for slightly different reasons, that were equally supportive.[27]

Sometimes, it was difficult for bands to manage the effects of media coverage internally, and this could lead to jealousy and occasionally exclusion. For instance, I was aware, playing bass in a mixed band, that the band received a certain amount of extra attention because of my presence. This led to jealousy and sometimes physical aggression, at the same time as rudeness from some quarters: on one occasion, *Sounds* sent a photographer to our house for a shoot, and he referred constantly to "the girl" without ever talking to me directly or using my name. None of the members of my band took him to task for this. Playing band-members off against each other was a constant tactic of the press especially, it seems, with mixed-gender bands, and often led to so much tension within the band that it split up. This was a problem across the spectrum. Nico, from The Velvet Underground, remarked, "They had some personality problems, they wanted to get rid of me because I had more attention in the press. Well, that's how it went";[28] a review of a gig by The Damned, The Adverts and Fruit-Eating Bears noted the following about TV Smith, guitarist and songwriter with The Adverts:

> [H]e has to keep moving, otherwise Gaye Advert [sic], in precarious black jacket and glowing trousers, smouldering motionless beside her amp at the back of the stage, would be the focus of attention.[29]

In yet another example, this time from Tony Parsons, a comparison is made between two artists who operate in different musical genres, seemingly just because they are women:

> ...Patti Smith is still unable to stifle her tiresome predilection for indulging in lengthy bouts of flagellatory calisthenics [sic] on that dreaded instrument of hers, her wretched guitar. Crouched over her dull axe like Quasimodo on a Bert Weedon course for butter-fingered beginners, Patti sadistically scrubs the cursed frets with such obsessive frenzy that...you conclude she's not trying to affirm her undisputable [sic] virtuosity, she's merely making sure Harry Debbie [sic] don't get too far ahead in the glamour stakes by having a manicure.[30]

The tensions of being in a band are great enough without external judgements upsetting the balance of power within a band, and this is exacerbated when there are gender issues to take into consideration as well as "normal" tensions. Lora Logic experienced the ill-effects of excessive media praise when Poly Styrene could not cope with sharing the limelight with another woman:

> Once this journalist called Jane Suck in Sounds, she wrote, "Lora Logic is X-Ray Spex," and that was it – I had to go after that one. The manager just wanted to keep her happy; it was working, it was a happening band, and I was quite dispensable. So they replaced me with a male saxophone-player, and I was devastated. It was my whole life. I was very, very upset, and so I was not going to have anything more to do with this horrible music business, so I went to St Martin's College of Art to study photography.[31]

This is an illustration of Potter's observation about competition for space. Gender politics are such that it is possible that Jane Suck may have known what the result of her review might have been; there is a very controlling relationship between rock reviewers and the bands they review, particularly when the band is relatively inexperienced. Luckily, Poly and Lora later resolved their differences and have worked together since.

It often seemed to me at the time that the people who came to interview the band I was in (The Chefs) wanted to actually be involved in the music itself as much as mediating it; perhaps the number of journalists who became performers reflects this factor (among others at this time, Chrissie Hynde, Giovanni Dadomo, Mark Perry).

The Radio

After gaining attention via the music press, the next step for most bands was to make a record and then try to attain radio play. Making a record, even on a small label, brought bands to a new audience and was a seal of approval that allowed them to move a stage further, whether this was more gigs, or radio play; there is an obvious symbiosis between youth music radio and records that reflect changes in youth culture. In order to achieve radio play, a recording must be made, whether this takes the form of a session (which may lead to a recording deal, as it did in the case of Siouxsie and the Banshees) or a record on a small label. Recordings were the passport to radio play, which would increase live audiences and therefore offers of gigs.[32] Sometimes this could be relatively easy. As Enid Williams says:

> We had an old friend who we met down the local youth club a few years earlier who started a little record label, as happened at that time, and he was very helpful in the sense that if we hadn't had that first record we wouldn't've gone on tour, but again it was kind of a business thing, it wasn't that he was rooting for us.[33]

The influence of Radio 1 DJ John Peel was tremendous for all punk and proto-punk bands, and especially so for the girls. John Peel and his producer John Walters regularly attended punk gigs at venues such as the Vortex and the Roxy, and were both aware that there was an unusual tolerance and support from the audience for girl bands at this time. As John Peel says:

> You were aware that it was the first time that it was possible for women to be in bands for reasons other than the fact that they looked cute. I mean obviously there had been women in bands prior to that, but they'd been there for novelty reasons as much as anything else I think. I suppose it was really seeing The Slits a couple of times, where you just thought... It was quite exciting really, not exciting in a sexual way, you just thought about time too, really.[34]

The music policy of the BBC as a publicly funded station had to be incorruptible, according to Peel. It was not linked to the market and did not have to show commercial success nor have to please advertisers, and by playing minority-interest music, Peel and Walters were fulfilling a remit *not* to follow market forces:

> We were lucky and remained lucky because of the BBC's strange position within the market: we've never had to worry about whether things were commercially viable or not. We just put them on because we thought they were worth hearing. So a lot of the things we put on you'd know perfectly well they'd got no commercial potential what-soever. Whereas Capital or somebody would have to take that into consideration.[35]

There was opposition to their choice of music:

> The controller of Radio 1 at the time, Derek Chinnery, called John Walters in...to get an assurance from him that we weren't playing, or had any plans to play, this punk music that he'd read about in the tabloids. Walters was very happy to tell him that the last two pro-grammes we'd done had been devoted to nothing but![36]

However, Derek Chinnery was well aware of John Peel's cult status; Peel was actually being paid a loyalty payment at this time to prevent him from leaving the station. Many of the women I interviewed would not have had any sort of radio exposure had it not been for Peel and Walters. Even high-profile bands like The Slits found their music effectively censored in the UK by being ignored in playlist terms, as manager Christine Robertson told me:

> The only person that would play their records was John Peel. None of the other so-called liberal stations in this country would play them. The minute it got onto the continent it was a different matter. Then the records were played. And even more when you got onto America, the records were played. Okay, it might have been on college radio stations and so on initially, but they were exposed.[37]

Once, Peel and Walters, by "plugging" a band they liked, became actively involved in getting the band signed. The band was Siouxsie and the Banshees:

> It was Walters and myself, particularly Walters really, that got Siouxsie and the Banshees signed. They'd done two sessions for the programme before Polydor signed them. I always wondered whether their reluc-tance to sign the band was because it was fronted by a rather stroppy woman (I mean, albeit one with good legs which would have been of interest to the tabloids). We just kept putting them on the radio and saying, "This is a band that should be signed." Whenever we talked

> to people from record companies we'd say there must be somebody
> at your company who's got sound judgement. And just mentioning
> their name and probably giving them copies of the sessions on tape.
> We did play our part in that respect as well. [We didn't do it with
> other bands because] it wasn't necessary...they [The Banshees] didn't
> want to bring out their own records, and they quite wanted record
> company support.[38]

This degree of power within the BBC gave Peel and Walters the confidence to allow bands to record whole series of sessions without breaking into the mainstream charts. However, as Rachel Bor explains, their support for female bands was not unremitting, as Dolly Mixture discovered:

> We did a John Peel roadshow with my brother's band; from there he
> gave us a a session which didn't get repeated because John Walters
> hated it; he said he thought we were a mixture of The Slits and The
> Nolans. It wasn't very cool at the time.[39]

Naturally, if bands were receiving a vote of confidence by DJs on a national radio station, there would be interest from smaller record companies even if the larger ones did not have the courage or inclination to enter into a working relationship with them. This is where the independent labels came into their own, and they were given a particular boost by the Cartel, a distribution network set up by Rough Trade Records, which facilitated access to radio play.

Record Distribution and Production

Any musician's autonomy depended on disrupting several factors controlled by major record companies; one of these was the record distribution system. As Paul Taylor remarks,

> Malcolm McLaren knows that the distribution of art in the post-
> Pop era is the secret to greatness, just as the town-planners who
> redesigned London's Oxford Street after the Gordon Riots knew that
> power lay in a web of invisible control over the masses.[40]

McLaren's solution to this was to sign The Sex Pistols to major record labels EMI and, later, Virgin; for various reasons, this was not an option for most bands. The Cartel was set up by Geoff Travis as a national association of like-minded small record labels, which agreed to distribute each other's products as well as other small label records and imports:

It just seemed that the way to organize that was to develop a distribution system where you could, in a countrywide way, give people access to this stuff. That was a clear, plain plan, really. And that's what we started working on. The way that we did that was we just identified, if you like, our kind of "allies" around the country, the people who had a very like-minded vision... It became obvious because, for example, if we bought 200 copies of a single – if we bought the Pere Ubu singles in, say – they would call up and say, could we get some of those, and by the fact that they were communicating with you, you knew they were interested in the same things. And so it was five or six people. So people at Rough Trade, Richard Scott, had the idea that why don't we try to encourage people to be regional distributors, not try to make it London-centric. Try to make it very regional and empower the regions and create the possibility that bands in those regions could have somewhere relatively local that they could go and say, "Look we need help, can we plug into the system," rather than, say, if you're in York, it's a long way to London, it would be impossible to get someone to listen to you, and it's a bit of an expensive journey if you can't get in at the front door.[41]

This encouraged local music-makers to become even more productive: the "outreach" attitude of Travis was unprecedented in Britain. Travis "joined the dots" of the local companies to create a national profile for independently produced music. For Peel, it meant that he

> ... got sent an enormous number of records because people realized that you didn't have to come down to London, or come up to London, to sign up with a record label and place your future completely in the hands of some bloke that you'd never met before.[42]

It is interesting to compare the attitudes of Peel and Travis, because so many of the later all-female bands (such as The Raincoats, The Mo-dettes, The Bodysnatchers and The Marine Girls) had taken the punk ethos and moved on with it. Travis and Peel respected each other, but there were differences in their musical taste that enabled a broadening of the genre that further increased access to the dual exposure of recording and broadcasting. Peel, for instance, told me:

> I've never been that impressed by musical competence anyway. We'd gone through that whole progressive rock period with all those awful people like ELP and Yes; people when they reviewed them would emphasize their enormous musical skills but frankly I think they were grossly exaggerated. What they did with those theoreti-cal musical skills is make pompous, overblown, and extraordinarily boring music.[43]

Travis agrees, though he stresses the difference in taste between the two:

> I think the bane of music is that most of the worst music is played by the people who think they can play the best. It's a kind of punk principle which is just not accepted by the normal world. It's much more interesting to be able to play three chords well – or even three chords badly – than to be able to play thirty-nine chords perfectly... I like to do my A&R as a fan, really; if I think it's exciting and I would pay money to go and see this a lot, I'd definitely listen to that record loads. And that's my main criteria. John Peel was a lot more obscurantist than I am – I think I've got a lot more populist streak in me. I'm just a normal English bloke, it's just having belief in your own judgement. Not many people have belief in their own judgement.[44]

Both Travis and Peel were far from being "normal English blokes" and it is arguable that Travis was just as obscurantist as Peel; however, since both men have achieved almost iconic status with regard to their support for more unusual bands, it is not surprising that they might want to differentiate their respective tastes in music.

There was a non-geographical problem with distribution – that of quantity. The inability of the small labels to manufacture enough records to meet demand was a constant problem and one that I had personal experience of.[45] A band could go so far independently, with media interest and potentially high promotional possibilities, but if the company was not capable of pressing and distributing the records, the media interest would recede: most journalists and DJs do not want to be seen to have failed by promoting a record that does not achieve chart success, and for a band such as The Gymslips this could cause problems:

> It was a bit of a struggle at the beginning. We had four John Peel Sessions. When we released a single it was played on Radio 1 quite a lot and we had a lot of interviews – one in *The Guardian*, quite a few in the music papers – and they were generally quite good. The thing that let us down was the record company, because the first single that we had was on Round Table, and they were playing it quite a lot on Radio 1 in the daytime, but it just wasn't in the shops because the record company just wasn't big enough and didn't have enough money to distribute it properly.[46]

The Au Pairs resorted to label-hopping in an effort to sustain their careers by charting a single, alongside retaining a degree of autonomy. As Lesley Woods commented, it was difficult to achieve a balance between both the control a small label allowed artists to retain and their distribution problems, and the commitment demanded by the majors who had much more marketing power:

> Most record companies offer only one-off single deals or else sign you for five years and everything. We knew what we wanted in a contract, and I don't think many major labels would have been prepared to do that sort of deal. When the last single started selling we suddenly got all these phone calls from major record companies who two months previously wouldn't touch us with a barge-pole.[47]

The band's first single sold over 30,000 copies, but they still did not manage to make an impact on the singles charts. Asked by Tony Fletcher if he thought the charts were important, Chris Youle of their record company, Human Records, replied:

> Yes, and I think The Au Pairs think so too. Many record shops only order what's in the charts, which is fair enough, but it means that once you're in the charts you sell more; and then you get more airplay.[48]

The necessity for a record producer caused other problems. Band psychology is defensive; generally, bands are close-knit groups of people who have defined roles within the group. Many, though not all, record producers regard themselves as auteurs, and this attitude is not surprising given the inexperience and lack of confidence in the studio of young bands. A record label taking a gamble, and believing that records must have a particular "sound" to get airplay, would pressurize the band to use a producer. Sometimes, the ambitions of the manager would manifest themselves in this situation, which was a problem experienced by The Mistakes:

> We were trying to do this recording. Initially we had a recording contract with Oval Records and then with Twist and Shout. The manager wanted to be the producer. There was division within the band: we were all arguing about producers, and we were all arguing about sound; there was a degree of dissension. Our manager actually just left – she just stomped off – but myself and Judy Parsons (her husband was a sound engineer)... did the final mix and it got played by John Peel.[49]

For the producers, the experience could be challenging, even if they had a longstanding relationship with the band. This is what Geoff Travis found with The Raincoats; but eventually:

> Although some of Ana's things are very powerful, some of the tune-
> lessness to my ears was quite difficult to take. It worked because it
> was counterbalanced by Vicki's violin and by Gina's more melodious
> tones... Her input was very, very important. Obviously that's what
> made it magical. When we were making that record, because Mayo
> Thompson [of Red Crayola] and I produced it, it was quite difficult
> some of the time, because of that.[50]

However, Travis's attitude was very different from the "auteur" producer that
other groups had problems with; his attitude was very much in keeping with
the independent label ethos. He continues:

> The thing is that also it was two sets of amateurs next to each other, we
> weren't professional producers: that was why people asked us, so there
> wasn't any kind of mystification by speaking in technical language to
> try and bamboozle them. We were doing what they wanted; we were
> trying to get their sound, rather than trying to change them.[51]

Bayton concluded from her research that, for a woman in the studio, "lack of
confidence may cause her to lose heart since a lack of technical knowledge
and techno-jargon puts her in a position of relative powerlessness in a world
where strange abbreviations abound."[52] As a traditional male domain, the
recording studio can be actively delineated by "Man Made Language"; therefore, the active rejection of jargon by Travis had a direct positive effect on the
production relationships in the studio. The inability to describe the sound a
musician wanted to achieve could prove frustrating, as Gaye Black found:

> Unfortunately, I never got the sound I wanted to achieve on record.
> I'm not sure why; I was trying to sound like Jean-Jacques Burnel and
> it just didn't really work. I used to get really angry – sometimes I'd be
> playing it and what I was listening to sounded fine, and then when
> you heard it back it just sounded horrible. I couldn't technically say
> to people, why don't you try doing this to get that... It seemed so sim-
> ple, but I know it's not simple; I'd get really, really angry and probably
> came across as a really horrible person. I was devastated that it never
> really sounded how I wanted it to. I was such a perfectionist... Possibly
> I wanted something that I wasn't capable of achieving, even with the
> right sound; I don't know.[53]

In contrast to the experience of The Raincoats with Travis and Thompson,
Dolly Mixture had a rude awakening when they came to make records. They
had previously been in control of their activities, but found that once they
signed with Chrysalis, which was a major label, their producer was chosen for
them and they were not permitted to release one of their own songs:

We got signed to Chrysalis in 1980 and we did one single which was disastrous and they dropped us. They wouldn't let us do one of our own songs – it was a bit weird because we were just doing our own songs really. It was produced by Eric Faulkner from The Bay City Rollers, and he wanted us to do "Baby It's You." So we recorded it just 'cos he wanted us to, and they bunged that out and it was just horrible. We realized that we had no control over it and they wanted us to be sort of glamorous and do covers. We had our own style and we just liked writing pop songs and we didn't really think about the direction or anything because we were just being what we were and enjoying what we were doing, and so when people started saying, you have to be like this or we're gonna drop you, it's like, "No thanks."[54]

The Raincoats (left to right: Palmolive, Vicky Aspinall, Ana da Silva, Gina Birch). Photographer Janette Beckman

It is hard to determine whether young women had worse experiences than young men because the (predominantly male) record company personnel they were dealing with expected them, because of their gender, to be malleable as well as inexperienced. Dolly Mixture, alongside many of the less aggressively presenting female bands, had a strong streak of irony throughout their lyrics, image and general presentation that was simply not understood by many of those men who worked with them. The degree of toughness that it had taken to remain focused on their band was overlooked. As Hester Smith explains:

> Basically we demanded so much and we were quite stroppy... We did have managers, but we fell foul of them because we wanted to do it all on our own terms. We would insist on going to the record company and saying we want total artistic control; no, we're not doing covers; no, we don't want our photographs on the front; no... I think we just blew a lot of things by being like that. We were so wary of being taken for a ride because so many people would warn us about being taken for a ride. It seemed so ridiculous really, because at the same time as we were doing all this and sort of blowing our chances, we were getting all this stuff in the press about The Dolly Mixture were a disgrace to women in music because of the way we looked, and 'cos we were writing pop songs and things like that – so we absolutely couldn't win.[55]

Repeated attempts by Dolly Mixture to release what they wanted led eventually to the demise of the band, which obviously still rankles its members today. Rachel continues:

> After that we just carried on loads and loads of gigs and doing supports and tour supports and we met The Jam, and Paul Weller really liked what we were doing and said he was starting up a label so we signed to him. We met Captain[56] at the same time and he wanted to produce us, and we did two singles on Respond Records which was our own thing but it didn't work for some reason. We got a bit of radio play, but I think we were probably a bit difficult as well. We didn't get on very well with their manager. So that didn't go anywhere. Perhaps he just didn't like what we were doing. Our songs were quite commercial, but our style and everything...maybe it wasn't what a big record company would want and he couldn't see it going any further. After that we signed to a distributor who paid for us to do another single with the Captain and they also put out a double album of all our demos, which was really fun to do but that didn't go anywhere and the distributor folded, went bankrupt or something, and that was the end of that really...and that was the end of our career.[57]

Lucy O'Brien also felt that lack of planning was an inevitable consequence of the sudden nature of success at this time:

> We did a few interviews with local fanzines and I think we got one review in *Sounds* – we had a couple of songs on a compilation album called *City Walls*. We were very unsavvy about things like that. If you

were seventeen, eighteen, today you'd be much more aware of how to work it all, but we weren't, it was all just sort of by accident really, and getting gigs through a friend of a friend. We didn't have a business plan or anything like that; it was much more spontaneous really.[58]

Siouxsie and the Banshees, however, managed to remain aloof from the machinations of record companies, largely because Siouxsie herself refused to set foot in their offices.[59] The Slits, too, had a strong and uncompromising attitude to record companies:

> We were one of the first people, not just women, but people, who put artistic control in the contract with the record company. We insisted from the get-go on artistic control. Which is why, when everyone called in '77 "We wanna sign The Slits, we wanna do something," there was tons of labels who were like, "No thank you," 'cos they either wanted to cash in on some stupid gimmick, let's do a quick trashy, "Oh, the punk girls," and cash in, or they wanted to actually change us and take every artistic thing that we were and turn it to be a sort of Charlie's Angel version of what we were.[60]

Ari feels in retrospect that it was a pity that their early music never saw the light of day on vinyl:

> We didn't sign until '79 – every other punk band was signed up and we weren't because we didn't get what we wanted; we were hindered from '77 right up to '79. They wanted us to completely change, or they wanted to cash in on a stupid, gimmicky, cheap-arse trashy girl-band image, sort of crap-image...the time it was '79 a whole musical period passed which was the early, raw, punky sort of thing, and we weren't in that state any more so it turned into something different and people missed out on the early nice Slits stuff, 'cos we couldn't get a deal the way we wanted it.[61]

When The Slits did progress to a record deal, there was friction with certain personnel at Island Records. Zoe Street-Howe reports an incident in which the photographer who documented many of the punk bands' early incarnations, and who was attached to Island Records at the time, actively tried to have Viv Albertine removed from the band.[62] At this point, Dennis Bovell, their producer, stepped in and pointed out that Viv's creative contribution was a vitally important component not only in the sound of the group, but also in the way they looked. As Viv reports:

> I did most of the visual steering of The Slits, what we looked like; quite a lot of it, if not all, came through me. Palmolive was Spanish and not

totally au fait with what was going on [style-wise]; Ari was about fifteen and Tessa was very quiet. I'd been to art school. I'd been hanging
with people a lot older than me, I was aware of lots of underground
films and music; for those days we were very conscious of how we'd
appear so I took an active interest in what the photograph might be;
this photographer didn't like that. What! A woman with a point of
view? He's a very old-fashioned sort of guy. He tried to get me thrown
out of the band. He went to Island and said "You should chuck Viv
Albertine out of the band." They had a big meeting about it to throw
me out, and luckily Dennis Bovell was at the meeting and said "Are you
fucking mad?" So this is one black guy against another; probably only
Dennis could have said that. He said "Viv is the one *running* the band.
Viv *is* the band, you can't throw her out."[63]

However, most women artists faced the same problems of artistic control
and lack of planning as many of the male groups who started performing as
a result of the punk moment, compounded by the fact that they always had
to pass male gatekeepers as they progressed upwards through the hierarchy
of the record business. Peel's support in providing a broadcasting platform
and Travis's support in terms of recording were unusual; both men showed
a strong degree of independent thinking, and Peel in particular was mentioned by almost every woman artist I interviewed, or who responded to
the questionnaire, as a DJ whose radio show they listened to and as the only
DJ who offered support in the form of playing their records and offering
sessions. Only one woman instrumentalist reported that he did not help
her band: Poison Girls' Vi Subversa said, "He did not like the band." Radio 1
eventually adopted the independent sector and for a while provided daytime
radio access to the post-punk bands who released material on small labels.
Even this had been debated at management level. When Tony Blackburn was
replaced as Breakfast Radio DJ in 1980, either Dave Lee Travis or Mike Read
was to be given the job. Dave Lee Travis was a fan of US disco music, and
the big record labels in the States were poised to release a large quantity of
disco music in Britain if he should be appointed. Read, on the other hand,
took his lead from John Peel and had been presenting an early evening show
on Radio 1 that featured many of the more musically conservative of the
punk-influenced bands, most of which recorded on small British independent labels. According to producer Pete Waterman, it was the appointment of
Read that led to the burgeoning of the small-label share of the market at this
time, in addition to the continued interest in the more unusual bands that
released their material via this outlet.[64]

Finally, the position of the female performer in relation to the media can
be summed up in these words from classical composer Nancy Van Der Vate:

> When you are young and unknown you don't get knocked down by
> the press, and of course you have all sorts of hopes. On the other end
> of the spectrum, if you are well established, the critics can be very
> chary. But in the middle ground...you don't have a big enough name
> yet that critics feel they have to treat you with any particular respect.
> So the increased attention not only is sometimes uncomfortable, it
> can even be devastating. You may decide it was better being anony-
> mous.[65]

The relationship between the cultural intermediaries that facilitated the
spread of the punk music ideal across the British Isles and the bands they promoted can be summarized by the following observation by Deena Weinstein
(albeit describing the US scene):

> It is not punk music but punk mediators that deconstruct the art-
> commerce binary: record labels giving total autonomy to their
> musicians, enabling them to record with the content and in the style
> that they choose, not what some suit thinks will sell. The free-form,
> underground FM stations in the United States in the mid-sixties,
> and their college-radio offspring, are another example of such pure
> mediators, playing music that did not follow a format designed to
> grab a large demographic... Genre mediators share the artists' own
> standards and thus erase the binary opposition between art and
> commerce.[66]

Industrial Hazards

In the music business, there is an industrial hazard that is accepted as part of
the territory. For women, the frequency with which most of them encounter
this hazard can lead them eventually to give up their careers altogether. This
hazard is sexual harassment.

> *Did you ever get hassled for being a woman in a band? If so, what form did*
> *it take and how did you deal with it?*
> One memorable gig at the [Brighton and Hove] Resources Centre,
> Peter and the Test Tube Babies got very abusive about lesbians and
> feminists and started wanking on stage! So we switched the electric-
> ity off.[67]

This incident displays a feisty attitude by an older woman towards onstage harassment! Although sexual harassment is not directed solely at
females in the pop and rock world, as the exploits of Jonathan King have
confirmed, the importance of sexual availability is another area of the
lucrative music business that is under-documented. The attempts by the

press and the industry to negotiate the new-found power of female artists at this time need to be documented here, as this was a moment at which the established mores could have been renegotiated to the artists' advantage. However, sexual control is embedded in the industrial structure of the music business to such an extent that this aspect of the business did not change during the gender renegotiations that appeared to be happening during this period.

By 1976, pictures of John Peel draped with naked women had stopped appearing in *Sounds*[68] although the paper made much of reporting in a titillating fashion the advertisements for heavy-metal band The Scorpions (whose album sleeve featured a naked female child with a cut across her genitals)[69] and *Boxer*, an album that featured a naked woman whose parted legs straddled a boxing glove that appeared to be heading towards her vagina.[70] Advertisers leapt at the chance to use images of females to sell their latest guitars; *Sounds* reported on the Frankfurt Trade Fair of 1977 using an image of a model (Deborah Vaughan) in leathers playing a Gibson guitar, with the guitar lead draped round her neck, under the heading "Hardware."[71] In the same issue, there is a photograph of two naked girls, one black, one white, with guitars entitled "Ecstasy at your fingertips," used to advertise Kasuga electric guitars.[72] In other words, as soon as girl guitar bands appeared, the idea was exploited in a sexual context by admen, and the unusual achievement of becoming an instrumentalist in a rock band was recuperated and sexualized. The stereotyped female punk image was also recuperated by the very sources that had amplified the moral panic aspects of punk: Page Three girls band Blonde on Blonde was launched in the summer of 1977, its cover featuring two blonde models wearing dog collars and studs, and although record reviewers were not particularly impressed with the music, the currency of the "punk" presentation alongside the sexuality of the women ensured press coverage.[73] Perhaps the most well-documented instance of *violent* imagery in conjunction with a woman used to advertise punk music was the "Ripped and Torn" advertisement, in which Debbie Harry of Blondie appeared next to the slogan, "Wouldn't you like to rip her to shreds?" This had not been approved by Ms Harry and was later withdrawn. However, some journalists appeared puzzled by what they seemed to regard as a mixed message; Tony Parsons challenged her in an interview, calling her current stage persona "cutesy," whereas before this, when she first played in Britain in 1976, she had "sneered at the Man Must Have His Mate misogyny, her voice thick with vitriolic contempt, proud and feisty as she rejected the servile role expected from her gender." Debbie replied:

> The difference in the media's attitude to a boy or girl on stage infuriates me... If a band full of men is on stage and an audience of girls are screaming at them then everything's as it should be...but if it's a girl on stage, then suddenly everything is cheap... I was furious when I saw that fuckin' ad! I told them not to put it out anymore – and they didn't.[74]

Gaye Black had a similar problem on a smaller scale, when Stiff Records attempted to advertise The Adverts by pasting a photograph of Gaye's head onto a picture of a naked body. Mark Perry, author of the prototype fanzine *Sniffin' Glue*, recalls:

> To show you how far the music scene had not progressed [in 1977], Stiff wanted to put an ad for the album in the *Glue* featuring a picture of a topless girl with Gaye Advert's [sic] head stuck on top of it. This was their idea of a laugh. I refused to print it, obviously, and was accused of all sorts of malpractices, including having an affair with Gaye.[75]

Perry's comments reflect a change in his own thinking, however; in the first issue of *Sniffin' Glue* he starts his review of US all-female rock band The Runaways' debut album by remarking, "I've always hated girl bands, singers, etc. Rock'n'roll's for blokes and I hope it stays that way."[76] Interestingly, journalist Julie Burchill attempted to articulate the commercial exploitation of the sexuality of young women musicians with reference to the same band:

> The Runaways are presented as sex-zombies whose every breath is drawn solely to screw with, the music the mere cherry on top. They come across as acting not like teenage girls, but as how dirty old men would like teenage girls to act... Veteran Blondies guitarist Lita Ford and drummer Sandy West prove that anything boys can do, we can do better... The blame for their "jailbait morons" image, which sets them up for such easy dismissal and ridicule, lies not with them but with old man Fowley [manager Kim Fowley]. He has already said "rock and roll is dead" – so he has no business mucking around with youngsters for whom playing clean rock and roll is possibly the most life-affirming experience known. He can only contaminate them with his own cynicism.[77]

In the rock world, the position of young women was as objects of desire; in reality, their function was to sexually satisfy the rock star after a gig. The pop world was more secretive about these activities. I found that it was common for DJs, record company personnel, managers and so on to proposition young female artists. This belies Suzi Quatro's comments when reviewing the TV series *Rock Follies*, which had featured attempts to seduce the "little ladies":

> We love what we do and struggle for at least 10 years to get that first "shot at the top" and when we see a movie about ourselves that's as phoney as this, it gets on our collective TITS... It reconfirms all the mug's fantasies of dirty ladies, casting couches and sex, without ever letting them know the real truth.[78]

The situation was not helped by the wilful naïvety of artists such as Kate Bush. A talented and influential mainstream artist, posters of her wearing a tight T-shirt with visible nipples appeared on buses, hoardings and in the press, very much emphasizing her sexuality in place of her musicianship. Occasionally, Kate would indicate that she wanted people to concentrate on her music, not her physical attributes. Challenged, she remarked somewhat disingenuously, I suppose the poster is reasonably sexy just "cause you can see my tits, but I think the vibe from the face is there."[79]

Sometimes the benefits and drawbacks of being "available" are only hinted at; for instance, a female interviewer (still a relative rarity) picked up on comments made by The Adverts' drummer, Laurie Driver, about possible reasons for the insulting comments made by other journalists about Gaye's playing abilities: "Laurie's convinced some of the slagging originated in one well-known punk commentator's failure to have his evil way with Gaye..."[80] In spite of the alleged equality *within* the punk scene, traditional male attitudes prevailed as soon as one entered the "outside world" of mainstream pop. I found an early interview with Siouxsie in *Sounds*, in which she describes the way a singer could be used as "bait" to acquire success for a band, regardless of her talent or lack of it:

> I went to some interviews from *Melody Maker* ads, record producers looking for singers, and it really put me off. They made me think I'd have to be a classical-type singer to be popular...so that the general public would like you. They gave me the impression that everyone who makes it has to sleep around... The fact that I could get work by that and be paid for it and nothing be expected of me (professionally), that was, you know...[81]

These incidents are mentioned here because they were an additional pressure on the women I interviewed; most of them wanted to remain anonymous when discussing serious sexual assault, which I believe reflects the fear that these assaults engendered in the victims, and some women I spoke to decided not to participate in this book because their remembered experiences were too painful to relive. This is a pity, for I believe that the frequency with which rapes and sexual assaults occurred were (and possibly still are) a major factor in the exclusion of girls and women from rock music; this will be discussed more deeply in Chapter 4, "Noise, Violence and Femininity."

Dolly Mixture. Photographer Laurie Lewis

The punk subculture itself was supposed to change the environment for girls and young women, but in fact it did not always do this. Johnny Rotten recalls:

> I don't think anybody actually looked down on women. They were equal, and everybody was as stupid as each other. You would sort of hit women the same way you would a guy if she was taking the piss at you [sic] or spilled your drink. But it wasn't an antisex attitude or a matter of acting puritanical. People just didn't give it the same importance as it had before... It was a rebellion against the lad ethic – get drunk, pull a bird, and get around the back, wherever. The punks believed they had some sort of intellectual capacity – each and every one of them – and didn't want to slip back into that rock thing.[82]

Despite the fact that he is reported as having beaten up Vivienne Westwood,[83] later in the same book he says, "During the Pistols era, women were out there playing with the men, taking us on in equal terms... It wasn't combative, but compatible."[84] This betrays a similarly sentimental memory as that of Mark Perry; for some women, the memory is rather different. The debate was alarmingly physical on the ground. Caroline Coon reported being raped, and demeaning assaults were common; a series of such assaults could build up to an unbearable pressure, such as that reported by one interviewee:

> I remember one gig in Holland or Germany and we were walking through a seated audience, who were sitting on the floor, and I had quite a short skirt on, it was summer, an open-air gig sort of thing. And somehow this bloke sitting on the floor managed to get his hand not only up my leg, but also right under my knickers. It was appalling. It got to the stage where I just couldn't handle it and I started really creating a fuss. And they [the band] were just really belittling this, just don't be so stupid and we'll talk about it afterwards. But I was feeling really violated! It was awful, really.[85]

Attempts to be assertive could be foiled by simple insulting acts. Dolly Mixture were able to appear on *Top of the Pops* when Rachel's then partner, ex-bass-player with The Damned, Captain Sensible, released a version of "Happy Talk," a song from the musical *South Pacific*. He had asked Dolly Mixture to sing backing vocals on the recording, and when his single charted they were asked to accompany him to *Top of the Pops* to perform it on television. Because the record company asked them to wear grass skirts, they insisted on wearing their guitars so that they could show the audience that they were more than backing-singers for a novelty single. The presenter approached Rachel as she was miming a chord and said, "That's an F"; Rachel corrected him, "No, it's a G." The presenter insisted that she was playing an F, and when she refused to capitulate, he put his hand inside her skirt and pinched her backside.[86]

I spoke with a woman musician who played keyboards with many well-known punk and new wave bands at this time. Her position was that she was employed to tour and record with these bands, and as such was never a full member; she was treated appallingly by many of them, and this almost invariably took the form of sexual harassment in some form. She describes an incident involving the manager of a very successful punk band at a party, for instance:

> He cornered me in a hotel bathroom. I actually lashed out at him! Not my style, but survival instinct kicked in, I guess. He emerged backwards into the party, glasses tipping off his face, and fell on the floor. People rushed up to see if I was OK and I did a line that I have enjoyed ever since: "I'm OK, but I'm not so sure about him."

> So I left with some dignity, but was very shaken up, and it meant that future work through that channel was a no-no.

Unpleasant approaches by other road crew and managers were made to this musician on other tours, and would always "make the rest of the tour very uncomfortable." Eventually, she stopped playing altogether, and says now:

> There was never any question about musicianship, but in telling these stories you always see that question mark rising over people's heads, or suspicion that I might be bringing it on myself, or that I was over-react-ing, or that it's just whingeing. So you stop mentioning anything, and they become a silent cancer eating away at your self-confidence and enjoyment. It has taken hindsight to be certain of how it really was.[87]

It is not surprising that throughout the history of women instrumental-ists, strange strategies have been developed to cope with unwanted sexual attention. For example, trumpeter/pianist Billy Tipton who died in 1989 had pretended to be a man all her life:

> Some male musicians felt that Billy Tipton didn't have to pose as a man with a wife and adopt children to get work. But his one-time "wife" referred to an unwritten code of ethics in the jazz world as the unequivocal reason for Tipton's masquerade.[88]

The complex relationship between the selling of sexuality and the selling of pop and rock music is almost impossible to disentangle. Caroline Coon feels that women are justified in using their sexuality to sell music, because men do, but that *not* using it then becomes a hindrance:

> It was easier for the solo woman artists, adopting an acceptable sexy guise was easier than if you were going to be part of the group of musicians...you can be really sexy if you're the front singer, [but] if you're going to be the lead guitarist or the bass-player you're not nec-essarily going to want to show too much flesh. Being the band, you're going to present yourself slightly differently. And that's absolutely unacceptable... Men would accept women who negotiated sexism by being sexy. And that is valid... I'm never going to put women down for using their sexuality as a negotiating tool in the workplace. But for the musicians who weren't going to go in that direction because they were playing guitars, then they were absolutely going to be excluded.[89]

Some women I spoke to used what they perceived as male weakness to their advantage. Mel Ritter, who joined The Mo-dettes on guitar after Kate Korus left, told me:

> I was never sexually harassed but I was hit on by every male industry exec (apart from the gay ones) I ever came in contact with. I think the myth that if you sleep with someone you will get ahead had been so perpetuated that the male execs were always hoping and expecting to get laid. They would always be very flirtatious and openly let it be known that they were available if you wanted them sexually. They were always hinting and hoping that you would think it would help your career. My way of handling it was to let them think they MIGHT (ha, ha) get lucky, in order to keep them on their toes, but I never felt obligated in any way.[90]

Many women told me that rumours on the "no smoke without a fire" basis caused them problems within the industry; just being seen talking intently with an industry executive could start a phantom relationship that became a more important talking-point within industry circles than the business in hand. There was always an undercurrent of threat, even in the best of situations. Rhoda Dakar described an extraordinary tour in which The Bodysnatchers took part in 1980:

> We toured with The Specials in the Seaside Tour, us and The Go-Go's – that's the only time I've ever been on tour with equal numbers of men and women, 'cos they had female roadies and a female manager. That was a really nice time, and it's never ever been like that, and it'll never be like that again. Even one of the lighting engineers was a woman... Maybe in the days of Motown that might have happened, but they wouldn't have been instrumentalists or roadies or managers, they wouldn't have been technical at all. It was great![91]

There was, however, a recurring incident that spoiled the tour; when asked if anything had happened to her that made her feel threatened or afraid, Bodysnatchers' guitarist Sarah-Jane Owen replied:

> During the tour, Belinda Carlisle was experiencing some weird mail from a very strange fan. Black dead roses would show up just before their gig. It was all very spooky and no one could work out who they were.[92]

In the course of interviewing people for this book, I had a strong feeling that I was not being told everything about the women's experiences of sexual harassment – who wants to go down in history as an abused woman? As "survivors," it is better to remember (and be remembered for) a positive rather than a negative personal history; incidents of harassment and violence are often overcome as part of the experience of pioneering a new "world." Indeed after the first edition of this book was published I received a call from one of the interviewees describing the rape, on separate occasions, of three of her band-members by a stranger, a rock journalist and a fellow musician respectively; another musician I spoke to was raped by her manager, and I was told of the rape of yet another by a group of young men in the back of a van on the way home from a gig. In Chapter 4 "Noise, Violence and Femininity," I will describe in more detail the violent environment in which all this music-making took place.

The next chapter describes the Brighton scene, and explores the context for music-making using a customized version of punk in a local setting.

3 The Brighton Scene

A vandal ain't no scandal We haven't any money
No matter what you think We have to steal and cheat
It's pretty hard to handle Scrawling our graffiti
In a town that stinks Up and down the street
A menace to the homeless! A menace to the students! A men-
ace to pensioners![1]

The same music and style will often produce not one but a
variety of responses on the part of young people to the particular local circumstances in which they find themselves, each
response being underpinned by a common set of base knowl-
edges relating to the local but using this knowledge in different
ways and to different ends.[2]

Context

One of the purposes of this local case study is to establish whether the
existence of local scenes facilitated the flow of young and inexperienced
women into performing in rock bands. This has not always been apparent in other analyses of scenes and "territories" (Finnegan,[3] Cohen,[4]
Straw,[5] Swiss, Sloop and Herman,[6] Lesley C. Gay Jnr,[7] Shank[8]). Some of
these are recent, and reflect globalization issues; however, I believe it is
possible to "work backwards" from these texts, using this hindsight to
identify characteristics of the punk phenomenon that may not have been
apparent at the time. Finnegan's study in particular shows the different
scenes in operation at a given locality at one time; this has encouraged a
focus in this study on mainly punk bands as opposed to women's bands
in general.

An underlying theme in the development of rock music sociology is
the concept of local "scenes" that act as greenhouses, where new bands
are nurtured and fine-tuned in an almost cosy environment, formed by
friends, surrounded by friends, and "rooted for" as they progress through
ever-increasing circles of success: was the security provided by friendly local
audiences a factor that boosted the confidence of young women instrumentalists and made them take to the stage with electronic instruments,
making noise like their male counterparts? Shank describes the music
scene in Austin, Texas, and how the support of the music community:

> ... escapes the encoding structures of everyday life and represents the possibility for the return of the repressed, those elements of the human overlooked in the enforcement of industrial organisation. In the inexpressible nature of collective musical pleasure can be found an implicit promise of something more, a potential that exceeds the competitive struggle for individual gain.[9]

Cohen's *Rock Culture in Liverpool*[10] is another landmark in the study of local music-making. Her methodology involved "hanging out" with two local bands and observing the minutiae of their existence; rather than becoming irritated by her, they grew to trust her and consult her opinion on occasion. Written in 1991, her work is interesting and relevant for many reasons. First, there is a debate about Liverpool's validity as a "punk city." Second (as Gay also found[11]), women are very much a side-issue to the (male) band scene in Cohen's study:

> Sometimes women were also used by bands (as well as other gimmicks such as leaving unusual objects scattered around on stage) to enhance their visual image, usually as backing vocalists dressed in glamorous outfits.[12]

Cohen's study also details very effectively the daily grind of being in a band. Other, more autobiographical, memoirs, such as that of Frank Cartledge,[13] give an evocative account of the moment, which emphasizes the importance of punk to different areas of the UK; however, again, the memoir is male and does not engage with the female experience. The aim in this chapter is to describe the music environment in a town that is not normally regarded as a "music city," but which had, and still has, a thriving music scene.

Punk Rock in Brighton: The Beginning of the Scene

The shrinking of scale brought about by local punk scenes greatly benefited young women who wanted to break out of their stereotyped existence. The application of punk values to other non-metropolitan localities, "customized" to the needs and attitudes of young people further afield, became an important and creative by-product of the original subculture. This chapter, in addition to giving an impression of the Brighton scene, will show how the increased access to recording and performing opportunities applied to punks in a "micro-subculture." Erstwhile manager of The Slits, Christine Robertson, sums up the importance of small scenes to aspiring punk musicians:

> Okay, your audience may not be global, it may not be national, but you can get an audience locally in your club and it can grow and be bigger. I think it [punk] broke down a lot of things, and it freed a lot of people to believe that other things were possible.[14]

It is easy to identify the beginning of the Brighton punk scene, as it started with the dissemination of punk music and ideas across the UK from late 1976 onwards; it is less easy to identify the end point. Although music scenes in local towns are continuously evolving, there was a particular, almost desperate, political flavour to the scene in Brighton in the late 1970s. Many of Finnegan's findings are applicable to Brighton – for instance "the somewhat startling fact that one of the interesting characteristics of local music organization is precisely the absence of an absolute distinction between 'the amateur' and 'the professional'."[15] Some of the musicians in the older, semi-professional and more established rock bands in Brighton deliberately changed their musical and visual style, and their names, in order to be incorporated into the new punk scene; others followed the more usual punk route of picking up instruments before they had learned to play them. There was mutual scorn: the former saw the latter as incompetent musically; the latter saw the former as bandwagon-jumpers. Joby, lead singer of Joby and the Hooligans, recalls:

> There was great rivalry between the bands because some had commercial aspirations and others remained true to an anarchic ideal (mainly due to lack of lucre). Slurs such as "Why don't The Depressions[16] appear with their wives and kids" etc. were rife.[17]

However, none of the bands in Brighton discussed here was fully professional at this time. The dole was a necessary part of many a musician's income, no matter how they defined themselves, and all of the bands had an interest in playing with each other at the same events in order to create the scene that justified their existence. Some band-members worked in the many clubs, hotels and bed-and-breakfasts that welcomed tourists in the holiday season, and others had mainly menial jobs. The aim was to survive – as one interviewee says, an essential ingredient of band membership, apart from rehearsal space and equipment, was "the dole being something you could live on – you lived in a squat and you signed on, and you could survive."[18]

The duration of the particular politicized "flavour" of the music made in Brighton at this time was finite, although a thriving music scene has always existed in Brighton. Punk arrived in Brighton in late 1976, when it had already been declared "over" in Chelsea.[19] Previously, its music scene had been dominated by small heavy-metal bands and blues bands, and the occasional Irish

folk band. The audience size for these gigs would be around ten to thirty people, depending on the night of the week; but as punk was "being declared
dead in London... [it was] springing to life in the provinces."[20] McKay describes
how it "brought life to the countryside and market towns."[21]

In Brighton, an appealing factor of punk gigs was that it was possible to
attend gigs free, by volunteering to collect money at the door of the venue,
by sneaking in through the lavatories (a common trick at pub venue the
Buccaneer), or simply by being in a band, being a fanzine writer, or generally being a "face" on the scene. Bands rarely expected to be paid, particularly earlier on in their career. They were often resigned to their own lack of
musicianship and, in Brighton at least, it was only when bands such as The
Piranhas started recording sessions for John Peel's Radio 1 show, and discovered that they had to be Musicians' Union members in order to do so, that
the concept of being paid for performance and recording was even taken
into consideration. Finnegan's findings underline the value of the *status* of
being a band-member:

> Even if they earned quite substantial fees and spent most of their time
> on activities related to their music, they could still end up substantially
> out of pocket and perhaps engaged in musical performance as much
> as for the enjoyment and the status of "musician" it gave them as for
> money.[22]

There was little understanding (or premeditation) by the bands of their
value as entertainment, or as a live experience, yet this was an area where
punk was at its strongest, as Hebdige noted.[23] For unemployed punk band-
members, the difference between being "unemployed" and "in a band, but
unpaid" was of tremendous importance.[24] With time on their hands, some
took part in direct political activity almost by default, by not opting out if it;
others just wanted fun. There were also people who had a determined and
formal political agenda, among them Attila the Stockbroker[25] and members
of the women's group based at the Brighton and Hove Resources Centre,
who had personnel in several bands. Generally, there was resistance from
band-members to joining formal political groupings, which were regarded as
predatory. The attitude of punks in Brighton was genuinely anarchic with all
its ironic implications: they were a group defined by their differences, who
frequently had to operate collectively as a defence against the police, rogue
landlords, the Conservative Council, Teds' violence and so on. So in Brighton,
the independent nature of the groups involved in the scene meant that some
wrote overtly political songs (Poison Girls, Brighton Riot Squad, Joby and the
Hooligans, Devil's Dykes) and others wrote whimsical songs (The Piranhas,

The Golinski Brothers, The Chefs, Peter and The Test Tube Babies). It was not uncommon for a variety of local bands across these parameters to appear together on stage to support (most frequently) Rock Against Racism (RAR) or another more local cause. The whole scene involved activity and action, as punk scenes did across the country, that included everything from fanzines which may or may not have had overtly political content, through attendance at the Rock Against Racism marches, through music, to simple attendance at gigs; the common factor for most of us was a feeling of personal pride and responsibility that had not been there before.

Brighton as a town had a strong musical environment even before punk music itself made an impact upon it: in this respect, it was primed to be receptive to a productive music subculture. Sara Furse, from pre-punk all-female band No Man's Band, describes it in this way:

> There was a real sense that Brighton was just buzzing – every corner, every pub you went in, everywhere you went somebody was thrashing out some form of music or other, and everywhere you were surrounded by people playing instruments and singing and busking in the streets.[26]

The Brighton *punk* scene, as opposed to the general music scene, grew out of a combination of smaller communities of young people that loosely revolved around several music venues in the centre of Brighton. In 1976, the Buccaneer hosted small bands and "fading stars" such as pre-comeback Shakin' Stevens; the Alhambra hosted Irish bands, blues revivalists and R&B bands in the style of The Rolling Stones. The promoters of these venues eventually allowed punk bands to play, driven by commercial necessity. Apart from the small-band community that was already in existence, audiences consisted of groups of art students and ex-art students, itinerant workers who had settled in Brighton because of its proximity to the sea and the seasonal work it afforded, a very politically active squatters' movement and the aforementioned women's group based at the Resources Centre in North Road. Later, local record shop Attrix started up its own label, also called Attrix, and released three compilation albums – Vaultage 78, Vaultage 19 and Vaultage 80 – that showcased some of the local bands and gave Brighton a collective musical identity. It also released singles by The Parrots, The Piranhas, The Chefs and others. Punks congregated in the Windsor Tavern, a tiny pub near the Resource Centre run by two elderly ladies, until the sight of punks eating their beer glasses when they had finished their pints and sitting there with blood running down their chins put them off. We shared the pub with a group of deaf people, who mocked us ceaselessly in sign language, and an elderly fence who tried to offload various stolen goods onto the punk community, including, on one memorable occasion, a lorry-load of bananas.

The fringes of the Brighton punk scene were criminal and violent: once I had to bind the arm of a girl who had slashed her arm with a razor blade during a concert at the Resources Centre; another time, a young woman was thrown to the floor and kicked in the face by her boyfriend.

Because of Brighton's relatively small centre and its relatively small population, it has been reasonably easy to delve into the nature of the Brighton scene even now, over thirty years later.[27] The following account consists of personal recollections interspersed with those of other participants in the scene, located mainly through Internet searches and word of mouth; there are also excerpts from local fanzines (spelling errors intact). Sometimes different versions contradict each other, but history has already been established as subjective. Starting from a general discussion about the experience of punk music and the punk scene in Brighton, I will go on to explore how bands were formed, the venues, getting gigs, negative aspects of the scene (jealousy and opposition within the scene, stealing, violence), subject-matter, politics, aesthetics and just having a good time. It is intended not only to reconstruct the variety of the Brighton scene, and to pinpoint the enabling factors for women instrumentalists, but also to identify aspects of the scene that made the environment difficult for them.

There were possibly two hundred people who regularly attended punk gigs by local bands in the main venues (the Alhambra, the Buccaneer, the Vault and the Richmond). Of these, around fifty were "full-timers"; around fifty were in bands; around twenty-five worked in "alternative" professions. A further fifty were students (school, college and university), although generally there was little overlap between the university and polytechnic students and the local punk community; the rest were mainly shop assistants, nurses and technicians. Some of the remainder were slightly odd people who sensed an accepting community. Visually extraordinary-looking people rubbed shoulders at gigs with relatively conservative-looking people. Punks occasionally attended the more upmarket discos; when the "big-name" punk bands played at venues such as the Kingswest Centre or the University of Sussex, the audience was even more mixed. As far as gender was concerned, the Brighton scene did not display the characteristics of Brake's comments regarding working-class and middle-class punk women; Brake talks of working-class women "being punk" and middle-class women "dressing punk."[28] My empirical view of this was that in Brighton exactly the opposite was the case. The punk women I knew who wore clothes from Westwood and McLaren's shop Seditionaries in the King's Road were working-class; in the bands, it was more common for the girls, regardless of class, to have come from disturbed or difficult family backgrounds, and for them to be involved in the scene because of its willingness to accept them in spite of this, than it was for them to belong to a particular social grouping.[29] McRobbie's interview with Michelle in Moseley[30] is representative of the experience for young women *and* young men in Brighton: "Why was punk important? For me it was like going to university. I got all my education there...there was so much mixing, people from different backgrounds...".[31]

Forming a Band

This section describes my personal situation in Brighton at the time of punk; the following section describes how I joined a punk band and, later, how other personnel in Brighton joined bands. Because it is not possible to write objectively about my own involvement, I have tried to merge my own experiences gradually with those of my contemporaries, until these experiences appear as quotations alongside those of the interviewees I spoke to. In several places, it is therefore possible to note that our experiences were contradictory in nature; in others, they were similar. I believe the tension between the similarities and differences of experience and memory show how important it is not to stereotype those involved in subcultural activity. In many respects, this personal memoir is typical of young women's experience at this time, and in writing this way I am following the precedent of Valerie Walkerdine, who uses her own experiences as a case study in her book *Daddy's Girl*[32] almost as a direct alternative to the quasi-objective stance taken by some writers (see Chapter 5).

In late 1977, the occupants of the basement of the squat I was living in started to become rather noisy. Two girls (they were very young, probably about fourteen) had moved in. They had run away from a children's home. One of them wore a dog-collar, a corset and suspenders, the other wore an old black jacket and a miniskirt, and they both wore lots of black eye makeup. A band had been formed and these girls were the backing vocalists. The name of the band was descriptive rather than ironic: they called themselves The Molesters. The only times the band stopped playing was when Social Services came round looking for the girls (they all sat in total silence behind the net curtains until they went away) and when someone wired up their door handles to the mains to attempt to give them a fatal electric shock as they entered their rehearsal room. They remained alive and noisy; at times, we used to bang the floors above their rooms with a hammer to try to shut them up.

They told us they were rehearsing until they were good enough to get some gigs. My boyfriend had started a new job working in Brighton and Hove Resources Centre, a community organization based in an old church hall.

We'd been to some strange parties in the crypt beneath the hall (transvestites in Alice-in-Wonderland drag mixing pancakes) and we knew that bands had started playing down there, playing punk music that was loud and unsettling. He arranged for The Molesters to play at the next gig, as a challenge, which they did not take up. So that is when we formed a band; our conversation went as follows:

> "What do you want to be?" "I want to be a guitarist." "So do I."
> "I want to be the lead singer." "But you can't sing." "So?"
> "Helen, you can play bass."
> "But I haven't got a bass guitar."
> "That doesn't matter."
> "All we've got to do is find a drummer."
> "Let's ask that boy from Punktuation."
> "Okay."
> "We'd better write some songs then." "Okay."

As our lead singer Joby wrote:

> Attila the Stockbroker had a band named Brighton Riot Squad who had a gig upcoming at the [Brighton and Hove] Resources Centre. I produced posters and they needed a support band. A bunch of art students (plus me) got together and threw a few songs into a set 3 days before the gig. I worked just as Mark P had stated "Here's a chord, here's another, now form a band."[33]

We bought a copy of *The Sun* and wrote three songs based on the day's stories, and played The Molesters' gig for them; afterwards, we found ourselves with several more bookings and became another of Brighton's sixty-three bands.

Once the Resources Centre had established a community printing-press upstairs, it became a thriving venue with publicity assets. Bands could rehearse, hang out, argue and help each other out in an uninterrupted, private way. The whole ethos of punk, the "do it yourself" part of it and the "encourage others to do it themselves" mentality, was fully taken on board, and the resources of the Centre facilitated this with its upstairs printing-press, its performance and rehearsal spaces, and, most importantly, its network of people with the requisite moral attitude to enabling others. Punk poet Attila started off in Brighton on the punk scene, which he describes here:

> We used to hang out together, and when punk started we formed a band, and as soon as we did, Joby did our posters for us without a question, The Poison Girls gave us a gig without even hearing us. If

Joby and the Hooligans in the Vault, Brighton. Photographer Ray Renolds

you turned up at a punk gig and said, "I'm a poet, can I do five minutes between the bands" and the bands wouldn't let you, they were an arsehole. It was the other way round from now. The unwritten law of punk was that if there was a little bit of space and someone wanted to do something you would let them do it and that was absolutely tailor-made for me... The most fundamental thing was not the music or the politics, it was that simple fact that everybody felt that they could get up and do something, and not just that; if you were denied the opportunity, then the people who were organizing the gig weren't true punks.[34]

Punk Bands in Brighton

The first punk band I had really noticed was Poison Girls. Lead guitarist and singer Vi Subversa was an engaging performer and they had a girl bass-player called Sue who had very long hair and played a semi-acoustic bass of good provenance (it used to belong to the Manchester punk band The Buzzcocks). It was this that she lent me for our first couple of gigs. Punktuation's thirteen-year-old drummer sat in; our first gig was a defiant two-fingers to the cowardly Molesters in the basement of our squat. After the first gig we were offered more straightaway. It was a matter of days before The Molesters, too, were performing on the Brighton circuit, and recording a John Peel session as well.

The Dandies, who were a sort of glam/punk group, used to help other bands start up, in a similar way to Poison Girls. Tom Maltby, the lead singer of Wrist Action, commented:

> We were the first punk band in Brighton and it was hard getting started – The Dandies were the only band that helped us – so now we like to help these new bands that are getting going – we've played with most of them y'know...[35]

Spontaneity was also a common factor in the generation of Brighton's bands. There *were* bands who had a "career plan" and who worked on their set and their song-writing skills from the start; it did not appear to matter to the audience whether the band they were watching was motivated by a desire to communicate or a desire to make a career. Many of the instrumentalists had little or no experience. Julie Blair, organ-player in The Mockingbirds, recalled:

> I joined the band in, I think, '78 or '79. I can't quite remember. We were four women... I was on keyboards, my friend Shirley was singing, another friend Rose played drums, a friend Hilary was playing bass. And I'm afraid someone's boyfriend played... But we did write our own material. And none of us had ever played an instrument before. We decided to form it one night in the Richmond having watched the Piranhas, I think, and Nicky and the Dots. I thought, We can do this, we can write songs, we can play a chord or two. It just seemed like a really inspiring thing to do at the time... I think it was a combination of things. I mean, obviously I was married to Rick and he was playing in a band and I've always enjoyed that. He encouraged me, or encouraged us. And I thought it was about time women got up and did it. So many subjects to talk about as a woman, to sing about.[36]

Kate Hayes, a guitarist who sang with The Objeks, took part in a seventeen-day sit-in at Brighton Art College when she was a student there; her experience illustrates the generation of a band from mutual political activity:

> During the occupation we decided to make this band called The
> Objeks and I sort of managed to muscle in as a sort of co-singer cum
> backing-singer – I don't think they would have liked the idea of any-
> one as a backing-singer because it wouldn't have been particularly
> equal, so we were co-singers although Dawn was the main singer.
> Paul couldn't play the guitar before he joined The Objeks – he had
> no idea how to play the guitar. He had no idea! And Dave didn't – he
> just went and bought a bass and decided to play it! We were art stu-
> dents, we weren't musicians at all apart from Heather and Stella. So
> we really were pick'n'mix, let's just do this, 'cos we've got something
> we want to say.[37]

Stella Clifford, another member of The Objeks, describes the feeling of
heightened energy she had and the way that affected her life:

> I remember it as being phenomenally exciting! We could all do things
> that you could never imagine doing. I was from the provinces and I'd
> never seen a band before I went to Brighton, I'd never even been to
> a gig. And to make your own band...and suddenly there was a record
> label as well and there was a chance that you could get somewhere,
> that you could be taken seriously. You could let off a lot of steam,
> dance about, scream, get onstage, get offstage, have people follow
> you around, follow people around and of course it was very sexy,
> wasn't it? Everyone was sleeping with everyone else.[38]

For some musicians there was a completely "chance" working relationship
with a performer. A technician at the University of Sussex who called himself
Dick Damage used to phone round to get a band together before his gigs. One
of the occasional bass-players told me that their rehearsals consisted of Dick
reading the chords out to him over the telephone about half an hour before
he left for the gig. However, Dick's gigs were immensely popular – he was
funny, amiable and unsophisticated (or a master of irony), and every person
I spoke to in conjunction with this work used to attend his gigs regularly. One
of these was Sue Bradley, who played violin with The Reward System and any
other band who asked her to; here, she describes the beginning of what was
to become a serious twenty-year career (in this, she was unlike many of the
other women I interviewed):

> I moved to Brighton in 1979 to come to Art College and joined The
> Reward System pretty quickly. I met Adam, who was the keyboard-
> player, at a Rock Against Racism gig in the Sallis Benney Hall. I can't
> remember who was playing... Adam was telling me he was form-
> ing a band and I sort of said hopefully, "I don't suppose you want a
> violin-player by any chance?," and he said, "Yeah, great," and I was

really surprised, shocked in fact, it was extraordinary, and he took me really seriously as well. It wasn't that he wanted a sort of girly, backing-singer, show-violinist at all, so it was absolutely brilliant. That was the first band. I also went on to be in The New Objeks, which was Dawn on vocals, Heather on drums, Dave Roughton on bass, Jeanie, she used to have lots of ribbons in her hair, on sax. I'm actually on the *Vaultage* album twice, once with The Reward System and again with The Objeks. I did a lot of guesting as well, with people like Dick Damage, and things like that.[39]

The ethos of the time is summed up by the fact that a friend of Jamie Reid[40] came down from London and met us in a pub; he had a bag full of new Sex Pistols albums which he gave out to each of us. I took one, but later gave it away; I did not need a Sex Pistols album because I was in a band myself.

The Venues: Gigs and Rehearsals

When punk music first started to be played by Brighton bands, there was a dearth of venues, as these two excerpts from a local fanzine illustrate:

> G: *Why do you think it's so difficult to get venues in Brighton?*
> DB: Well the whole towns [sic] run by a few old geezers who want to present Brighton in a different image to what's really happening. They want it to be a holiday town. Not much fun for those who live here. They don't want to see scruffy guys playing in bands, they want 'em smart with dickie bows y'know?[41]

> I told lead guitar player Dan Dadandan that Flesh were fast becoming known as a good punk band particularly in view of the fact that Keith Hurley, of Alhambra fame, told us when approached about Flesh doing a gig that they were a punk band and people who claimed to have seen them had said they were outrageous & obscene and he didn't want *that*. "People who come into the Alhambra want to listen."[42]

At one point, the local council tried to restrict live music in many pubs.[43] However, promoters soon realized that putting on punk bands would draw crowds. There was always a "circuit" of sorts: two seafront pubs, the Buccaneer and the Alhambra, were already live music venues, and their promoters recognized that the best way to pack them out with people was to accept punk bands whether they liked them or not. For example, although my band Joby and the Hooligans never made any recordings (we were a bit too anarchic for Attrix at that stage), the live gigs always drew large audiences. The promoter of the Alhambra, Keith Hurley, once said: "I fucking hate your band, but every time you play here it's packed, and that's why I keep booking you." The music was not regarded as aesthetically pleasing, and the local press also did not understand the attraction of the new sounds. The Molesters were described thus:

> They have been reported as sounding like a pub brawl, but they have been voted one of Britain's top 12 new bands.[44]

And Fan Club's music aroused similar sentiments:

> Friends say their original style is sixties pop with the added energy of the seventies. Enemies say it's a loud, horrible noise.[45]

The Buccaneer was "rough," featuring boxing as a regular attraction; it often hosted "trouble" between Punks and Teds.[46] The Alhambra, however, was more relaxed and it was possible to make a few quid by "doing the door." It was very dilapidated: an audience member at the time recalls that she "never paid to get in cos the windows were always broken so you could hear the bands from outside."[47] The Concorde, formerly a seafront soul club, joined the circuit, as did the Crypt, a bar at the university.[48] The basement bar of the art college had been a disco, and put on the odd gig; later, a large pub called the Richmond became a regular venue. Later still, around 1979, other venues opened – for instance, the Bombay Bar, a "tropical paradise" in Kemp Town; the Ice Rink; and the Cage (a skate park on the seafront). There was a constant stream of new venues opening, as others closed due to bad relationships with punk audiences:

> I...promoted bands at the Sussex Sports centre in Queen Square above the Ice Rink. We had such gems as The Chefs, The Vandells, The Golinski Brothers, The Vogue, Woody and the Splinters and loads more until Dame "someone or other" had us shut down. After that I put on The Piranhas in their "Tom Hark" era at the Cinescene cinema at the top of North Street, supported by Daddy Yum Yum. We had several more planned in the following weeks at the Cinescene including Wreckless Eric and Bad Manners, but there was some minor vandalism and the owner lost his bottle.[49]

By far the most important venue, however, was the Vault, at the Brighton Resources Centre, originally set up as a venue by Vi Subversa, guitarist and vocalist with the band Poison Girls:

> My active years were 1972–1977, in the Brighton scene, laying some of the foundations for what happened later. For me the "punk" scene began when we got permission from the church elders to run rehearsal

rooms in the vaults [of the Resources Centre]. I got on to the management committee of a community group involving the church elders.
And perhaps because I was middle-aged they trusted me! The Brighton
Resources Centre above The Vault was a political community project
and housed many groups such as Shelter, Gay Rights, Women's Centre,
and offered practical help and resources such as screen printing. I was
the first employed member of this project and the main link between
the political community groups housed on the ground floor of the
church and the Vaults [sic], which were, of course, below ground.[50]

The Vault attracted punks from London as well as hosting a gig by Manchester band The Buzzcocks. Although it had no mod cons (no toilet, no bar,
no fire escapes), it was easy to run a gig there – you just carried the PA down-
stairs from the Resources Centre, brought your equipment through from your
rehearsal room, and asked a couple of people to take money on the door, with
or without a knife to persuade punters to part with (not very much) cash. It
was a centre for gigs, borrowing and lending of equipment, and a place to go
if you wanted to find out what was happening that week; it was a centre for
anarchy, but also had a macabre charm:

> We used to get cans of beer from the off licence over the road and
> get pissed – also remember the old bill raiding it one night, cause we
> were letting off fire extinguishers from the car park next door. They
> took a look at us inside sweatin' drunk and the noise from the band
> and just left.[51]

> We did about four gigs altogether, the main one was supporting
> Poison Girls at The Vault. It must have been June '77. When I was
> around we'd rehearse in The Vault regularly...the amazing thing about
> the place was it was a burial vault with Huguenot graves boarded
> up with hardboard round the sides and with all the jumping around
> and things, the vibrations caused the boarding-up bits to move and
> the hardboard to come down, and by '77 there were literally bodies
> coming through the wall. I remember there was this little baby's lead
> coffin just lying there with all these bones in one end, no inscription or
> anything, and reverentially I pushed the bones up the other end and
> used the other end as a till to collect the money.[52]

There is no doubt that the grim aesthetics of performing in an environment such as the Vault had an effect on the type of music and behaviour
that emanated from it: the music performed by many Brighton bands became
notably more cheerful as the scene eventually moved to other venues.

Stith Bennett's study on the way in which rock bands function underlines
the fact that the physical constraints that rock rehearsal demands are respon-

sible for "actually determining the scheduling and total amount of practice time, the ability to chemically alter the consciousness, and most importantly the sound power which is available during practice."[53] The amount of access to rehearsal time seemed infinite and allowed us to produce a large quantity of material; some band-members actually lived in the Vault, sleeping on an old doctor's examination couch and rising for band rehearsals when the rest of the band turned up. It was possible for anyone to "hang out" in the Vault all day, watching bands and sharing cider, amphetamines and gossip during breaks. However, as Julie Blair remarks, there was one crucial fact about the Vault and the staff of the Resources Centre upstairs:

> That is one of the most crucial things, affordable rehearsal space. I think we shared our arch with three bands. Several bands had one arch, didn't they: and we knew all the people in the Resources Centre anyway, so it was always, ah, we owe you a couple of quid, pay you at the end of the month, you know.[54]

This was confirmed by Steve Bassam, later leader of Brighton Council ("Basso") and now a member of the House of Lords: "I don't remember any money entering the accounts."[55]

Jealousy and Inter-Band Rivalry

There was sometimes a volatile atmosphere, described here by Kate:

> I myself would get quite aggressive – not towards other people, but things – I'd smash things up, generally by accident, but there was an awful lot of pent-up feelings. Brighton seemed like an absolute cauldron: whatever emotion you were experiencing, it would get completely exaggerated, so if you were in love it would just be amazing, or if you were sad you'd be absolutely devastated. Nothing ever seemed to ever find a balance, everything was exaggerated; wherever you were in yourself, it would get completely amplified by everything around you. It made it a very creative place to be, but also potentially very, very dangerous.[56]

There were arguments about authenticity: who was a true punk – the person who bought clothes from the King's Road, the London epicentre of punk style, or the person who played in a punk band, inspired by The Sex Pistols and The Clash, whose exhortations were encouraging bands all over Britain?[57] For instance, at a punk gig at the University of Sussex a very large punk girl, "D," came up to the band and started "slagging us." She picked on me particularly, saying what a poseur I was in my leather jacket and sunglasses. I pulled the tag out from her T-shirt and the label read "BOY," which was a sub-Seditionaries shop on King's Road. Shouting ensued, and as she flounced off I kicked her in the backside, prompted by our lead singer Joby. Two or three days later, a friend of hers went into a shop that Joby's girlfriend worked in and said that "D" was going to kill me. Later that week, some friends who lived in a squat on the other side of Brighton, where "D" thought I lived, said that she had sprayed some graffiti about me opposite their house. I went up there to take a look. "I'm going to kill that fucking tart Helen from Joby and the Hooligans," it read. I started carrying a small knife in my pocket. A few days later at a gig at the Resources Centre she came up behind me and started trying to pull off the rubber dinosaurs I'd sewn on to the fur shorts I'd made to wear at our gig that night. I turned round and shouted, "Why don't you just FUCK OFF!" And she did not trouble me again.[58]

Sometimes, the problem was an interloper from another subculture, who dared to cross the boundaries of political opinion and sartorial style:

> We had a huge row with The Molesters: those two girls, they came down and said, "How can you be a punk band? You've got a Ted drummer." (He was a right-wing Ted as well – he wasn't a fascist or anything, his parents were Hungarian emigres or something and he'd grown up with that whole right-wing attitude.) I'd say, "Leave it out; it doesn't affect our music."[59]

There were disagreements within bands, with personality clashes:

> Basically, I know Steve thought I was a prat and couldn't stand to be in the same room as me. I thought Joby was a prat and could have done without seeing his bollocks through his stage tights. It was a relief all round when Chris Dousley dragged me away to be in a more middle-of-the-road pop group.[60]

Joby and the Hooligans had a strong rivalry with The Molesters, who were never part of the Vault scene, and had their sights set very much on success in London. We disliked them because they kept us awake night after night (there is no official bedtime in a lawless squat) and had also smashed our guitarist's window by throwing a brick through it – they were angry that we had shown them up, and they particularly did not like him. One of The Molesters "stole" this guitarist's girlfriend, who was one of their backing vocalists, and married her "just to get my own back."[61]

A local punk started the Anti-Piranha League (or APL) as The Piranhas became successful outside Brighton, signing first to Virgin and later to Sire Records.[62] He made badges which he pressurized people to wear. Some were slightly scared of him, others relied on him to score speed, and the movement took off. In retrospect, this was part of a "big fish in a small pond"-type power struggle for control of the scene; The Piranhas' manager was involved in many of the venues by now, as local bands began to have a radio and recording profile.

As bands became more successful, and developed fanbases outside Brighton, this could result in a jealous possessiveness on the part of the early fans.[63] The APL manufactured badges, and a sizeable proportion of the audience at local gigs by other bands could be seen wearing these. In spite of the fact that The Piranhas remained loyal to Brighton, this would seem to contradict Bennett's findings regarding the "forms of local pride [that] are also attached to local bands and musicians who have become internationally established artists and who rarely, if ever, return to their original locality."[64] Jealousy was not uncommon in local music-making in other towns: for instance, Hester from Dolly Mixture reported that the group lost their friends as they became more successful outside their locality, and they became isolated:

> We were loathed in Cambridge by most people once we started getting somewhere – really badly, it was horrible. I think it was partly jealousy. It's pretty horrible when it happens. So very quickly we became our own best friends, sort of thing, and just seeing people who were to do with the music business.[65]

Lucy O'Brien's local scene did not include any other girls in music-making, and this too led to a feeling of remoteness:

> I think we felt that we were a bit isolated. It was quite different being in the regions, and being in a town that was off the map. We were just very aware that we were the only girls doing it for miles around. We would have loved for there to be other girls on the scene, because we did find it quite difficult at times, difficult to be taken seriously, and we did encounter quite a bit of opposition and aggression from different subcultural tribal groups.[66]

Stealing

There was as much stealing as there was lending. Bands regularly lost smaller items of equipment, especially guitar leads, but sometimes larger items.

In 1979, The Chefs played an open-air gig at Sussex University in aid of Rock Against Racism. The band Gong were also performing, and their set went on interminably. Our guitarist, who was rather hot-headed, leapt up on stage to tell them to get off. It looked as though there was going to be a fight, so I leaned my just-bought second-hand semi-acoustic bass onto a nearby car and followed him to try to pull him away. When I returned, the bass was gone. Other bands were supportive; The Golinski Brothers' bass-player offered to lend me his. Someone called the shop where I was working to say that the police had accused him of stealing it, because he had an identical one. Eventually, "L," a local drug dealer, told me he thought the Hell's Angels had it, and if I had not reported it to the police I could get it back. I pretended that I hadn't told the police, and started hanging around outside the bikers' pub in Kemp Town. I told "L" to pass it through the grapevine that not only had I practically starved myself to pay for the guitar (£85 was a lot of money to me) but it would be impossible to sell, as it was so distinctive. We had a gig at the Art College Basement Club one night soon afterwards, and I was sitting and sulking in the Norfolk pub next door when my brother walked in, holding my guitar. He'd been on his way home before the gig to get changed, and had seen a woman walking into the police station with it. He rushed up to her, persuading her not to hand it in so I could use it that night. She had been sunbathing in the park and had found it under a bush.

Sometimes bands would capitalize on the misfortunes of others; eccentric band Fan Club was always on the lookout for a way to appear in the local press. When the band who shared their arch (where they rehearsed at the Vault), The Dodgems, had a break-in and lost all of their equipment, reports in the *Evening Argus* said that both Fan Club and The Dodgems had had gear stolen. Fan Club had somehow intercepted the press report and managed to include themselves in the story, although they had lost nothing. They achieved the desired effect of being mentioned in the article:

> Brighton rock bands could play benefit concerts to raise cash for Fan Club and the Dodgems who this week had equipment worth more than £3000 stolen. The Dodgems were hardest hit and lost almost everything when raiders forced their way into the basement at the Brighton Resources Centre and carried away drums, keyboards, guitars, amplifiers, speakers and lighting gear.[67]

A riot at The Buzzcocks' 1979 gig at Brighton's Top Rank Suite provided an amplifier for university-based band Emil and the Detectives and cymbals for the drummer of town-based band Midnight & the Lemon Boys, after a large-scale fight erupted in front of the stage halfway through the gig. Another incident involved the roadie of Joby and the Hooligans stealing our amplifiers and selling them to a local second-hand musical equipment store while we were away for a few days. He enthusiastically joined in our search for our gear, and was arrested while eating dinner at our house. Due to other offences, he was sent to Borstal, from where he wrote to us asking if he could roadie again for the band on his release.

Politics

The Brighton scene embraced every sort of punk from the hyper-political to fashion-followers, sometimes within the same band and always within the same pub. Whether or not you thought someone was an idiot, the scene had moved on before you had time to consolidate an opinion. The amount of talking was incredible; this must have been due partly to the amount of amphetamine sulphate we consumed, but a considerable amount of this talk was productive, leading to fanzines, records, political demonstrations and high-profile activities like the Jubilee Squat in 1977, in which a combination of squatters and punks moved into an empty office building close to the station, Britannia House, just for the day. There seemed to be a mixture of disaffected middle-class students, waiters (Tom Maltby from Wrist Action, Dave MacDonald and Pete Smith from Fan Club), community workers and girls who had run away from care homes in the bands. Political involvement would vary according to the beliefs and feelings of the band-members. For instance, the Hooligans did squatters, Rock Against Racism, gay and local community benefits, but did not play women's benefits. Some bands did every benefit going; others did none.

One of the earliest punk bands in Brighton was The Depressions, whose album is cited by Stuart Home as "simply brilliantly empty 'teenage' posturing."[68] He divides punk music into "Punk Rock" and "punk rock," the former being the type of music being made by those who would have been in bands anyway, whether or not the punk moment had happened, and the latter being the type of music made by enthusiasts, carried away by the excitement of the moment (Home's punks are rarely female). An interview from a local fanzine illustrates the priorities of bass-player Dave Barnard:

> G: *What about your involvement in your lyrics, you write about doll* [sic]
> *queues and youngsters but how much do you really care about that?*
> DB: My part is to write about it. I'm not a member of the Sqatters
> [*sic*] Union or anything like that, I couldn't be an active member of
> that, I don't have the time because I play my music. My involvement
> is to write about it. I don't think we are accepted as a pank [*sic*] band
> in Brighton by other bands. I don't know why, I think we are nearer to
> it than other bands in the way we are. I have been through it and still
> am, contract or not.[69]

Another early Brighton punk band, Wrist Action, was fronted by Tom Maltby, who was clearly into it for a good time:

> At the Art College gig I looked round and found the rest of em were playing a different song – but people seemed to enjoy it tho – by the way I got 7p from the Art College gig, enough to buy a pack of peanuts – playing for peanuts ha! – we're different tho – politics is shit – the last thing we want to do is preach politics...[70]

This was in great contrast to Attila the Stockbroker, who was committed to the hard left:

> *Did you feel there was "No Future"?*
> For me it was absolutely the opposite. There were two sorts of punks – there were Clash punks and Sex Pistols punks. The Sex Pistols punks were precisely ones who thought no future; and we were all highly politically motivated, antifascist, communist – I was in the Socialist Workers' Party, very involved with Rock Against Racism. Red Saunders actually recorded one of my very early gigs and I said, "Who's going to listen to that?," and he sent it to John Peel and he played it hundreds of times. I was terribly involved in the Rock Against Racism. At university I was involved in putting on all sorts of gigs, not just your lot. We put on Misty and the Black Enchanters, and Steel Pulse. For me, one of the great things about punk was the punk/reggae crossover. The day I saw The Clash I knew exactly what I wanted to do; when I saw them on stage I thought, that's me. That just focused everything; everything culturally made sense. I saw them about twenty-five times that year, and it literally changed my life.[71]

The lead singer of Joby and the Hooligans was involved in squatting, and enthusiastically embraced the idea of performing:

> *How did you become involved in punk?*
> It was the socio-political aspect of a subculture that kicked ass & disrupted a complacent music scene but was also perceived as a threat by the political establishment. This was later realised by SWP who organised "Rock Against Racism" gigs to further their objectives but also provided an opportunity for bands to be heard. As a careerist squatter the ethos suited my anarchic lifestyle. Until that time my greatest achievements had been cracking squats & a band would be a great medium for egotistic expression particularly if named Joby & the Hooligans.[72]

There was a strong political element in music that was made by some of the "art-college" punks, as Kate Hayes said when asked if her band played any benefit gigs:

> Yeah, always – that was mainly what the gigs were that we did. I don't think we ever got paid for a gig. Rock Against Racism, we'd do benefits for community-based stuff, for the nurses. We were hugely politically motivated. We didn't quite fit into the norm in that way – we did care about what we were singing about hugely, and we did care about what we aligned ourselves with, 'cos as a group, those of us who were at art school, our work was very political...we were very much wanting to make a statement with our work. So we wouldn't probably have seen making money as a good thing to have done, in our naïve approach to what we were doing – we really thought we were at the heart of a revolution; we wanted to really change how people thought and felt about things, which may explain why I wasn't that interested in what other bands were doing, because the industry bit of it wasn't the language I was speaking at the time. It was much more about supporting things that we wanted to add our voice to.[73]

When asked if she thought music and politics were tied to each other in Brighton at this time, Sue Bradley, another of the art-school punks,[74] replied:

> Yes they were tied, in a way that it doesn't seem to be now. I got into my first band because I was at a Rock Against Racism gig, and I think there were ever such a lot of political viewpoints being expressed through the songs – people like The Golinski Brothers. Just indirectly generally left-wing politics were going on. You just would know that none of these bands would ever be playing the Conservative club – it would just not be done. In fact I remember The Pookies being offered a gig at the Conservative Club and not doing it.[75]

However, one of the most successful bands in Brighton, The Piranhas, were cynical about "good cause" gigs, and discussed their feelings in a fanzine interview:

> Johnny: The point is, before the tour, we'd already done about twenty RAR gigs in Brighton, which nobody outside the area would have even heard about.
> Bob: I think that, as a band, our first thought was that it was a gig. We wouldn't have done it if it had conflicted with our beliefs, but I must admit I never thought about it consciously. Racism was a new word to me: I've never had anything against anybody. We're not into RAR just because it's a fashion.
> Zoot: RAR's UNfashionable [sic] in a way now and we're still doing it. All the little bands do it just to get their names heard.
> Interviewer: That's why I asked the question.
> Bob: Well, as I said, we did it for the gigs, but we wouldn't have if it was in support of something against our principles.

> Mick Dwyer: There was...an agreeable lack of carefully thought-out collective world-view... During the interview they frequently disagreed with each other and argued amongst themselves, and that can only be a good thing the way I see it.[76]

The ambivalence shown by The Piranhas may have been a "front" for the interviewer; as Bob says above, nearly all of the bands had principles that guided their choice of audience. Sometimes, the level of political activity of certain members of a band would cause others to feel uncomfortable, and they would leave; an ex-guitarist told me his reasons for leaving Joby and the Hooligans:

> [It was] a lot to do with you and the other guitarist going to Grunwick[77] and living in the squat at Lansdowne Place. All too political and right-on working-class for a typical middle-class dreamer like me. I just wanted to be in Talking Heads while The Hooligans wanted to be The Ramones![78]

Sometimes, a band's name alone would cause controversy. Brighton was a conservative town with a Conservative council, and this was reflected in the attitudes of some of the local promoters; the musicians themselves were defiant, however:

> Brighton rock band The Lillettes refuse to change their name. Some agents and landlords will not book them because it's risque. But the five-piece neo-punk outfit say the name must stay. "Those people who know us and like us would see it as a piece of blatant commercialism if we were to change the name to suit the establishment," said manager Steve Hall.[79]

Other aspects of the subculture were found objectionable by the council; all of the gigs were promoted by fly posting, nearly all of which were printed on the presses at the Resources Centre. A local fanzine urged bands to poster over the council's stickers, and had this to say about fly posting:

> It's illegal but the police can only prosecute after a complaint from the offended party (i.e. property owners). But the Council threatened the Alhambra because bands playing there had fly posted the town, and a friend was heavied by some over zealous officers with threats of ripping his coat to bits in search of drugs (!!??) The council inspired "Bill Posters will be Prosecuted" stickers that are providing a more frequent eyesore to the town, is an attempt to stop us communicating; cover one over tonight; right![80]

By the time Attrix Records began in 1979, the relationship between bands and radical politics had mellowed, and is best described by Julie Blair who outlines her attitude to her band, The Mockingbirds, and their attitude to politics:

> It was purely for fun – I always knew that it would be short-lived. And it was an intense and very enjoyable time. If they can do it, we can, in the sense of one-chord wonders. A lot of people started to do things musically because they could see it was possible. I don't think many of the bands were politically motivated. There was a lot of political interest skirting round it... I don't think even in terms of having a political message. Often the gigs were CND and things like that; often they had a political resonance. A lot of people in the bands were political animals, but I don't think it affected the music. I don't think that the music reflected that political interest. There was an overall sense that we all had, sort of, political beliefs along similar lines, demos, anti-establishment. Attrix was so much the heart of music at the time. Rick had done so much to encourage young bands.[81]

Attrix Records

Attrix Records was set up by a local musician, Rick Blair, in 1978, initially to release recordings by his band (also named Attrix).[82] In 1978, Attrix released a compilation LP of Brighton bands who were based at the Vault, entitled *Vaultage 78*. The album had a real "homemade" feel with a silkscreened cover designed by The Piranhas' sax-player, Zoot. Rick Blair was a natural facilitator rather than a pushy businessman, and this made local bands trust Attrix as a conduit for their material. Rick's family had a continuous financial struggle that matched that of their protégés (their flat was often lit by candlelight when they could not afford to pay their electricity bill), and he understood the underlying desperation of many of the punk musicians in Brighton.[83] In 1979, he opened a record shop in Brighton's Sydney Street to sell records from other independent companies. Staff member Stuart Jones recalls his involvement with the first Attrix release, and the release of the second compilation, coinciding with the opening of the shop:

> For me, it was amazing: I was chatting to Someone Who Had Made A Real Record! Who had put the whole thing together! Who played fantastic guitar, wrote fantastic songs, who sang just like Lou Reed! That night I helped them sleeve-up hundreds of copies of *Vaultage 78*. I was in heaven! I felt I had become Part Of The New Wave!
>
> [In 1979] We all stayed up for most of that first Friday night, still painting the shop! The second compilation album, *Vaultage 79*, was

released that very Saturday the shop opened it's [sic] doors...the local press arrived, pictures were taken, and we sold hundreds of copies of the album.[84]

I asked Julie whether she felt that the bands on these albums had anything in common:

It was very open [as a scene]. You think of the range of stuff that was on the *Vaultage* albums – it was very hard putting those together and sorting out a running order, because there wasn't a definable type of music. But in common – only that they sang about what mattered to them.[85]

When asked if she thought that the output of the Brighton bands on Attrix Records seemed lightweight in comparison to other post-punk bands (often, the music seemed comical while the lyrics contained a serious message), she answered:

I'm not sure how that would have panned out from other record companies or from the listening public, but I've got a whole folder of letters that we used to get from running Attrix from all over the place saying how fantastic they thought this song was or that song was, and how it meant so much to them and how they could relate to this. There was one referring to your "Twenty Four Hours" one that brought a couple together from out of nowhere. I always thought that was the fantastic thing about the lyrics, although the music was so catchy and poppy. I've always gone for lyrics and I wondered if that was what made the Brighton sound so interesting. It was always called the Brighton Sound, but I don't think there was such a thing really – it was a sort of job lot of individuals. Which is a contradiction in terms. But the lyrics were always important, and interesting.[86]

Attrix performed a function that effectively consolidated the fact that Brighton had a scene of its own. There were the same tensions between Attrix and the industry at large as there were between other, much larger labels who wanted to build on their stables of bands; Reynolds describes this tension in Manchester, where there was a debate between Tony Wilson at Factory Records and other more financially ambitious labels about whether or not to capitalize on their protégés, and how to do this effectively.[87]

Opportunities for Female Instrumentalists

An entry in my diary of 22 April 1977 describes my friend Barbara's (nearly) all-female band, No Man's Band, playing what must have been one of the very first gigs in the Vault. They had formed because Barbara was fed up with following her partner's band, the Irish folk band Moonfleet, and wanted to do something herself. This was before punk had stamped a seal of approval on the participation of women in rock music-making, but No Man's Band had a rough sound, a feisty attitude, and enough friends to create a sizeable audience for their gigs; they were also all squatters, and their formation was punk in concept:

> We were hanging around with a band called Moonfleet at the time and Mufti was going out with the guitarist...and there was a bunch of us that just got fed up with hanging around the band and decided one day, well, if they can do it, we can do it, we'll learn to play and form a band ourselves, and that's what we did, isn't it? And we got one guy to teach us all how to play the instruments 'cos none of us could play at the time, we were completely hopeless. He really enjoyed it – he used to dress in drag for gigs and he looked pretty ridiculous 'cos he's six foot two with a great big long beard and long hair and size fourteen policeman's boots with a frock...it was easy because it was such a scene; it seemed like everyone we knew played music, so you'd just mention it, and play a gig here, play a gig there...[88]

No Man's Band benefited from the fact that, in their squat, musical equipment was permanently set up, making rehearsal an easy and relaxed affair; and they lived in a big, old house with thick walls that prevented the noise levels from causing problems with their neighbours.

As with the London scene, the willingness to lend equipment, offers of gigs and general encouragement that was part of the punk mentality directly affected the gender make-up of the bands in Brighton. I can recall very little active exclusion of women by male musicians, and, as above, a considerable amount of informal mentoring, alongside an "I can do this" feeling by women who might previously have been put off by the level of skill required to take on the mantle of, say, Joni Mitchell, or even the level of coyness (for instance, Karen Carpenter).

Heather de Lyon, the drummer with The Devil's Dykes (and several other bands afterwards) describes the way she was helped in different ways by several different (male) drummers:

> The Piranhas' drummer would show me stuff, and Nicky & the Dots' drummer showed me how to do paradiddles. Russell from The Parrots lent me his old kit and helped me to buy a new one. Everybody showed me different things, and I'd watch people playing and copy them.[89]

The bravery of Vi Subversa, lead guitarist and singer with Poison Girls, cannot be underestimated; in effect, Poison Girls were a whole punk family (at least three of them were related sexually or genetically), and although their lifestyle had a hippyish flavour, their punk attitude was apparent in their actions. They did not want to include other musicians in their "family"; instead, they encouraged other people to set up their own bands, whether or not they agreed with their political views, and in this they were anarchic. It would have been unlikely for them to have come across extreme right-wing views among the bands, and I assume that this is where they would have drawn the line. However, the sight and sound of loud, raw, aggressive (and amateurish) music coming from a family was very impressive; how could one not want to be involved in this outlet for one's anger, whatever their gender? As Frances says:

> In those days, the sound of a power chord and the buzz of the live gig [were] heady thrills – compared to having to explain myself or even making sense.[90]

Frances was hassled from time to time for being a woman in a band. She continues:

> I ignored it as much as I could. I got to be very "assertive," but I actually hated having to deal with it. By nature I am quite sensitive and rather reserved, but I felt I needed to "come out" as a woman and not just be supportive. Other members of the band were encouraging me as well. Actually, I was hassled as much for my *age* as for being a woman in the band. Cries of "get em off" were heard, interspersed with references to "old age pensioner." It seemed that to start, as I did, aged 40 was more unacceptable than my gender.[91]

Visual image, of course, was an issue. For the lesbian bands, who developed as a consciousness-raising expression from the Brighton Women's Centre (based in the upstairs part of the Resources Centre), there was a deliberate decision to "dress down."[92] Others, like Sue Bradley, had difficulty in making the transition from punk neutrality to "new wave" gender issues:

> I always found the sexuality thing difficult. I never knew whether I was supposed to be a boy or a girl clothes-wise and looks-wise. It was quite easy when it was punk because you had a very particular style and makeup which wasn't to do with looking attractive, it was to do with a particular look. But once that started to die out a bit in '82, '83, I started thinking, should I be wearing a dress to gigs, should I be wearing trousers, do I want to look attractive or not? Usually, it was

safer to *not*. It was to do with my own confidence, and also to do with being taken seriously.[93]

There was an understanding among those in the punk subculture that sexualized clothing was worn as an ironic statement. However, in Brighton there were "hangers-on" who were intrigued by the scene for various reasons, and the non-exclusive nature of the scene could lead to misunderstandings.[94] It was actually more comfortable to wear "male" clothing, particularly when setting up the gear, and one was not excused from this activity on account of one's gender. Bayton discusses aspects of this in *Frock Rock*.[95] Guitars are heavy and large, made for men's bodies and men's arm-spans; playing in a dress can be a nuisance.

Some women instrumentalists had an uneasy relationship with the lesbian community, also based at the Resources Centre. There was an attempt by the lesbian community to co-opt the visible empowerment of women playing an instrument on stage. This is later referred to as "colonizing" by Steve Beresford (see Chapter 7).[96] Some of the women from the women's group drew me aside after one of the gigs and asked me if I knew what I was singing, and how the lyrics degraded women. I did know what I was singing – I sang the degrading lyrics in unison with Joby; this made them utter nonsense. There was an element of out-machoing the male members of the group in this (personal recuperation, perhaps), but I was so angry about everything that I did not care. I knew how to change fuses in my amplifier, change the strings on my bass, and tune it; many of those in the women's bands did not know these things, and I did actually see one woman bass-player hand her guitar-lead to a man, for him to plug it into the amplifier. It seemed that an element of the audience wanted a parallel to the band hierarchy in the "real world." My experience was echoed by that of Julie; when I asked her about whether The Mockingbirds attracted a good audience at all-female gigs, she responded:

> Yeah. We had a lot of feminists who were deeply disappointed to find out that I was married with two children and Shirley was married with one.[97]

One of the best things about being a girl in a band, however, was the fact that nobody could accuse you of being a groupie. Previously, if you had shown a strong interest in bands and gone backstage, the etiquette of rock'n'roll dictated that you were there to service the band-members sexually. This point was noted by French all-female band The Lous in 1977, who were interviewed for *Sounds* by Caroline Coon:

Women are much more curious about us than men. They like what we're doing. We're showing them another aspect of living and they are encouraged to take up instruments themselves. Before, they couldn't believe women were capable of playing rock'n'roll. But if we can do it in France, then women over here, with all the opportunities, have no excuse. Groupies must become musicians.[98]

I experienced this change personally when a journalist from a paper in Worthing came over to do an interview with The Chefs. The band we shared rehearsal space with, Midnight & the Lemon Boys, were determined to muscle in on the interview, as they felt they were more seriously ambitious than The Chefs. They showed off, interrupted and so on, until the journalist turned to me and asked, "Are these your groupies?" A few weeks later, in a reversal of the rock'n'roll norm, a female journalist from *Sounds* came to see them play at the Richmond. Both she and their lead singer disappeared early in the evening, and the rest of the band were frantically looking for them so they could go on stage. They returned from the beach, where she had taken him to have sex, as he was young and relatively good-looking. After the gig, the band looked for her to find out if she would be giving the gig a good review. She had returned to London before they began to play, having had a satisfactory evening already. Although these appear to be funny anecdotes, at the time they seemed to affirm a change in the whole rock'n'roll idiom!

Many of the younger female participants in Brighton bands took on the role of backing-singer: The Molesters, The Accents, and The Smartees all had at least one female backing-singer. The Lillettes were led by a woman who played guitar on their recordings but restricted herself to vocals on stage until she had gained enough confidence to play keyboards as well.[99] However, after Frances on guitar and Sue on bass in Poison Girls came The Devil's Dykes (all-female band), The Bright Girls (all-female band), Sue Bradley on violin/keyboards (in The Reward System, The New Objeks and Pookiesnackenburger), Laurie on sax (in Birds with Ears), The Mockingbirds (all female apart from male guitarist), The Objeks (female guitarist, female sax-player, two female lead singers), myself on bass (in Joby and the Hooligans, The Smartees and The Chefs), and other younger bands, who played non-licensed venues such as the Skate Park on the Brighton seafront. Being able to play an instrument did not necessarily mean that the instrument was played on stage; Kate Hayes told me:

My confidence was not very good at all, even though I could play guitar and had played guitar for years even before going to Brighton. I could probably play guitar better than anyone else in the band, to be honest, 'cos I'd had more practice and used to play more songs and things.[100]

Groups of musicians have to negotiate the distribution of power within their bands, and in Kate's case she felt the necessity to "fit in" was more important than asserting her right to play an instrument.

In general, there was an enabling atmosphere in the Brighton punk scene that made it easy for girls to take to the stage. This was not brought about just by the availability of cheap or free rehearsal space, gigs, and encouraging female role models; the attitude of the young men in bands was very encouraging, to the extent that Brighton's most successful band at this time, The Piranhas, sang several songs with lyrics that were about empowering women. This point was made by The Devil's Dykes' Heather, who said that in retrospect some of their songs were a "brash" attempt at "doing politics through singing, when it's a political statement being in a womens' band anyway."[101]

The Disintegration of the Brighton Punk Scene

The burning down of the Resources Centre in October 1980 had a profound effect on the morale of the band scene in Brighton. The *Evening Argus* reported the number of bands who had been rehearsing there:

> One of the worst affected sections will be the 64 punk, new wave, mod and rock bands which use the centre for rehearsals and performances. Firemen saved thousands of pounds worth of equipment from serious damage by moving it away from flooded areas of the basement.[102]

As one of the members of No Man's Band puts it:

> The practice is an essential thing, having somewhere to practise...when the Resources Centre got burnt down, that completely decimated the music scene in Brighton. Where else do you practise drums? Where do you go now? It was free! And I really think that was crucial – that's why it got torched basically, because it was so successful.[103]

Attila the Stockbroker believes the Centre was burned down by right-wing activists, who had identified it as a place frequented by those of a left-wing persuasion; the factionalism among young people's subcultures at this time was underlined by this extreme act:

> I remember...hearing on the radio, that there was a fire. Nobody actually knew who burnt it down. The police said they didn't know. I mean "B," he was a fascist, he was a skinhead who still goes to Albion. He used to boast about it, I don't know if he actually did it; various people claimed to it. The police knew all about it, but didn't do anything because the place was a thorn in their side.[104]

Kate Hayes had temporarily left Brighton to try to find work in New York, but the news reached her there:

> I remember when I was in New York...being absolutely despairing that the Resources Centre had been firebombed by the National Front. And for me that was like the end of the world – what's happened? That's where everything creative came from, that's where I believed all of the revolutionary stuff, all of the hope for change, was focused there. And to have it firebombed by the National Front, that was the end of the music scene for Brighton, that people wouldn't be able to share their equipment and spaces any more. It felt very destructive and depressing when that happened. I found the fascism the most depressing thing in Brighton.[105]

The Vault underneath the Resources Centre had allowed for a mixture of ideologies, genders, genres and communities to co-exist; this is why rumour had it that the National Front had burned it down because of the anti-Nazi benefits it supported. The Resources Centre itself had provided a venue for the local Tory councillors' surgery, as well as tap-dancing classes (Dawn Jordan's School of Dance), keep-fit, and various left-wing and anarchic activities. As Steve Bassam remarked:

> [It was] more of a gathering-point for people who were political; it didn't have an overarching political ideal – I think in its constitution it wasn't allowed to. Some of the people in bands were involved in squatting and social action; some were artists; it also inspired this whole poster culture.[106]

By the time the Vault was burned down, The Piranhas were relatively successful and had shown that there was a way of translating a local audience into a national one, if a band could use the interest in punk bands and local music-making to their advantage. However, the self-deprecating humour of The Piranhas defined the expected style of the Brighton bands, who came to be seen as twee in the "outside world" of the music business.[107] As Julie Blair says:

> It got toy-towny, Noddy – that's how it came over in the media. John Peel latched on to that wacky thing about it. He really liked us, and he played our song that was on the *Vaultage* album loads of times. He rang me up a couple of times to tell me how much he liked it, 'cos he did a lot of studio work with the Attrix bands.[108]

Throughout, The Piranhas had been among the most well-organized and musically competent of the bands, with a persistent manager, enough band-members in employment and earning money to ensure that their equipment worked, and generally good relationships with other bands. They were not overtly political, their personnel was relatively stable, and they must have seemed marketable. An unwritten contract must have existed between their manager and Attrix Records' owner Rick Blair, for as soon as The Piranhas made contacts in London that led to their leaving Attrix for Sire Records,[109] other bands on Attrix started to have meetings with record labels that had been set up by their manager. In many respects, the relative success and later failure of The Piranhas in terms of national impact provided a blueprint for other Brighton bands to learn from.

Basically, the Brighton punk music scene had developed as a customized version of what had begun in London: it developed out of a need for activity for a pool of unemployed and dispirited young people (including a small group of students and low-paid workers), and a parallel need for somewhere for their friends and contemporaries to go in order to "belong." In this respect, the micro-subculture of Brighton punk very much follows Willis's observations in *Profane Culture*:

> Having posited itself, shown its existence, manifested an identity in concrete worldly items, the social group has a degree of conscious and unconscious security. It does not have the same struggle with the void of possibilities its culture and identity might have been. And with this stored and coded image safely locked up within cultural items the social group can then, in a reverse dialectical moment, learn from and be influenced by its own cultural field and develop its feelings, attitude and taste in relation to perhaps a widening circle of art forms, cultural items and objects – in particular directions first instituted by itself and its own needs.[110]

The "widening circle" that resulted in local customization also brought about the commercialization process that eventually destroyed not only the political element of the new music (albeit after its development into Two Tone with its high profile for anti-racist songs in terms of radio-play and chart placing), but also its local identity in many cases. This was particularly apparent in Brighton, whose bands included very few indigenous personnel. As a seaside town, it was prone to an itinerant population (and the Tory government at one point attempted to prevent young people settling in resort towns), and this, in conjunction with the shifting student population, meant that the town did not inspire the same loyalty in its bands and their audiences as, say, Manchester or Liverpool.

Finally, although the Brighton band scene had many women protagonists right from the start, this did not necessarily give them any advantage over men. In a small town, it is easy to overestimate the importance of any activity. Carola Dibbell, writing about the US, comments that, even over there:

> It may well have been at the local level that women in punk or punk-influenced bands, some of whom were even less than sidemen and many of whom never even made records, had the most impact.[111]

And local music-making, in spite of all the attempts by its supporters not just at local level but also at national level (John Peel and Geoff Travis) sometimes remained stubbornly local, in spite of frequent gigs in London. Pauline Murray of Durham band Penetration observed: "It was frustrating. Bands were getting on in London and we were working harder and not. It was basically geography."[112] I was very aware of the "pull" of the Brighton audience to remain local and to "belong"; this became stifling, and in 1979 my band The Chefs moved to London, although we continued to release material on Attrix Records. We did lose a proportion of our local audience when we returned to play gigs in Brighton.

To conclude this chapter, it is revealing to report the fact that when I approached the local studies library in Brighton to seek information for my research, I was directed to a male member of staff "who had been to loads of Brighton punk gigs at that time." He assured me that "There were no women in punk bands in Brighton – if there were I would have known about it, because I went to see bands all the time." This authoritative reply indicates how complete the "forgetting" of women's roles in male-gendered activities can be. It is perfectly possible that he was not *aware* of more than fifteen female instrumentalists, let alone lead and backing vocalists, in bands in Brighton, given the parallel nature of musical activities there, but it is most unlikely that he never saw a punk band with a female presence in it.

4 Noise, Violence and Femininity

Go 'way, I hate you, hate you, hate you
Go 'way I hate you, far across the sea![1]

Maleness and the Expression of Adolescent Anger through Rock

When Hebdige writes, "Subcultures represent 'noise' (as opposed to sound),"[2] he is referring to the way in which subcultures at their point of inception, before assimilation, grate on the consciousness of mainstream society. Sound can be interpreted; noise annoys. In this chapter, I will explore the ways in which this subcultural noise has manifested itself in rock music, and how this noise and music are identified with maleness to such an extent that women have difficulty in using the "enemy language" in a coherent way in order to externalize their inner noise. Rock music started as a male youth form of expression and rebellion; what is interesting is that it is still one of the last bastions of inequality, a symbolic resistance to change in the gender relations of young people – perhaps a rather depressing thought considering the fact that young people are often charged with the responsibility for social progress. The moment under scrutiny appeared to be heralding change in the way rock music "worked." However, as Holly Kruse remarks in her essay "Abandoning the Absolute":

> The problem we encounter is in fact the way popular critics
> define rock, because hand-in-hand with intimations that rock
> *is* primarily a mode of male expression and understanding is
> the assumption that rock is governed by a more or less tran-
> scendental aesthetic, which, it therefore follows, only men can
> comprehend.[3]

Mediated mostly by male critics, it is not surprising that male values predominate. However, a remarkable number of female writers at the time took on "male" attitudes when reviewing female artists.[4]

Male/female writing teams also reiterated the girls-in-a-men's-world stance – for instance Julie Burchill and Tony Parsons:

> Rock is a pedestal sport, as is being a Monarch – wherever
> possible a boy inherits the throne – females are not thought

of to be the stuff worship/idols are made for/of. Girls are expected to grovel in the mezzanine while the stud struts his stuff up there, while a girl with the audacity to go on stage is jeered, sneered and leered up to – rock and roll is very missionary, very religious, very repressive. A guitar in the hands of a man boasts "cock" – the same instrument in female hands (to a warped mind) screams "castration."[5]

Burchill and Parsons thus identify rock fandom as akin to the worship of a deity – a ritualistic, ceremonial system that reflects the natural order of gender relations as we know and accept them.[6] Reynolds and Press, another male/female team, reiterate the castration theme:

Punk, in fact, was a sort of asexual relative of metal: cock-rock, with the cock replaced by a sort of castration-paranoia (society's to blame). Musically, punk suppressed the remnants of R&B's syncopation that endured in heavy metal, and turned rock into a martial beat for those at war with the status quo.[7]

Perhaps in this context it is interesting to note how many of the female-based punk groups were influenced strongly by reggae, The Slits and The Raincoats being the most influenced and influential of these; their double outsider-dom (being both punk outlaws and women) perhaps gave them more affinity with black male musicians and their music than with white men of their own punk community. Although The Clash reflected their West London locality by using reggae rhythms in many of their tracks, their output falls much more into the realism of rock, and this genre assured their longevity, as we will see later.

Reynolds and Press examine at great length the military imagery and attitudes taken on by young (and not so young) rock musicians in their historical account of rock attitudes; they scorn what they see as half-hearted attempts by female punk rock musicians to counteract the misogyny and sexism of rock bands and their lyrics.[8] Simultaneously, they trounce the macho posturing of male rockers, and emphasize the differences between rebellion, which they say is ultimately self-serving and futile, and revolution, which they claim is rarely associated with rock music.[9] Discussing the "wartime settings and martial imagery" used by The Clash,[10] they continue:

Forming a rock band or joining the Army are often the only alternatives to a service sector job or unemployment. Like rock'n'roll, the military offers a life of adventure, the chance to live like a man rather than a minion.[11]

In an interview, John Peel told me how well boarding school had prepared him for National Service, and how National Service had provided him and his contemporaries with "scam" skills that proved to be very useful in later life: he considered similar skills necessary to start a band, and keep it going, during the punk moment as akin to this.[12] Does this mean that being in a band is akin to warfare for young western men, with all its implications of male camaraderie, risk-taking and survival? What are the implications, if this is so, for the rebellious or restless young women whose rite of passage now includes similar freedoms to that of their male contemporaries? What is it that has prevented them from achieving parity of protest?

Sonic territory is marked by loud music; the pure *volume* of rock music is an oppositional weapon, according to Lawrence Grossberg, who writes this about Bruce Springsteen:

> Rock and roll substitutes style for authenticity (making the latter into another style), finds pleasure in the very structures of noise and repetition that are so oppressive in the straight world. Quite literally, somehow, noise feels good rather than painful. Rock and roll takes its content and form from outside of its own boundaries and in the very process of appropriating them (for instance in its musical practices, its fashion statements, and so on), it forces the straight world to organise itself in opposition to the rock and roll culture.[13]

The noise of rock music encapsulates the anger of young men, packages it and uses it as a weapon against the older generation, in particular their mothers,[14] according to Frith, who believes that "youthful bohemia begins...as a revolt against women who are identified with the home as mothers, sisters, potential domesticators."[15] In this respect, a rock gig has much in common with a football match, says Frith, "reminiscent of football games and other occasions of male camaraderie – the euphoria experienced depends on the relative absence of women."[16] This causes the first problem for young women who want to articulate their own anger through rock music; rock speaks out against society, it is loudly oppositional, but it is lyrically, and some would claim sonically, misogynistic.[17] The male version of the role of women is sometimes overtly, often blatantly, embedded in traditional rock. For instance, to return to the example of Springsteen:[18]

> Springsteen's women do not exist as characters in their own right but as signifiers of domesticity and commitment against which men define their masculinity. Men's right to "fool around" becomes part of their self-definition. The good times are celebrated in numbers like "Sherry Darlin" and "Born to Run" which show women offering sen-

sual delights. Here Springsteen expresses a true blue-collar authentic sexuality – "Lovin' you is a man's job." In these moments the hero is at one with a million rock stars demonstrating their commitment to a primitive model of sexual politics. At the risk of overstating the case, when Springsteen is rockin', his lyrics display increasing levels of crudity. It's almost as if the crowd-pleasers are designed with simple pictures in mind. Simply wrapping this up in a humorous package smuggles in the mythology propelling it.[19]

Gareth Palmer's use of the word "smuggles" sums up the way in which rock music perpetuates misogynistic values and entrenches them in the minds of young music lovers. Springsteen's pedagogical approach to song-writing (educator of the white working-class American male) displays a disheartening attitude towards women in his underlining of male-defined attitudes to them.

There is an acceptance, therefore, that rock music affirms gender relations in a conservative reflection of mainstream society, hidden beneath a cacophonic shield that coerces listeners into a "with us or against us" stance. Some writers believe that this oppositional position is defensive; in relation to the heavy-metal scene and its associated subcultures, Deena Weinstein observes:

> In light of the fact that music-based masculine subcultures came into their own at approximately the same time as the late-twentieth century women's movement was reaching its peak, one should not dismiss the idea that these subcultures have a defensive nature...heavy metal music celebrates the very qualities that boys must sacrifice in order to become adult members of society.[20]

Walser, however, posits the opposite of this, saying that: "although behaviour changes, the same patriarchal ideals are largely held in common by both 'boys' and 'adult members of society'."[21] While heavy metal plays with the male gender stereotype, challenging images of female sexuality in dress codes and even singing styles,[22] "blue-collar" rock music, such as Springsteen's, confirms it.

From an aesthetic point of view, Attali equates all music with the position that ritual sacrifice used to take in primitive societies, and the power of noise in rock music certainly appears to bind the aggression of its audiences into a therapeutic and oppositional whole. The following passage seems apt:

> Music responds to the terror of noise, recreating differences between sounds and repressing the tragic dimension of lasting dissonance – just as sacrifice responds to the terror of violence. Music has been, from its origin, a simulacrum of the monopolization of the power to kill, a simulacrum of ritual murder. A necessary attribute of power, it

GOWER COLLEGE SWANSEA
LEARNING RESOURCE CENTRE
LLWYN-Y-BRYN
77 WALTER ROAD

has the same form power has: something emitted from the singular center of an imposed, purely syntactic discourse, a discourse capable of making its audience conscious of a commonality – but also of turning its audience against it.[23]

Women Like Rock Music

Although male commentators and consumers alike define the world of rock music as male, the sounds and excitement generated by the music has often appealed to girls and young women. There is a well-known passage in Sheila Rowbotham's account of her gradually emerging feminism in which she describes the physical effect that rock music had on her:

> Every rock record simply was. The words were subordinate to the rhythm and the music went straight to your cunt and hit the bottom of your spine. They were like a great release after all the super-consolation romantic ballads.[24]

Barbara O'Dair, editor of *The Rolling Stone Book of Women in Rock*, writes of her own difficulty in rationalizing how she *felt* when she listened to rock music, with how she *thought*:

> I include myself among the legions of female fans who empowered male rock stars for embodying our own wild desires...it became less accessible to me...as I grew older, as it grew clear that much of the grittier stuff I loved was not meant, or at least not made, for me. As I tried to shake off adolescence, it seemed strange to stay fixated on the guitar gods of my youth.[25]

The lyrics and attitude behind male rock music thus engendered a sort of admiring indignation in some women. Mavis Bayton gave me an account of the inappropriateness of rock lyrics to the new social situation of the early 1970s:

> Since the early 1970s the Women's Liberation movement had had women-only socials. They played records initially. I remember there was one when we were all having a jolly dance to The Rolling Stones and I remember thinking, hold on, look at that stupid girl dancing to "Under my Thumb"... The contradictions of dancing to those lyrics![26]

There was therefore a *need* for a different sort of rock music. This need had been overlooked by McRobbie as she studied teenyboppers who listened to safe pop music in their home environment, and was pointed out by Rumsey and Little in 1979:

GOWER COLLEGE SWANSEA
LEARNING RESOURCE CENTRE
LLWYN-Y-BRYN
77 WALTER ROAD

> Feminists know that if rock/pop was really revolutionary, they would
> be embraced as the greatest rebels of all – real rebels, the genuine
> article, not just another piece in the jigsaw of popular ephemera...
> When they're fourteen, girl fans attract a lot of study and analysis...
> But what happens when we grow up and become a minority in the
> audience for "serious music"?[27]

In other words, the assumption made by rock critics that all girls liked pop and
did not like rock, and all boys liked rock and did not like pop, was too simplistic. As Kembrew McLeod succinctly puts it: "...what is talked about and how
it is talked about influences who feels comfortable enough to come out and
play – how certain cliques form."[28] McLeod discusses violence, maleness and
aggression in music, and how the very language used by rock critics bestows
approval or disapproval on the music reviewed, placing it in the "male" or
"female" domain.[29] On the other hand, Susan McClary had written an optimistic Afterword to Attali's book, in which she placed great faith in what she
described as "New Wave" music and its openness to female rock instrumentalists:

> The music is often aggressively simple syntactically, but at its best
> it conveys most effectively the raw energy of its social and musical
> protest. It bristles with genuine sonic noise (most of it maintains a
> decibel level physically painful to the uninitiated), and its style incor-
> porates other features that qualify as cultural noise: the bizarre visual
> appearance of many of its proponents, texts which express political
> content, and deliberate inclusion of blacks and of women (not as the
> traditional "dumb chicks" singing to attract the libidinous attention of
> the audience, but – taboo of taboos – as competent musicians *playing
> instruments*, even drums).[30]

Bayton commented: "The problem was that so much music had been labelled
'male' that only the folk area was considered ideologically safe. Paradoxically,
then, the feminist challenge looked likely to result in retreat from rock and
amplified music altogether".[31] There was, continued Bayton, a continuous
debate about noisy music and women:

> This debate, which came to the boil in the early 1980s and which
> still lingers on, is an interesting manifestation of the wider con-
> tradiction within feminism of, on the one hand, wanting to do
> what men do, and, on the other, wanting to create something
> altogether different, which expresses women's "femaleness." This
> is currently called the "sameness/difference" or "equality/differ-
> ence" debate...[32]

It is interesting that several of the women that I spoke to were inspired to learn rock instruments by old-school male rock musicians: Gaye Black said that she was inspired by Jean-Jacques Burnel of The Stranglers: she "just couldn't get enough of him"; and Shanne Bradley said:

> I used to go to loads of gigs [in London] from the age of about thirteen: I saw Hawkwind, so there was Lemmy, Thin Lizzie (Phil Lynott): I saw just about everyone in the Seventies. I saw The Faces... The train was 32p return from Hertford where I lived.
> I just used to play some chords, I could play basic power chords. I taught myself playing to Hawkwind on Spanish Guitar and then I switched to bass.[33]

The complex structures of rock also inspired the young Ros Allen, of The Mekons (and later, Delta 5) before she left home:

> We were fourteen and it was amazing. I swapped some boots for a guitar and tried to play along to my Hendrix records...ambitious, I know. It was easier to follow the bass lines and I managed to stumble through "Hey Joe" and "Manic Depression," but I was always a closet bassist. It wasn't until I joined The Mekons that I got a real chance to play in a band.[34]

Punk's "Responsibility" to Women

According to Lucy Green, the concept of rebellion in the mid-1970s was still defined by male ideas of girls and sexuality; the task of punk was therefore to define this concept for girls who wanted to join in. Even today:

> Girls are...seen to avoid performance on electric or very loud instruments, especially those associated with popular music, most notably electric guitars and drums. Contrastingly, boys are depicted as flocking to these instruments, and to active involvement with popular music.[35]

Punk music was therefore entrusted with a socio-political responsibility that was to be tremendously difficult to exercise. Laing noted the low incidence of love, or "love," songs in punk music.[36] Although they were often replaced by polemical hate songs, arguably also using aggressive and male-associated vocabulary, I believe there was enough of a shift towards gender neutrality in these lyrics *not* to exclude female listeners and participants. Burchill and Parsons, however they felt about female instrumentalists, pointed out at the time that there was a shift away from defining girls and women as "picturesque topics and targets for songs."[37]

In critiques such as Reynolds and Press's *The Sex Revolts*, the authors fail to underline the difference between the stereotyping of males (who are operating from a position of relative power in society) and that of females (whose relative power is much less, particularly because the access they have to communication opportunities is controlled by the other gender). Their disgust at some women's attempts to rework pop (as opposed to rock), in order to empower themselves within what is assumed to be the more feminine commercial music form, is palpable. For Reynolds and Press, there is "a no win situation" for women. Here, they amplify a comment made by Frith and McRobbie:

> We should probably admit that we don't find representations of "strength" in pop particularly compelling. The autonomy of figures like Lennox and Joan Armatrading has the reek of mental hygiene and health-and-efficiency. As Simon Frith and Angela McRobbie wrote of the soft-core feminism of Helen Reddy's "I Am Woman": "What you hear is the voice of the idealised consumer, if the commodity for consumption in this instance is a packaged version of women's liberation." The posture of tyrannical, marauding omnipotence is pure rock'n'roll; benign self-empowerment isn't.[38]

Reynolds and Press fall into the trap of reinforcing stereotypes rather than exploring different grades of sexuality, and their book is a fine example of the rock ethos being presented through an aggressive style of writing.[39] As they assert, rock's attitudes have become entrenched and made into rules, and this makes it difficult to revolutionize.[40]

The bias against women's musical activities is infinitely older and broader, however. From George Upton, who asserted, "Man controls his emotions, and can give an outward expression of them. In woman, they are the dominating element, and so long as they are dominant she absorbs music,"[41] through Adorno, criticism of women who move across the amateur/professional divide is rife. Barbara Engh discusses Adorno's assertion that a woman's singing voice cannot be recorded well because it demands the presence of her body, whereas a man's can, because "his self is identical to his voice; his body disappears";[42] this early prejudice persists today, and is analysed at length by Shepherd in *Music as Social Text*,[43] where he identifies the stereotypes in rock and pop to which women (and men) conform in order to sound "good" on record.

However, in punk, female singers dispensed with the "female in rock" and "female in pop" stereotypes, and the rules of skill and stereotype that applied to each; *different* vocal styles were presented on stage and on record. Dave Laing labels the two main styles of rock and pop vocals as "confidential" and "declamatory" modes of singing:[44] punk singing was almost exclusively declamatory, as practised by Poly Styrene, Siouxsie, Ari Up of The Slits, Pauline of Penetration, and many others. The emphasis was not on craft, but on feeling.[45] Artists such as these featured vocal performances that consisted of screeching, shouting and chanting reminiscent of girls' playground rhymes (in particular The Slits and Delta 5) that bore no relation to the myth of the Siren. The following exchange between Lucy Toothpaste and Siouxsie of the Banshees illustrates the confidence that Siouxsie had in her role as vocalist with her band (and her own negative attitude to female instrumentalists!):

> Lucy: Can you play any instruments, Siouxsie?
> Siouxsie: I played the piano on "Staircase" [their latest single].
> Lucy: But you don't play it on stage.
> Siouxsie: I "play" the vocals.
> Lucy: There aren't many women instrumentalists and I think that's because of women's general lack of confidence – there aren't any models. It's much easier for a woman to visualise herself as a singer than as a guitarist or drummer...
> Siouxsie: I don't like females emulating a male instrumentalist. There have always been female instrumentalists, but it's always been a male interpretation. Then female singers have to be soft, enticing, with the spotlight...
> Lucy: So they're not expressing their own experience, but just the male fantasy.[46]

In addition, the subject-matter of many female-based punk bands did not lend itself to any of the stereotyped vocal timbres observed by Shepherd; Joy Press describes The Au Pairs as "didactic"[47] – whether this is an accurate description or not probably depends on one's political convictions. Greil Marcus admires the very characteristics that Press finds objectionable;[48] and Angela McRobbie, who knew the band in Birmingham, also admired and understood the rationale behind their attitude: "The idea was to create a band which injected into traditional left and feminist politics a sense of pleasure, mystery and eroticism."[49]

The revolution in the sound of female vocals was to be short-lived, but the shock of the sound of these voices, even heard out of context today, shows how oppositional they were. Simon Frith had written in 1975 that, even in US protest music in the 1960s, unfair rules applied:

Ari Up, The Slits. Photographer Desmond Coy

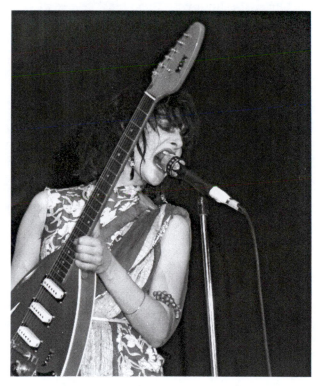

An unusual photograph of Siouxsie playing the guitar. Photograph Michael Ochs Archives;
© Getty Images

> Of the newly furrowed genres, folk was the most accessible to a young white woman – she could do it by herself. But there were special rules here too: in one corner we had Joan Baez, pure voiced, classical, cool, in the other sat Bob Dylan, impure, clumsy, and full of anger... Guess who was the genius...and who the lovely lady.[50]

Angry women, according to Frith, still had to sound nice as they made their political protest. He talks in the same article about Joni Mitchell's "chopped, emotionless" style of singing that *"isn't* easy on the ear"; it was this style of singing that was adapted by Siouxsie in the context of punk.

The voices of punk women and the music that accompanied them were not *for men.* They were *from women.* As such, they communicated in a different way from rock vocals *(from men for men* or *women for men)* or pop vocals *(women for women* or *men for women).* They bore an oblique relation to Hall's and Jefferson's definition of female defence/aggression, where "both the defensive and the aggressive responses are structured in reaction against a situation where masculine definitions...are in dominance."[51] In their research, they report girls giggling in groups as defensive, and inappropriate sexual titillation (for instance, at school with male teachers) as aggressive.[52] The punk bands presented a confusing text regardless of their gender, none more so than The Slits, who Caroline Coon described as a "radical step forward for women in rock'n'roll."[53] The review below shows how a male reporter from *NME* rationalized a performance by The Slits:

> St Trinian's tantrums dubbed over an oblique, hippy-ish malevolence... Rock has traditionally denied women certain positions through an inbuilt, narcissistic, repressive apparatus which wields stereotype and asinine implication, but in performance, The Slits suggest a new space; potential... The degree of control over the meaning of what they're doing and what they're coming up against (press, managers, clubs, etc.) is minimal. The onstage music maximises minimalism; the offstage manner minimalises the implications of the music.[54]

Penman is uncomfortable as the group "parody sexuality to the point where it becomes a...teasing, inverted approximation of the norm."[55] They refuse to engage with the audience:[56]

> Such wilful detachment sets up the conditions for violence, profit and apathy – as bad as The Clash "Who care about their fans" continuing to play the Music Machine time after time.[57]

Arguably The Slits, for Penman at least, have succeeded in creating anarchy on stage; the inappropriate sexual titillation that they engage in leaves him mystified. Later, the same reviewer follows up this point as he reviews one of The Raincoats' first gigs at the Acklam Hall in Notting Hill, saying that the group were "playing music and not male-comforting roles."[58]

Many women were conscious of breaking away from how music played on electronic rock-defined instruments should sound, and this was a feature of The Raincoats' music. As Gina Birch commented:

> [We were] pretty cut off from the mainstream at that time. I think I despised anything that wasn't what I was doing, because what I was doing was a revolution. We were revolutionaries as far as I was concerned and we were on a mission and what was going on outside was really just irrelevant.[59]

Frith's definition of authenticity cited earlier ("truth to self rather than truth to a movement or audience") should be applied to the way women performers operated in punk and post-punk, but the sort of authenticity Frith means applies only to men, as it is defined by men. Caroline Coon talked to me about the attitudes of the (male) journalists among whom she worked:

> I'd noticed the way the music press was treating women. The women that the music press liked were the tragic victims – Billie Holliday, Mama Cass, any of the women that had tried to break through into the system who actually had died, that was legitimate.[60]

It is not surprising, therefore, that music with vocal performances like this could not survive long in the mainstream. With male gatekeepers in control, "unsexual" female vocalists were unengaging; male concerns were not being addressed or nurtured. The different aesthetic rules they made meant that oppositional music made by females was doubly oppositional: against hegemony (as was male rock sound), and offensive to aesthetic ideals (there was no sonic oppositional ideal for women[61]). While it was not being deliberately exclusive (and thus stirring up some sort of oppositional furore that could be capitalized upon), the male viewpoint was negated. The authenticity of the female punks' aggression was also unquestionable and, as Ari remarked, had more extreme connotations for a woman musician than for a man:

> If boys were rebellious, it was okay – they're boys, they *can* be rebellious. But if it was women, that was like a totally different situation. It was a different planet. It was so taboo – we absolutely threatened the world. It's easy to be a woman who's all dressed up on stage and looking punky and rebellious on stage, and then when they come off the stage they look all dainty and camouflaged again. Let them walk around in all the real shit the way we did at the time.[62]

In our society, girls were expected to be respectable. Iain Chambers tries to pinpoint the reason why women who do not fit into the pop stereotype were so disturbing – "The concept of 'romance' is obviously central to the *whole cultural economy of pop*" – and speculates that, for teenyboppers, the gap between being "trapped between the sexual brutality of boys their own age and the seeming unavoidance of future domesticity"[63] has to be filled by some sort of fantasy. This fantasy is not permitted to be physical; it has to be cerebral. Barbara Bradby attributes the belief that girls can't and mustn't rock to the fact that:

> Rock's rhythmic insistence can be heard as a sexual insistence, and girls have always been thought by mass moralists to be especially at risk; the music so obviously denies the concept of feminine respectability.[64]

Susan McClary also modified her views on the liberation of women musicians, and warns of the dangers of succumbing to the dominating and containing beat of male producers:

> The options available to a woman musician in rock music are especially constrictive, for this musical discourse is typically characterised by its phallic backbeat. It is possible to try and downplay that beat, to attempt to defuse that energy – but this strategy often results in music that sounds enervated or stereotypically "feminine." It is also possible to appropriate the phallic energy of rock and to demonstrate (as Chrissie Hynde, Joan Jett and Lita Ford do so well) that boys don't have any corner on that market. But that beat can always threaten to overwhelm: witness Janet Jackson's containment by producers Jimmy Jam and Terry Lewis in (ironically) her song "Control."[65]

Therefore, there were assumptions to do with lyrics, and also sound, that a female rock instrumentalist had to overcome in order to undertake and enjoy her experience in a band. There was also a much more difficult problem to engage with: that of visual image and stereotype, explored with great skill by Bayton in *Frock Rock*.[66] For as Green observes:

> The sight and sound of the woman singing...affirms the correctness of the fact of what is absent: the unsuitability of any serious and lasting connection between woman and instrument, woman and technology...her real ability to manipulate technology is temporarily effaced.[67]

Aggression and Exclusion/Exclusivity

There can be a marked determination by young men to exclude women from their activities. Mica Nava describes a youth club where there was a strong hostility to the attendance of girls; girls-only nights (held once a week only) were started to allow the young women in the community to attend the club because male hostility was preventing them from doing so. These nights in turn were castigated by the boys and men, leading to their cancellation.[68] Nava articulates the dilemma that young women face and, perhaps in doing this, identifies why punk's opportunities for young women were embraced so avidly; she comments that:

> [fifteen-year-old girls] experience the fact of being judged by two, incongruent sets of expectations as the feeling that whatever they do, it is always wrong; a correct impression since so often if they are ful-filling the expectations of femininity they will be disappointing those of adolescence, and vice versa.[69]

This form of gatekeeping was much more direct than the "filtering" activities of the press; and the violence that attached itself to the punk scene rapidly after the tabloid reaction to it was not directed exclusively towards male bands. It is difficult to describe how polarized the different youth groups were at this time: punks were under threat from Teds (a second-generation version of Teddy Boys), straights and skinheads. Skinheads, in particular, took on the role of "gender-guardians" in addition to their racist disruption of gigs, and are often mentioned by reviewers and bands alike.[70] Straights disparaged everyone; football hooligans threatened everyone.

In the previous chapter, I discussed sexual harassment as an industrial hazard faced by women instrumentalists, and indeed many women musicians, and not just in this subculture. I have chosen deliberately to separate the harassment they faced as musicians from the violence they faced as punk performers. I have done this for several reasons: first, in case any reader has a feeling that sexual harassment is justified in any way by the incorporation of a woman's sexuality into her performing persona; second, because if I were to discuss the different ways that men's anger was displayed across both the social and the performing spectra in one chapter, the negative impression given would exceed the positive and productive experiences of these women, and possibly cloud their legacy; and, lastly, because as a performer I understand the desire to persist with the right to express oneself creatively, while also having had far too much direct experience of aggressive opposition myself.

The sheer senselessness of some of the violence was astounding. Ari here describes an incident that could have been fatal:

> Ari: I was stabbed for looking the way we looked. Some disco guy stabbed me, some John Travolta guy.
> Tessa: She had loads of layers of clothes on and he came up behind her with a knife and said, "Here's a Slit for YOU." But she had so many layers of clothes on, she was OK, she was only scratched.
> Ari: And by the time we turned round he had gone. There's no way we could go to the police, are you kidding me? Do you think people like us could go to the police at the time? We were harassed by police as well.[71]

Ari and Tessa went on to describe an incident where the police forcibly ejected them from a party and threw one of their female friends down an escalator.

Lucy O'Brien, keyboard-player of all-women Southampton band The Catholic Girls, also experienced direct physical opposition to what the band were doing, after a gig in a pub:

> We had no idea before we got there that it was a skinhead pub... skinheads just hated us; it ended in complete disaster because they were throwing cans and bottles at us when we were on stage and when we came off stage they followed us round to our van where we were loading up instruments and just collectively beat everyone up.[72]

In Lucy's case, the skinheads were objecting to the fact that the band was all-female, doing something they did not believe girls should be doing. The Mo-dettes had a strategy for dealing with skinheads, says June Miles-Kingston:

> When they used to come up on stage or throw things, I'd come down the front with the sticks and say, "Look, pack it up, shut up and just deal with it." They gain respect for you then. It's like anything – if the bully pushes and pushes, you've gotta push back, and then they stop.
> We ended up becoming such good friends with the skinheads that they became our followers, and two of them became our roadies. And they were actually our official roadies for years.[73]

Sometimes, though, the audience could feel intimidated by the proprietorial behaviour of these fans; a gig review by Paul Du Noyer remarks on the "unimpressive yobbery" at a Mo-dettes gig at the Marquee where fireworks and stink-bombs were let off after a stage invasion.[74] There was an element of "regulation" and control by their fans that must have been difficult for the band to extricate themselves from.

Racism was also rife, not only formally in right-wing organizations that attempted to recruit from all youth subcultures, but also informally. For instance, The Bodysnatchers, an all-female mixed-race band, were interviewed for *Spare Rib* by Lucy Toothpaste, who reported:

> When I saw them at Dingwalls...it was very noticeable that the burly male skinheads commandeered most of the area just in front of the stage. Nearly all the women gradually got pushed back or to the sides... With monotonous regularity, every time they play, like the other racially mixed bands on the Two-Tone label, they have to put up with a handful of skinheads Sieg-Heiling. "It's best to ignore them and in between numbers take the mick out of them," says Nicky.[75]

Things eventually came to a head for The Bodysnatchers, as lead singer Rhoda Dakar told me:

> My brother and his mate used to roadie for us and sell T-shirts. We were in Middlesbrough; they were a real hardcore racist crowd. What they were doing at our gig, I don't know. They wrecked the vans; the police had to be called. My brother and his friend had to be escorted out by the police. There were about twenty people [who] wanted to kill them. Terrible. I thought, I'm not talking to this audience, I'm not interested. It wasn't fear, they were just pigs. Stella went and spoke to them afterwards and said, "How can you hold these views and come and see us? What about Rhoda, then?," and they said, "She's all right, she's a tart, isn't she?," and I just thought, yeah, whatever. And they tried to follow us back to the hotel so we had to drive round for about half an hour just to lose them.[76]

Political extremism was a factor that was very much to the forefront at this time; skinheads aligned themselves with the Right, but other groups were even more direct. Delta 5 were beaten up by eight British Movement men who followed them from a bar – they recognized Ros as a "Communist Witch," resulting from an attitude here described by Greil Marcus:

> Leeds is also the home of the fascist British Movement, which is distinguished from its more famous parent, the National Front, by a complete lack of embarrassment at its Nazi origins. Unemployment and the dole underlie not only bohemia, but also the great no-future trumpeted in 1977, and the ideology of no-future has made it easy for the British Movement, setting up drinks all around, to recruit plenty of punks specifically to harass "Communist" bands. Add an extremely

well-focused consciousness of sexism on the left and a bitter reasser-
tion of male dominance among threatened young men on the right,
and the result is violence.[77]

Even older female artists respected as precursors of punk could be unsafe
on stage. Mark Ellen reported the following during a performance by Nico,
the ex-singer from The Velvet Underground, now touring as a solo artist and
playing harmonium on stage: "Had she ended with 'Deutschland Uber Alles,'
and not kept going, we would have been spared the spectacle of a bunch of
barbaric jerks driving her off stage by lobbing beer mugs."[78] This was quite
apart from the heckling reported by many of the women I spoke to.

Violence against women by men could also be of a sexual nature as discussed in an earlier chapter. This did not happen to every woman band-
member I spoke to, but it was a common enough phenomenon to cause
disquiet; sometimes the co-option of sexual clothing that was claimed to be
empowering by Caroline Coon[79] was not always seen as an ironic statement,
particularly in the less sophisticated provinces. The problem was that some
women were punished not just for being women, but also for being punks:
could this be what led to the gang-rape of one woman musician's sister, a
punk, by thirteen skinheads in Canning Town, East London?

There is also the issue of male violence from *within* the punk subculture to
consider. Most of the sociological work in this area seems to have taken place
in the US and Canada, where the punk subculture is still very much in evidence. This research concentrates on the situation of young women as outsiders; in the case of Lauraine Leblanc,[80] who put herself outside the world of her
school contemporaries in what can be defined as a deviant way, auto-ethnog-
raphy combines with a similar type of research to that undertaken by Cohen
in the Liverpool music world, although Cohen was much more an observer
and less embedded in the culture of her subjects. Leblanc discovered stories of
abuse in the home; other researchers, such as Roman,[81] describe how young
women join in the "slam dancing" in the "mosh pit" at gigs – a violent but, it
seems, cathartic experience. Eventually, they often have to create their own
spaces for slam-dancing at the peripheries of the male "mosh-pit." However,
the levels of group violence that included women, described in particular by
Roman, have not been reported in the British punk scene in the period of this
study; the violence experienced by my interviewees or their associates was
much more personal in nature, as noted in the earlier section on Industrial
Hazards (see Chapter 3) and will also be explored in later sections of this work.
Another aggressive activity was spitting, purported to have been started by
The Damned's drummer, Rat Scabies; women were not excused from being

the targets of "gobbing," but, as the following incident shows, could often look after themselves, as reported by the Shrewsbury fanzine, *Guttersnipe*:

> On came The Slits, all the lads were shouting abuse, the wankers were making me sick. The Slits started... They all started spitting and Ari told the band to stop. She told one of the audience to come and get on stage and when he did she gobbed a greenie right on his face. Good one Ari, he almost fell off the stage with shock, I don't know what he was expecting.[82]

Any female musician had to show a high degree of resilience; the "atmosphere" could be hostile throughout, from the personal life to the stage. Shanne Bradley describes her early experiences thus:

> I had people trying to stop me playing – lots of people. When I first was trying to play guitar someone came up and just cut the strings off to stop me playing. People just used to laugh if you were a girl trying to play guitar: they just didn't take you seriously. When I started doing gigs the roadies used to make comments and be laughing behind their hands: sexual things, and just thinking the idea that I was playing was a joke. It just made me more determined and angry. It was someone in a band. And Captain Sensible [bass player with The Damned] smashed up my Spanish guitar once, 'cos it wasn't cool. He smashed up my room and my Spanish guitar. He plugged in an iron and came at me with it, all "in the spirit of punk."[83]

Additionally, the volatile atmosphere of punk led to the occasional fracas even involving women as active participants. The politics of this time were constantly under review and discussion on the ground; this was part of the everyday experience for many young people. Discussions about racism, homophobia or misogyny could often lead to violence. For instance, Liverpool band The Accelerators, who had a female rhythm guitarist, were involved in an incident that grew from the male drummer of the band becoming annoyed with a women's group for criticizing his girlfriend for wearing sexy clothes. In retaliation, he wore a patch on his clothes saying "All Women's Libbers are Cunts" at a benefit gig for two local people who had been busted. A member of the local Women's Action Group, annoyed also by the volume of the music the band was playing, rushed the stage with some others and tipped a pint of beer over his head. The drummer then hit one of the woman attackers, and in the resulting melee another woman's face was cut on a broken beer glass, necessitating twenty stitches. Guitarist Kathy Apathy wrote to *Spare Rib*, after a report in the paper about the gig by the women concerned commented, "the sounds and mannerisms of punk rock are an expression of fascism in music and we want nothing whatever to do with it." She responded to the report that "[the woman's] face was cut, either by the glass she was originally holding, or by one held by one of her friends," writing that "No-one in the band was holding a glass." Consequently, a picket line was organized by the Women's Action Group to urge people not to watch "the sexist Accelerators" at a Rock Against Racism gig.[84] In the previous chapter on the Brighton scene there were some further examples of this sort of melting-pot of outlaw sensibilities being played out in the scenario of political action, and resulting in similar situations of impasse.

This fluidity of behaviour patterns meant that punk moved in and out of favour among the various formal political groupings at the time that it spoke to, as observed by the journalist Lucy Toothpaste (see Chapter 2).

Militarism in the Early 1980s

Rock music has many of the characteristics of National Service: leadership, noise, "desirable" phallic weapons, male camaraderie, capture of and expansion of territory,[85] power struggles and a distance in relationships to the opposite sex (women); it also takes on the role of expressing anger for *all* young people, just as war consists of national representatives sent to vent anger on other peoples in other locations. As with warfare, the representatives of dissatisfaction were predominantly young men; in rock music terms, young men signify anger and unrest, and young women signify peace and tranquillity. Margaret Thatcher's Britain of 1983 had a new, militaristic set of values, with Thatcher herself as the "Britannia"-style figurehead, as Marina Warner observes:

> The identification of the Prime Minister with the renewed military grandeur of Great Britain was accomplished in part through the language of female representation; it was natural, as it were, to see Mrs Thatcher as the embodiment of the spirit of Britain in travail and then in triumph, because of the way that spirit of Britain has been characterized, through its famous great queens on one hand, and the convention of Britannia on the other.[86]

Did The Sex Pistols clear the way for the anarchic and anti-royalist thought that allowed Margaret Thatcher to challenge and take over the iconic role of Queen of England? Was traditional maleness reinstated by the Falklands War of 1982 and pop music relegated to the feminized pursuit of showbiz? Chambers writes:

> Punk proclaimed the necessity of violating the quiet, everyday script
> of "common sense." It proposed a macabre parody of the underlying
> idealism of "Englishness" – that dour pragmatism that sees no future
> beyond the present, and no present except that inherited, apparently
> unmodified, from the past.[87]

The chaos symbolized by punk and the disruption caused to "common sense" was superseded by the "principled nationalism"[88] of the Falklands War. Ironically, the army-chic promoted by The Clash may have prepared a section of the unemployed British youth for army life. As Reynolds and Press observe: "Perhaps The Clash's real lament was that they longed for a Britain that was truly Great, a country that deserved their pride and fervour, a country worth dying for."[89]

It is interesting to note that as electronic, synthesizer pop developed in the early 1980s (a feminized male performance genre, *sans* phallus), and the war began, "real men" went off to fight the "Argies." This war, which lasted only three months, had a huge impact on Britain: first, the country had not been officially at war since the 1940s, and the impression we had of ourselves as a generally peace-loving nation was swept away; second, "national pride" was reinstated, jingoism re-emerged, and the identity of Britain reverted to that of an aggressive and proactive nation, rather than one in the grip of recession and industrial stagnation. The crisis that was expressed by the punks was thus superseded by an external crisis that some said had been manufactured precisely to consolidate Thatcher's government and marginalize Britain's internal ailments.

The influx of women into rock bands that had appeared to both terrify and sexually excite male commentators began to ebb, and they returned to their decorative roles as vocalists, allowing men to claim back their technology and the power that went with it. In a stroke of genius, Thatcher had already co-opted the entrepreneurial part of punk, detached it from its political meaning, and recreated it as enterprise culture. As Jon Savage observes:

> The Conservatives' victory did mark an end to the period of social
> unrest which Punk had charted so intimately. The post-war consensus
> was now over. "Try it": now people had. The very freedom which Punk
> had not only sung about, but enacted in every possible sense, was
> now hijacked by the New Right to mean something quite different: an
> inequality that was not only institutionalised but installed as a ruling
> cultural and social principle.[90]

Under Thatcher, the Conservative Party had been changed to appeal to a populace who regarded themselves as estranged individuals rather than a body of the discontented working class.[91] The increasing violence of punk gigs, fuelled by tabloid "moral panics,"[92] proved divisive for the punk subculture. It became necessary for some bands to rationalize their activities as small businesses, with self-employed personnel, and as such to focus on money-making over communication, on giving pleasure rather than provocation. As punk developed into more commercial forms of music, women were pushed aside and their disturbing presence was almost eradicated from the market. Punk rock, which for many men had been just another development of the rock genre, had for women given unprecedented access to a voice and a platform. Willis observes that the hippies did not "secure the conditions for their own continuance"[93] and that is why their longed-for revolution did not happen; the same could be said of the girls who joined bands at this time, probably because they carried responsibility for social change alongside their awareness of their marginalization in "outer" society; the boys could "have a good time with one eye on a deal" – and this in addition to the "social responsibility" mentioned earlier.

It seems that in peacetime there must be non-military sites for the expression and dispersal of surplus male energy,[94] and in the late 1970s the cultural phenomenon of punk served this purpose; the difference from other such "sites" was the awareness of equal opportunities brought about by changes in the law, and also the unemployed and bohemian nature of the associated subculture, unlike most earlier subcultures which were based in the leisure-time of employed male and female young people. Punk expressed the anger felt by both genders, and this is what gave it its unusual and radical elements. When the Falklands War began, militarism returned as the repository for male energy and aggression, and punk was consequently replaced as a musical trend by what Savage identified as the return of the feminine in New Romanticism – although it was a femininity reserved for males. Should this theory of the re-establishment of national maleness seem far-fetched, Christopher Ballantyne's study of the music of South Africa from 1948 to 1960 shows this happening in African culture as a result of migrancy after the assertion of apartheid, with the same collusion by the press in the stifling of music-making by empowered women. Men had to find "strategies for rehabilitating masculinity" that "handicapped women by limiting them to carriers of sexual frisson for men's groups."[95] From the 1930s onwards, there had been active all-female music troupes, and these all but vanished to be replaced by groups in which the female members were hired for their decorative and sensual value above anything else.[96]

Paradoxically, this was the exact opposite experience from that of The Ivy Benson Band, who were an all-female brass band during and after the Second World War. They had become the BBC house band, as the war took so many men players off to the front to defend their country. An opportunity arose for female musicians not only to work alongside men, but to actually replace them, as the army required so many of Britain's young men to join up and fight for their country. Benson's band were not only unthreatening to the public, but they were welcome. After the war, however, they were stripped of their privileges and the window of opportunity was closed to them.[97] The difference between their situation and that of the women discussed in this book is in the subcultural, youth-oriented nature of rock music, situated in opposition to the mainstream public taste. Although rock music is entertainment for young people, it has not always been so for older people, and punk in particular served as an abrasive reminder that all was not well in British society. The purpose of Benson's musicians during the Second World War was as escapist entertainment, to soothe the nation's nerves; the purpose of punk music was to express the angry feelings of a disaffected generation, and to empower them, regardless of their gender.

Historically, opportunities for women instrumentalists have tended to come about when there have been shortages of skills, such as in times of war,[98] or when men's interest is diverted towards other areas; in the final chapter, we will see how this happens in rock music.

Finally, Lucy Green points out that musical meanings are gendered, not only in the outside world (society), but also in the inside world (here she cites school; I suggest also the home):

> Gendered musical meanings are not only handed down through history; they persist in the organisation of musical production and reception in present-day society at large, and they are also re-enacted daily in the life of the music classroom as a dynamic, microcosmic version of the wider society.[99]

So from the classroom to the mediated outside world (as Kruse observed at the beginning of this chapter), the impact of gender determinism is impossible to escape for female players. To this can be added another observation by Attali about music: "Its order simulates the social order, and its dissonances express marginalities. *The code of music simulates the accepted rules of society.*"[100]

If we apply Attali's words to the "dissonance" of rock music, we could infer that rock fans see themselves as belonging to the margins of society; but still, this society has rules, and these rules often apply as much at the margins as at the centre. Changing the rules of music at the margins, where there are stress points with hegemonic culture, is as difficult as changing those at the centre of society, and this will be discussed at greater length in the next chapter.

To close this chapter in a way that will return us to the moment in question, I will return to the vernacular, and include the exchange between a female bass-player (used in an earlier chapter) and a female rock fan, printed in *Sounds* in 1976:

> I'm a bass guitarist who would like to play good, heavy rock (i.e. Sabs, Fairies), but because I'm a girl, no one's interested... You see I just want to stand on stage and play bass and that is (at the moment) unacceptable because I know (from experience) that men don't like the idea that girls can play as well, if not better, than them (I'm no women's libber – I'm talking about musical ability). I don't believe I'm the only person who feels this way, but if I am, surely I've not been devoting my life to an ambition which is doomed to failure just because I'm "the wrong sex" for a bassist? Maybe the answer lies in mixed bands... (Joy [the ferret], Carpenders Park, Watford, Herts).

And the reply:

> [T]he reason why all-female rock bands have not yet made it in the business is (1) because rock music has always been associated with lads therefore all-female bands are regarded as a joke, (2) because 90% of rock audiences consist of male chauvinist pigs who are not prepared to give such bands a chance. Margie, Newcastle Upon Tyne, Tyne and Wear.[101]

5 The Aftermath

> Pop's anti-intellectualism, it's [sic] rejection of a cultural herit-
> age in favour of instant creativity, means that its executants rely
> entirely on their instincts...given such inspiration, it can move
> brilliantly and rapidly along a path but eventually it finds itself
> facing a brick wall without the means to climb over it.[1]

Already, we have seen that the political mood of Britain changed immensely with the election of Margaret Thatcher's government in 1979,
and how this affected the context of the subcultural activity surrounding
punk. We have also seen how violence within the scene directed not just
at women in bands and in the audience, but also at punks in general (the
burning down of the Brighton and Hove Resource Centre, for instance)
was successful in suppressing and containing changes that the subculture could have brought about in the mainstream, particularly in terms
of empowering female instrumentalists in the music industry.

The ending of the moment is as difficult to pinpoint as the beginning. Muggleton describes how one of his "subculturalists" infers that
the moment of punk began with the infamous interview of The Sex Pistols by Bill Grundy on Thames Television on 1 December 1976, in which
the band and their followers swore on live TV, goaded by a drunken
Grundy.[2] Before this, Muggleton quotes his source, who claims, "'nobody
knew what a punk was'." The phenomenon had begun months before
this, underground; the end of punk happened just as gradually and, with
it, the end of the subcultural social privileges enjoyed by participants in
the scene. The music press, in particular the *New Musical Express*, was
acknowledging feminism and bands with strong female participants to
a degree never seen previously; "post-punk"[3] bands such as The Au Pairs
and Delta 5 were articulating new attitudes to music-making in interviews that were respectful rather than mocking in tone.

However, I found much evidence in the press of the assimilation of
the palatable elements of the subculture, discarding its revolutionary
core. According to Laing, the "exclusivist" tendencies of punk meant that
any music produced under its umbrella risked becoming alienated from
new audiences unless a positive attempt was made to engage with them.[4]
Laing, Hebdige and Frith are unanimous in their observations regarding
the recuperation of street lifestyles and music by the mainstream and

their conversion into commodities. However, I would not go so far as the writers of the pamphlet *The End of Music*, who blamed Malcolm McLaren himself not only for the emasculation of The Situationists but also for the perpetuation of the pop myth through punk:

> McLaren had helped to recuperate the situationist critique which, "after being suitably doctored" [*sic*], was used as a force able to keep pop music kicking as pacification agent of the young proletariat both in terms of channelling energy into hierarchical aspiration, fake liberation from drudgery and the goal of a higher level of wage slavery with all its alluring but alienated sexual appeal. T-shirts bearing slogans like "Be reasonable, demand the impossible," now meant "buy some of my kinky gear...and help make me a rich man."[5]

The activities of McLaren after the demise of The Sex Pistols, which will be discussed later in this chapter, certainly signalled a "separation" from the ideology of punk. Ironically perhaps, there were elements of Thatcher's ideology that struck a chord with those of the punks who valued independence over separation; the "independence" Laing describes was identified by Margaret Thatcher as "enterprise." Part of Thatcher's plan concerned the importance of small businesses as a route out of Britain's economic recession and increasingly evident unemployment problem that for some was embodied in the visibility of the punk subculture on the streets of every town in Britain. It was almost as though she was inspired by the shake-up that McLaren's activities had given the major record labels and used the model of the independents to develop the Enterprise Allowance Scheme, which formally recognized and rewarded those who wished to start up small businesses of their own. If this was the case, her skills of incorporation and the accompanying "emasculation" of subcultural meaning were consummate, as Jon Savage has noted (see Chapter 4). June Miles-Kingston agrees:

> About 1979/80, it all fell flat. It was because of Thatcher...it was, "England is a great place, a land of opportunity." Punk wasn't about that – it was about, "The kids have got nothing, we're going to show off about that and do something about it." They were very clever about it in a way, because the government turned it round and said, "Go out and get yourself a job and you can have the biggest car and the biggest telly," and it completely ruined the country as far as I can tell.[6]

Punk, in common with other subcultures, had incorporated alienation as well as independence. The time had been right for a seemingly oppositional youth movement: a general weariness of young people with formal politics and culture seems to have been in the air towards the end of the 1970s and the beginning of the 1980s. To the young unemployed person, the battles between the trade unions and the Heath and Callaghan governments meant nothing; disengagement from mainstream politics resulted from a feeling of rejection from society. Both the unions and the incumbent Labour government ignored the frustrations of the unemployed, proposing crisis-management strategies rather than long-term solutions. It was an environment in which pressure from parents to conform made little sense, especially if those parents were also unemployed.[7] Peter York remarked on the confusion of subcultural styles caused by this blurring of distinctions between parent and offspring: "A substantial group of teenagers…no longer believed in the future, but they'd lost any real links with the past. There weren't any *real* traditional styles left. The fact that you could 'revive' a style meant that it was dead at the roots."[8] Punk had provided a nihilistic novelty of style that matched the mood of its participants. Punks themselves tended to be either anarchic, or apolitical; it was these apolitical punks, unaligned to concepts of working-class struggle, whose activities were "recuperated" into Thatcherite ideology.

Equality in Unemployment equals Equality of *Lack* of Opportunity

The recession in the United Kingdom in the 1970s particularly affected young people of school-leaving age. Later it was to gather pace, resulting in 3 million unemployed people of all ages by 1981. It had an oddly levelling effect across gender boundaries. Michael Brake discusses the effect of this unemployment on young working-class women in Britain, with reference to an Australian study by Presdee in 1982; the girls displayed resentment at being forced by patriarchal assumptions into a subordinate role in the home:

> They presented the same contradictory sentiments found in studies of their young working class male counterparts. Fatalism was mixed with anger, resignation with revolt, ignorance with worldly wisdom, all "underpinned by a deadening material poverty"… Young women are not only infantilised by unemployment, but become forcibly recruited into the domestic labour role of housewife.[9]

Frith reiterates this:

> Mass youth unemployment has been, unexpectedly, a more aggravating problem for girls than boys: working-class girls, leaving school at sixteen, have always used full-time work as a means to temporary independence, a way of getting out of the home during work and leisure; on the dole, they find themselves still treated by their parents as dependent, expected to work in the home instead. Boys, by contrast, get the freedom of the streets whether they're working or not.[10]

However, the situation was hardly more tolerable for young men. The implications of the recession on the rite of passage from adolescence to adulthood, pinpointing the raising of the school-leaving age in the early 1970s as an additional factor in the frustration of young people, are described thus by Mica Nava:

> The decline in the material power of young people has led to a decline in their importance as consumers. Since so few jobs are available, "adult" comportment and "respectable" appearance become increasingly irrelevant... Not only are people increasingly disassociated from the culture of employment and from financial resources of their own, they are confined to the local street and family culture of their schooldays. This process of infantilisation which has occurred over recent years has increased the relative importance of the informal activities and relations of the street, of leisure, the youth club and the domestic sphere.[11]

Individualism as Personal Politics

As Muggleton observed with all of the "subculturalists" he interviewed, "Subcultures can...be understood, somewhat paradoxically, as collective expressions and celebrations of individualism."[12] The lack of a plan for the future (for there was "no future") allowed the reinterpretation of so many of its characteristics to be kidnapped by Thatcherism. The incorporation of style that had happened in the world of pop music, as described by Laing above, now happened to the ideals and outlook of those who lived the life. This had occurred before, although not perhaps in such an extreme way, but Paul Willis, who studied hippy culture, remarked of the ending of its influence:

> The detailed, informal and lived can enjoy its victory in a larger failure. The reproduction of more complex forms of social organization may even take the form of ideological inversions and experimentations in local cultural politics. If it is to even maintain its own existence, never mind its subversion into complex forms of its opposite, the detailed dialectics of cultural transformation and personal liberation must also stretch to a dialectic with political and material structures.[13]

The hippies' rejection of, and lack of engagement with, the world at large had led to complete introversion and no "strategies of passage from one to the other."[14] The situation regarding punk was slightly different, in that its DIY ideology apparently became transformed by Thatcher's policies into enterprise culture. Additionally, the effects of moral panic meant that in order to be in a punk band, and in particular to be a female in one, you had to make a decision: to carry on as a sort of outlaw (which had always been the case with the Crass Collective that included Poison Girls, Rubella Ballet and Honey Bane) or to attempt to assimilate (as did Gina Birch, who signed to a major label). Some decided to give up altogether (as did The Au Pairs and many of the instrumentalists in the local bands I spoke to).

After The Sex Pistols ceased to exist in 1978, there was still an upsurge of visible strong female performers, but the debate and friction became polarized. Because there was no longer a high-profile anti-major stance in the music business (the small labels had set up an alternative business that catered for many different types of music and their small audiences), this was an alternative arrangement and not an oppositional one, and all sides could feel they had won; each major label had a moderate stable of "punk" acts as well as new-wave groups who were less abrasive – although, naturally, the investment by the majors came to favour the less controversial acts. The small labels were "preaching to the converted" rather than evangelizing to the many, presumably a condition of the essential small-business work ethic. With the ending of the enabling ethic of punk came the ending of the progress of female instrumentalists as anything other than a novelty. Instead, new technology became the gimmick, both on- and offstage.

The Excitement Wanes

In the early 1980s, there was a change in the scene that led to the disintegration of many of the bands with strong female personnel. For Gina Birch, this was brought about by a marked change of attitude by a band at the heart of Rough Trade Records, her world:

> I remember Green from Scritti Politti declaring that the group was no longer a democracy: he was in charge, and for me that was an enormous turning-point. We made a big deal about equality within the group, and everybody contributed, everybody took credit, payment exactly the same. At Rough Trade, for example, whatever job you did, you got the same salary. And then Scritti Politti changed their way, and of course Gang of Four, heart of the beast, they signed to EMI. I suppose the Pistols had done that already, but we were in a more left field area.[15]

This change was felt across the country: Pauline Murray describes what happened in the north-east:

> This is the problem really: because all the ambitious people came along on the bandwagon of it, your Stings and all these people who were using it to get to where they wanted to be. I can remember

coming up to the invisible line with The Invisible Girls thing, and there is a line to cross if you want to get to that next [stage]. It's to do with abandoning people you know, your family, and your principles, I wasn't prepared to cross that line. I wasn't ambitious enough to cross that line to become all these people I'm talking about. You can pick them all out [the bands] who crossed the line. I never crossed it, and I have no regrets about it, even though I know that I can sing and I know I can perform and I know that I could do all right.

With the music business, there's no set rules, there's no set pattern, you can't say that I'm going from A to B, it's just elusive, and I didn't like that, where it's all based on someone else's whim.[16]

With the commercialization of music comes the demand from the record company for standards that will place the music in an arena that the public can evaluate according to precedent. Enid Williams found herself sacked from Girlschool because she was too fat; Two Tone band The Bodysnatchers metamorphosed into the more showbiz Belle Stars. Record companies tried to mirror more malleable "acts" that were having commercial success. This is what happened to The Mo-dettes:

It was the time of Bananarama, and that's what everybody wanted to promote, and we wouldn't go down that road. The worst thing we did, we made a single with Decca that had a pop producer, and that was the demise of it, really. They chucked [guitarist] Kate out, much to my disgust...and I thought, well what do I do? If I leave, that's The Mo-dettes finished... Put into a little box, you've gotta look like this, sound like this – the worst thing was we went in one day they'd put this session musician playing guitar on it. And that was the last straw for me and I said, "That's it, I've had enough," and [bassist] Jane said, "Yeah, so have I." I was really sad actually – five years of your life, when you've been doing something like that and it's so important in that whole scheme of things. Although we were in no way a great band and no way brilliant music, there was just something about the whole spirit of it that I totally loved, and didn't want to let go of![17]

This was a classic example of record company manipulation, as they attempted to capitalize on the commercial aspect of a punk band by severing it from the grass roots. Then, as Gina says:

Everyone just started to fade away, and I'm not sure if they faded away or the opportunities for them to be visible disappeared. But this kind of huge power and passion just kind of fizzled out. I remember

taking all of my punk rock records, all the ones that people had personally given to me and done drawings on, down the Record and Tape
Exchange.[18] I just felt that this is a phoney load of crap: I came down to
earth with a bang. I really felt this sense of being conned.[19]

This exhaustion of energy was echoed by Miranda, of The Bodysnatchers:
"The whole idea of 2-Tone was to break down all the barriers imposed by
big rock bands. But now it's [sic] energy has gone – it's like flogging a dead
horse."[20] Even The Slits, who had a good relationship with their major label
CBS, found that the realities of being female caught up with some of the
personnel in the band, just as their years of work were about to consolidate.
Asked if she ever advised the band against anything, their manager, Christine, replied:

> Yes, I advised them against splitting up. They split up in early '82, but
> they were in a uniquely strong position at that point, even though
> they'd released the LP on CBS that wasn't particularly commercially
> successful. But CBS were totally into them. They'd got the top man
> at CBS and Muff Winwood thinking the sun shone out of their arses.
> Their next LP, they could have taken six months off, they didn't have
> to just say, "It's over." The other sad thing about that was that they
> were going to go to South America to record, somewhere they hadn't
> been. They were going to be produced by a Salsa producer, and CBS
> were going to pay for it. To me this was just the maddest thing really:
> they were already into world music and they had a few songs and
> hopefully they could bring something up while they were there. So
> that went, and so did all the visits to the Far East.[21]

"Burnout" was cited over and over again as a reason for quitting. In Lora
Logic's case, a mistrust of the music business led to her doing everything for
the band, and she became overwhelmed and exhausted by the responsibilities. An alternative way of life was offered to her, and she decided to stop:

> My best friend at school moved into the Krishna temple in Soho
> Street. One day she came to see me and she told me about her new
> life. I went to visit her and I thought, this is what I want. I want to
> live like this too. It's not that I wanted to give music up altogether,
> but I needed a break; I'd been doing it night and day since I was
> fifteen. I was very young and it was a lot to take on my shoulders.
> I was managing the band, and writing all the songs, and keeping
> the boys together... There was five boys and me... I just thought,
> It's time for a big change, and so I split the band up, which they
> didn't like at all, we'd got to a certain stage and there was a tour
> of America in the pipeline. We'd worked so hard to get where we

were and then I just said, "OK, that's it." I don't think they were very happy with me.[22]

Hester Smith describes the constant round of disappointment and hope that eventually ground down her optimism:

> I wouldn't go through that again. It does your head in...the worst thing about it is constantly being disappointed, things coming up that raise your hopes and then just not working out. I couldn't go through that. All that pushing yourself at people you have to do, I'm so squeamish about that. Trying to get gigs, trying to get people interested in you, all that being dependent on someone else liking you...or they do like you, and then suddenly they just don't. All that stuff, it's horrible.[23]

For some of the other women I spoke to, their environment changed as they moved away. Lucy O'Brien left Southampton to go to Leeds University to study journalism, and it was not until she got there and played in other bands that she realized "just how good The Catholic Girls had been."[24] Kate Hayes from Brighton band The Objeks explained that her band had been very much a product of the art college:

> We'd finished – we'd finished our courses, we'd finished *why* we were in Brighton. Paul was going to London. It was through lack of knowing where to go with it really. Either we were going to all live together and make this thing a happening thing, where we were always in a group, or it was going to fall apart... And it fell apart because we weren't going to be living together. We weren't going to be thrown together in that way.[25]

Another problem that occurred was addiction to drugs: many punks used amphetamine sulphate to facilitate their twenty-four-hour existence, and this is evident in the speed(!) of their music. Others used other substances. Lora Logic cited overuse of cannabis as one of the reasons she withdrew from the music business. I was also told of heroin addiction by more than one interviewee; the invasion of heroin as a preferred recreational drug, replacing amphetamine sulphate, is regarded as "the beginning of the end" for the punk scene.[26] Tessa Pollitt, in an interview with *3:AM Magazine*, said:

> I had a problem with heroin, and I have theories about it: it seems London was flooded with heroin around the time punk was losing direction, and it seems to me to be no coincidence. It almost felt to me as though there was a conspiracy to sedate people.[27]

She told me her reasons for using the drug:

> When you have been busy from the age of seventeen to however old
> I was then, twenty-one, twenty-two, it's a real...not disappointment,
> but you feel invalid, suddenly; you have been so busy, so creative, you
> feel a bit empty.[28]

Palmolive's feelings were similar, although she followed a religious route to
conquer the emptiness she felt: "We were expressing a crisis we were going
through, but there has to be something. That's what I felt. There has to be
something beyond this, you know?"[29]

Because of the lack of precedent, even simple things like saying "No" to gigs
and tours did not occur to some bands; The Bodysnatchers toured constantly,
and eventually exhausted themselves:

> We were tired – we were in the middle of a tour; we came off tour
> for a couple of days to record a single. We did loads of gigs; The Body-
> snatchers gigged so much. We were offered them and it just never
> occurred to anybody to say, "No, we don't want to do it" – we just did
> everything we were offered, pretty much.[30]

Constant touring and the resulting fatigue could also mean that song-
writing suffered, with the consequence that a band did not refresh their set
frequently enough, as The Mo-dettes discovered:

> We didn't do any song-writing when we were touring – that's the
> other thing, we never ever moved on as a band, that was the problem.
> I don't think we could be bothered – we had a reasonable set together,
> and if we had one new song or two new songs every time we went off
> on a mini-tour, we were happy with that. I just don't think there was
> the motivation there, really.[31]

Lesley Woods became exhausted and lost her voice:

> When The Au Pairs finished I lost my voice, which meant my confi-
> dence took a very big knock. It was a culmination of factors. All the
> politics merged with the reality.
> I got into a violent relationship with a woman. It didn't last very
> long but it had a very profound effect on me. It was a determining
> factor in why the band split up. Partly as a result of that I became
> unable to function. I probably lost my voice through just abusing
> it.[32]

The Boyfriend Factor

I first played bass in a band because my boyfriend at the time (along with some friends) persuaded me to. This was a common factor, particularly in mixed bands such as The Adverts. It could also be a factor in the exit of young women from the band scene – though often not their men:

> *What did your partner think?*
> He was the singer!
> *Why did you stop?*
> Split up with the singer![33]

However, if Hugh Cornwell's comments at the time are representative of how male rock performers feel, it is the women's emotions that ruin the band, not the men's:

> *Would he ever consider giving a woman the opportunity to play alongside him in a band?*
> No, I don't think so. I don't think I really want to play music with women. They always end up getting involved with someone in the band and then the band is finished. Why? Because then two people have got something that the others haven't got. It's lost its democratic feel. I think women are more emotional than men. And emotional people are very difficult to work with. I'm a real chauvinist. Totally.[34]

These comments are remarkable in the similarity of their tone to those made by George Upton almost a century previously. However, they are contradicted by the comments of one of the women who replied to my questionnaire who told me how the *emotions* of her new boyfriend prevented her from performing any more:

> *Why did you first form a band?*
> My partner at the time was in a band and I got the bug from him.
> *Do you still play in a band?*
> I dabbled for a while in 85/86...by this time I had a new partner who was insanely jealous of my success in my previous band and he refused to let me talk about it.[35]

Another told me how her boyfriend's emotions led to his trying to prevent her from joining a band in the first place:

> *What did your partner think?*
> He hated it! I think he was jealous. He wouldn't look after the babies, so I took them with me to rehearsals.[36]

And Jane Munro's experience of playing in a band with her boyfriend led to her giving up playing bass altogether to escape from her relationship with him:

> I got into a relationship with a guy who played keyboards on our second album. And he was really, really manipulative; he hated me going away on tour and was pathologically jealous and seemed to imagine I'd be leaping into bed with any passing bloke (which I actually wasn't at all). The combination of the atmosphere within the band degenerating and the pressure that I was getting from him, I just thought "Oh God, I can't be doing with this any more." So I left in the end. [I carried on playing] in a band with him, which was absolutely unbearable; it was dreadful because I was with him twenty-four hours a day. He was also an ex-bass player, but a very technically adept one, and just completely undermined me. It was one of the worst periods of my life. I gave up playing because it was a way of getting away from him. I didn't want to be in a band with him, and it was part of my exit strategy from the relationship; it just completely finished me in terms of playing.[37]

Sexual relationships between opposite sexes within bands are not always destructive: Suzi Quatro toured for years with her partner, although she was occasionally criticized in the music press for this. Neither are same-sex relationships within bands necessarily constructive.[38]

As a rather amusing aside, I was told by one band-member of her frustration at one of the principal songwriter's changes of musical direction according to the types of bands her different boyfriends performed in, leading her to exclaim, "I don't want to sing your boyfriends!" Bands can split up for many reasons, and tend to encourage factions and strong emotional feelings purely because of the intensity of the experience. Female performers are unique in one way, however, and when some of the members of The Slits found themselves pregnant, this signalled the end of their careers:

> They had been touring too much – fatigue; Ari was pregnant, I was pregnant. At that point I think Viv really decided she'd had enough. I did try to talk them out of it. But there was no way to talk Viv out of it; she'd made her mind up and that was it, and everybody else just had to fall in line.[39]

Reversion to Stereotype: The Industry Recuperates

Malcolm McLaren had diverted his attention to the potential of the Sony Walkman, and the issue of home taping that was troubling the majors, with the romantic notion of piracy as a new political polemic. It is hard to overestimate the difference this small device made to the consumption of music. Previously, portability meant hoisting a beatbox onto the shoulders and broadcasting one's taste in music to surrounding people; the 1982 debut of the Walkman enabled the "closing-off" of personal space and a marked increase in music-for-me as opposed to music-for-sharing. It perfectly mirrored the Thatcherite philosophy that "there is no such thing as society." As Judith Williamson wrote at the time: "The Walkman is primarily a way of escaping from a *shared* experience or environment. It produces a privatized sound, in the public domain: a weapon of the individual against the communal."[40]

McLaren leaped on this new technology and the record industry's panics about home taping[41] and formed Bow Wow Wow, a band whose claim to controversy was the fact that their lead singer Annabella Lwin was fourteen, and was photographed naked for the album sleeve in a mock-up of Manet's painting, *Le dejeuner sur l'herbe*.[42] Annabella also made many pseudo-sexual vocal noises on the band's recordings and appears to have been very naïve about what she had been asked to do, as the following exchanges from an interview in style magazine *The Face* imply. One of their songs was entitled "Sexy Eiffel Tower," and Lwin's mother was reportedly shocked on hearing her daughter gasping in such a way:

> ...I explained to her that I was meant to be falling. I know everyone thinks it was Malcolm's idea to get a sexual kind of turn on because I was breathing like having orgasms or something, but the actual thing is that I was supposed to be falling off the Eiffel Tower. That's what I'm actually singing about. Truthfully...I get a real happy feeling 'cos I imagine how I'm falling.[43]

The interviewer then goes on to enquire about song-writing royalties in order to inform the reader that Annabella is being exploited in this way too, for without song-writing credits she will stand to make less money than other members of the band, or their manager if he has contributed to the songs:[44]

> *But if you're into gold, you're not going to get as much as the others, because you don't have any songwriting credits, do you?*
> No, not as far as the songwriting goes. I've written lyrics myself, poems, right?... When I joined the group I used to say "How about singing this poem that's about me?" But that's the whole thing, what you have to do is include everybody. You want everyone to join in and that's how I began to realise that the songs were done to aim not just at one person but at quite a few people.[45]

The message from McLaren had therefore changed dramatically, from exploiting what he implied was the pomposity of the established music business, to exploiting a young and vulnerable girl. This was not the first time McLaren had tried to exploit female sexuality in pop music: Reynolds and Press describe his intention to make a semi-porn film starring The Slits, in which they would have become striptease dancers in Mexico after finding themselves unable to perform as musicians due to Mexican misogyny, eventually marrying and becoming disco stars.[46] This was revealed by McLaren in an interview in *Melody Maker* in 1979; McLaren "still gets excited as he outlines his idea."[47] It is not surprising that the band rejected his management advances, which failed on a musical front before anything else. As Ari says:

> I remember him coming into the rehearsal rooms and that was the end of it then, because when he started saying he wanted musical input, it didn't work. We wanted him to manage us, not tell us how to play. He wanted us to be like the female Pistols. He was saying, "Oh you know, it's got to be guitar-orientated, because in punk bands, it's all about guitar, the guitar is the main thing in the front. Blah, blah, blah, play the guitar in the front." And we *were* playing the guitar in the front – that's the irony. So there was a heavy bass sound: it was, to him, "Oh, there's too much bass already. Don't play it like that!" But we wouldn't have been The Slits if we hadn't stuck to our sound![48]

Other bands, too, encouraged their women personnel into more traditional roles, albeit less controversially, notably The Human League, a band who had only moderate success until they introduced two young women to the band, who, according to Jon Savage, acted as taste arbiters, bringing the dance floor to the band. The girls had been "discovered" (a clever marketing ploy which would appeal greatly to other young girls) while dancing in a nightclub. Savage describes them "dancing and singing with the gleefulness of the suddenly empowered."[49] However, in an interview (again in *The Face*) Joanne Catherall and Suzanne Sulley report the conditional nature of their empowerment:

> S (Suzanne): The thing is with The Human League – nobody's really delegated to do anything. Nobody has said to us that we've got to sing and dance. If we wanted to play keyboards, we could...
> J (Joanne): If we learned how...
> The obvious question – don't they want to write as well?
> J: I don't know. It frightens me, the thought of having to go to Philip or Ian or Jo and say "I've got this idea." They're all so "we know it all because we've been in the business three years" and they've got this attitude that we can't really know anything yet because we've only been in the group a year and we can't *really* know what we're talk-

ing about... Like Philip said, they do know a lot more because they've worked at it, and they've had failures.

S: It's very difficult for us because we're in a position where we don't really have to learn. We don't have to do anything if we don't want to, except look nice...[50]

By the early 1980s, feisty girls, such as fun band Bananarama, were acceptable in chart terms[51] so long as they were "pop"- rather than "rock"-oriented, and their lyrics did not deal with "sensitive" issues.

Censorship

The Au Pairs experienced direct censorship – Martin Cloonan reports an interview in *NME* with BBC producer Roger Casstles after they recorded two songs for BBC 2's *Look, Hear* programme, which was broadcast in the early evening. One of the songs was "Come Again," a song about faking orgasm, and this song was barred from broadcast. Casstles's concern was that parents would understand the lyrics and cause the programme to be taken off the air. As Cloonan writes,

> ...it is not that the song causes harm to children, but rather their **parents** [*sic*] complaints, that is the worry. The fact that the lyrics would have probably passed the vast majority of the audience by was unimportant – the **potential** response was enough to get the song censored.[52]

Later in the same interview, Casstles has the following exchange with journalist Graham Lock:

> "The popular media just aren't ready for those kind of lyrics yet. Look, we need *support* from you people. All we're trying to do is provide a platform for young people to air their views."

> "But not about sexual problems, presumably?"

> "If we're gonna get this sort of hassle from you people, I'm gonna play safe and only book bands from big labels: is that what you want? I mean, we're trying to *help* local bands."[53]

Cloonan notes that this implies that bigger labels are more likely to be able to "bring bands into line" and that the BBC is only likely to televise bands that are not too "independently minded" to control. Although it would be naïve to suggest that the BBC ended The Au Pairs' career (Cloonan's book deals overwhelmingly with censorship by the media of *male* rock bands), songs dealing with subjects that concerned women (and that did not romanticize their relationship with men) were still being suppressed by this action. Lesley Woods felt that the censorship was almost a "claim to fame."

The Au Pairs weren't allowed to sing "Come Again" on the television, the same way that Lou Reed wasn't allowed to sing "Walk on the Wild Side" on *Top of the Pops*.

> I don't think that those lyrics now would be considered that radical. We didn't have the power of the big boys behind us, and all that money behind us: you can transgress censorship if you've got big money behind you and people who can go and give a backhander to a radio DJ on Radio One. The Au Pairs didn't have any sort of that backing so when they got up and sang a song about "Come Again," they got censored. It's like a red rag to a bull isn't it: it didn't stop Lou Reed from carrying on, from "Walk on the Wild Side" becoming an amazing classic song, because of a line about "giving head."[54]

Later, The Au Pairs had trouble again with their song "Armagh," which dealt with the poor treatment of women in prison in Northern Ireland; this led to the refusal of major distributors in Northern Ireland to handle the album that the track was on, *Playing with a Different Sex*.[55]

Perhaps the strongest *visible* barometer of the change in mood was the evolution of The Bodysnatchers into The Belle Stars. Although both bands were exclusively female and therefore featured women playing every instrument in their line-up, The Bodysnatchers had a political edge that was entirely lacking in the later band. Their second single, "Too Experienced," featured a track in which the band changed the lyrics of a cover version so that it was sung from a woman's point of view, "Too experienced to be taken for a ride," making the lyrics empowering rather than derogatory. Their lead singer Rhoda Dakar (who left to join Two Tone band The Special AKA) was taken to task by the music press for her rendition of a song about rape, entitled "The Boiler," which was later released as a solo single in 1982.[56] This song had originally been part of The Bodysnatchers' set. As Lucy Toothpaste, who interviewed the band for *Spare Rib*, pointed out, "It's very disconcerting at a live performance, because you've been dancing around to all their other numbers, and you suddenly find you're dancing to a horror story."[57] In 1983, one year later, The Belle Stars had a hit with "Iko Iko," the well-known good-time song, thus proving that you could succeed as female instrumentalists if your material was uncontroversial and you looked pretty; this was in spite of UB40's string of more political hit songs at the same time. Essentially, the metamorphosis of the canny, feminist-informed Bodysnatchers (who recorded for Two Tone, the record label famed

Lesley Woods, The Au Pairs. Photographer Karen Yarnell

for its multiracial attitude and politicized artists), into the glamorous and flirtatious Belle Stars (who made hit records on novelty label Stiff Records), was an embodiment of the recuperation of women instrumentalists by the mainstream industry for popular consumption.[58] This pressure did not come just from outside the band; Rhoda Dakar felt that attitudes *within* the band to risk-taking had been a cause of The Bodysnatchers' demise, and these attitudes were essentially to do with class background:

> The pressures...were upbringing – that's what you brought to the table, how you were brought up and whether you adhered to being working class or middle class or whatever. That made more difference

than anything. I think if you feel you've got a lot to lose then you don't want to upset the applecart, you know. If you've got nothing to lose, it doesn't matter what you say, you say what you think, you say what you want to say. When your parents pop their clogs there's not going to be any money so you don't care what people think.[59]

Being controversial for women bands was a problem, whereas it could be the opposite for a male band. I asked Christine Robertson whether she thought The Slits had been *deliberately* excluded from the normal routes to success provided by British TV and radio, and her answer was emphatic:

In this country there was an absolute media block, or brick wall, which could not be penetrated, because they were girls, and because they were outrageous, because their sexuality was confrontational. Because the name of the group was semi-rude-confrontational although it was never named with that in mind: that was something that other people put on to it... The reputation which preceded them which in a lot of cases was not actually accurate, i.e. that they were wild, wild, wild. Well yeah, they were wild but...so were The Rolling Stones...[60] And I think there was a media bar because they were too dangerous to be exposed... We got top name pluggers that could get your record on to Radio 1, on the Breakfast Show. Did it work for them? No, it didn't work for them! Were they ever invited on to any BBC music shows? No! Is there much film footage of The Slits being filmed as a subsequent of media companies asking for it to be filmed? No! It speaks for itself.[61]

Also, notably, there was apparently only space in the nation's heart for one all-girl group at a time; for instance, in the 1980s, all-girl Hillbilly band The Shillelagh Sisters fell foul of record company manipulation as their label tried to transform them into a soul band, jettisoning those band-members who were not willing to comply with their plans.[62] Once again, this fits in with Sally Potter's observation, quoted earlier, that "as more women achieve in a given area they are forced to compete with each other for the same space rather than the space itself expanding."[63] Indeed, throughout the 1980s there was a series of all-female rock bands – for instance, the reggae-based Amazulu, who seemed to take on the role of tokens in the pop/rock world. The "survivors" as far as profile and longevity in the music business were concerned tended to be keyboard-players in mixed bands, such as Gillian Gilbert of New Order and Una Baines of The Fall. Interviews with these bands would concentrate predominantly on the male members of the band; the musical skills of female players were very much downplayed when they were acknowledged by the press and other members of their bands, as the following exchange from 1983 shows:

> Gillian Gilbert, whose only previous brush with the stage was in a short-lived punk escapade called The Inadequates, was at Stockport Tech doing graphic design at the time. "But I didn't want to be a graphic artist. It was just something to do. I didn't really have any ambitions. I didn't want to be in a group – it was just a dream. They approached me."
> *Did she have to audition?*
> "Yes!"
> "We won't tell you what she had to do!"
> "She had to play Stairway to Heaven...backwards!"
> "I think I'm still auditioning, really..."[64]

Given the fact that the piano (hence keyboards) is very much perceived to be a "female" instrument,[65] one would expect that the replacement of guitar-based bands with bands that used new technology propelled by keyboard-players would automatically include more women instrumentalists, given the "space" created for them in public awareness (or at least, inky weekly press awareness). The "problem" of "unnatural" female guitar-players should no longer exist; women should have taken up their "natural" places in the New Romantic bands as a matter of course. However, this was not to be the case; what actually happened was not women's liberation, but more men's liberation. It became more acceptable for men to display femininity and indeed to dress as women, as did Boy George and Marilyn; this has never been noted as a distraction from the potential new roles for women in bands. In *Rebel Rock*, for instance, John Street includes a discussion about The Mistakes and The Au Pairs, and on the next page continues:

> Post-punk electronic technology, for example, has allowed for the emergence of a new type of performer. The posturing guitar hero, wrestling his guitar in phony sexual passion, was replaced by the computer operator, standing studiously over the keyboard.[66]

Street fails to note the abrupt ending of his section on women instrumentalists and its supercession by writing on yet more music controlled by and fronted by men, this time "playing with sexuality";[67] his explanation for this is that performers like Marc Almond and Boy George "wanted popular success" whereas for bands like The Mistakes, the "restrictions and conditions imposed by the musical form, the industry and the broadcasters...was an unacceptable cost."[68] It is surprising that this does not warrant further analysis in an otherwise thoughtful book, because once more not only gender, but also capital cost, had become integral to the creation and performance of pop and rock music. This cost was not only monetary, it was also temporal, for in order to learn how to operate new technology, one must have a teacher, however informal, and time in which to learn, both of which (as Bayton has noted) are usually in short supply for women performers. Andrew Goodwin explores the impact of new technologies on rock and pop around this time in his essay "Rationalization and Democratization in the New Technologies of Popular Music," and addresses the issue that the supposed democracy instigated by the influx of cheap(er) technological inventions did not extend to women, remarking that he has only seen "one major female star who appears to operate the technology itself: Betty Boo." He goes on to say:

> For now, it needs to be said that...the democratizing function of the new technologies of pop seem to stop short of opening up the new forms of composition and engineering to women – probably for socially complex reasons having to do with the identification of technology with masculinity. In other words, it is the boys, still, who are playing with the toys.[69]

The milieu of sharing skills diminished with the rapid recuperation of bands, who sometimes moved from shaky first performances to recording contracts before they had completed a set of self-composed material – this is what happened to The Bodysnatchers. For some players, this was successful. However, although Chrissie Hynde had a hit with The Pretenders' first album, the live performances of the band were often heavily criticized by the press; nevertheless, she has managed to sustain her career and remain an interesting performer. She reported her misgivings about her playing ability in interviews, specifically with *NME*; however, her co-guitarist, James Honeyman-Scott, praised her skills publicly, thus validating her role as a guitarist. Viv Albertine cited Hynde as an inspiration and speculates about the atmosphere of "Made in Britain" xenophobia she may possibly have experienced:

> Chrissie Hynde had been a bit of a gate-opener for me because she came already able to play. She, after Suzi Quatro and Patti Smith, was someone I could look at and say "Yeah I like the way she holds the guitar." And although she was a bit old-fashioned in the way that she could sing and play properly, she looked cool and she managed to hold the guitar and not look awkward with it which I found quite inspiring, actually. I saw her play a lot, just in rehearsal quite often with Steve Jones [guitarist with The Sex Pistols]. She was so desperate to get into a band. No one would have her. It was awful: we were sort of anti-American. We had to be so fierce about what we were creating

that The Heartbreakers and anyone coming in [from the USA], were considered old school, you know anyone with an American accent. It was like an English thing even though Malcolm had brought a load of ideas in from America, Richard Hell and all that; we didn't know that: we felt it was *our* thing.

[Perhaps] she put herself down because she was too good. None of us was any good and she realized it put her out on a limb so she may have undercut it for years. She could sing great, she could play great, better than the boys. How many girls have to put themselves down so they don't overshadow the boys?[70]

Other, later bands, notably The Bodysnatchers, suffered in the press because of their lack of playing skill; it appears from music press reports of female instrumentalists that the writers became *obsessed* with the concept of women players and their lack of skill, simultaneously praising the assumed lack of skill of The Slits (who had the advantage of being relatively established) and criticizing the lack of skill of Dolly Mixture, or The Bodysnatchers.

Far more important, though, was the reintroduction of camp into emerging pop bands. Jon Savage's article on androgyny in *The Face* in 1983 pointed out that punks' concerns were so sternly political that there was no place for camp:

What the punks were concerned with – at first rightly, and later to their cost – was a moral, political view of a world that was rotting and on the edge of collapse: love, gender and matters of sex were simply not an issue – what with all the amphetamine, there was simply not time nor inclination for it (although, paradoxically, it was through this lack of stress that a rash of gender integrated groups occurred).[71]

Savage omits to mention in this article the debates about sexuality and gender that the mixed-gender and all-female bands generated both among themselves and their audiences: concerns with realism in the lyrics of even spectacular bands like The Slits precluded their performances from being regarded in any way as camp,[72] and even bands who possessed visually sartorial style, such as The Mo-dettes, had a roughness of sound that belied their arch appearance.

As discussed earlier, the vocal timbres of punk and post-punk singers were unappealing to those expecting entertainment rather than proselytization from their pop music.[73] Lyrical content often challenged male hegemony or, conversely, concentrated on the female experience, which may have included subjects that men found distasteful. For an audience perhaps desiring escapist pop to distract them from the realities of the recession and the Falklands War, this was not apt. Some performers delighted feminists ("You hear this *sound* on the radio often. But these kind of lyrics? Not often enough"[74]) and critics such as Greil Marcus:

> The music wasn't aimed at a mass audience, and it didn't seem likely to reach one. It did speak with a disoriented passion and an undisguised critical intelligence strong enough to lead new audiences to identify themselves with it: ideally, audiences sufficiently passionate and critical to keep the musicians questioning their work.[75]
>
> ...verbal slap in the songs – most of them constructed like quarrels...there's hardly a line in their tunes that suggests a given character is male or another female...there's not a hint that the songs are confessional – that is, in pop terms, heartfelt statements protected by the high school homily that if what you say is an expression of your own feelings, no-one can criticise it. Delta 5 make critical music, and it is precisely this assumption the band criticises.[76]

However, Savage correctly identifies punk's seriousness as a factor that "boxed it(self) into a corner." He also reiterates a point discussed in the last chapter, commenting:

> ...it was as heartening as it was amusing to see Marc Almond and Boy George mincing about all over the nation's TV screens – with as much courage as self-absorption – at a time when "Our Boys" were warring with the "Argies." Small beer, yet their manifest camping was a relief from all the bellicosity that I, for one, refused to believe in... Punk's furious belligerence was a direct response to the cultural and social vacuum it appeared to face under the Callaghan government. Now we have the strong, rigidly masculine government of Thatcher, it's perhaps not surprising to find feminine virtues being reasserted in pop music, not least the quasi-feminine image of the love object, whatever the gender.[77]

He does not, however, mention the implicit misogyny of transvestism and the implications of the fact that the female presence in rock was overshadowed by an influx of male cross-dressers.[78] Nevertheless, Williamson writes of:

> [the] imbalance of power in both sexual relations and society at large, which makes the equation of men dressing up as women, and women dressing up as men, less even than it may seem: drag is not simply a reversible phenomenon.[79]

Savage mentions Annie Lennox and Grace Jones, both of whom had a strong impact at the time, but for both of these artists their strength was as much visual as conceptual: the debates around the sexuality of their presentation were a distraction from the sonic and lyrical inroads made by artists like The Slits, The Raincoats, The Au Pairs and Delta 5,[80] who existed in the smaller and more politicized sphere. As Gina Birch remarks:

> I do know when it was all over there was a sudden sense of deathly silence...you know, there was Madonna and Annie Lennox, kind of Cindy Sherman-esque, "I can be who I choose to be, with my leather pants on one day and my overalls on another day."[81]

There is a difference between male–female transvestism and female–male transvestism, since female–male transvestites are enabled to operate in a world of greater power by cross-dressing, but it should be noted that aside from the early punk uniform of jackets and ties adopted by both genders as a parody of the business establishment at the beginning of the punk moment, most of the female instrumentalists discussed in this study did not use trans-vestism as a style statement: they were visually anti-style in dress. To reiterate John Peel's alleged comment that "punk opened the door for fat women in dungarees to get up on stage and play in bands,"[82] it certainly allowed *some* women to be "neutral" for a short space of time, but as the subculture petered out, so did the lack of self-consciousness of female performers, as Sue Bradley pointed out (see Chapter 3).

Some artists tried to adapt to the new pop mentality, not always success-fully. Gina Birch describes how, after the final Raincoats album was finished, she tried to rethink her career and signed to a major label:

> I turned the screw in my own destruction, really. In 1985–86, Vicky[83] and I formed Dorothy and did the total pop bit. It was quite a trauma though, 'cos I thought I could handle pop culture, that we could have some kind of control over it and be whatever we wanted to be... In fact you get very consumed by it, [the idea of] selling records. It was a nightmare.[84]

The triumvirate of music papers that had incorporated punk rock were slow to appreciate this return to pop values. Demographically, it was inevitable that the new young generation would want music of their own; they also wanted a music press that reflected their escapist taste, and the new paper *Smash Hits* capitalized on glossy new acts that had, in some cases, evolved from the old ones.[85] *Smash Hits* soon overtook *NME* in readership.[86] This leads on to the role of music video in "weeding out" subversive ideas from pop music. The focus was not on activity or beliefs, but on appearance. Bands that included older or less physically attractive members were less appealing to record companies, who now knew that the medium of video, with its facility for repeated viewing, would not forgive artists who were not glamorous or who could not convey some sort of mystique to the camera. Enid Williams was thrown out of her band for being overweight:

> It was all quite nasty at the time. They didn't want me to be in the band any more because I was very different to them. I put on a lot of weight and there was all sorts of pressure about us not selling records because I didn't look right. I didn't look skinny and anorexic.[87]

At rock gigs, particularly because of the "it could be *me* up there!" ethos of punk, an audience would forgive a nervous or clumsy performer; even Debbie Harry was noted for her apparent physical stiffness at early gigs by Blondie.[88] The shambolic nature of the bands discussed here was a badge of authenticity. Pop video, particularly the cheaper performance video, required choreography, self-awareness and an ability to "act" the rock star that was anathema to some artists.

Pop Video: The Return of the Showbiz Ethos and Gender Delineations – for Women

As Kaplan says, "The creation of a marketable self has been a primary reason for the production of music videos by record companies and performers."[89] Artists had started making videos before MTV became so influential in the US and, later, the developed world, but it was the expansion of MTV in the 1980s that has cast the role of youth music in the mould of "showbiz" versions of itself, saleable to a wide audience. The profile of the punk mediators and their role in drawing the public's attention to this genre of music diminished. As Weinstein remarks:

> It is not punk music but punk mediators that deconstruct the art/commerce binary: record labels giving total autonomy to their musicians, enabling them to record with the content and in the style that they choose, not what some suit thinks will sell. The free-form, underground FM stations in the United States in the mid-sixties, and their college-radio offspring, are another example of such pure mediators, playing music that did not follow a format designed to grab a large demographic.[90]

MTV contributed also to the cycle of stereotyping and role models which maintained the status quo of gender representation; for women instrumentalists, pop video with its emphasis on physical beauty, and its requirement for financial investment, became the equivalent of progressive rock with its emphasis on technological expertise and financial investment. The stereotyping factor is explored by Kaplan, who puts even US rock instrumentalists such as Pat Benatar into groupings within a very small percentage of females who appeared in rock videos as "central figures" in the mid-1980s.[91] She also describes what she calls the "postmodern feminism" of Madonna:

> In some sense...Madonna represents the postmodern feminist heroine in that she combines unabashed seductiveness with a gutsy kind of independence. She is neither particularly male or female identified, and seems mainly out for herself.[92]

Once again, Thatcher's policy was reflected in consumer culture, with Madonna's self-interest reflecting the spirit of the times. Madonna had been a big fan of The Slits – Christine recalled seeing her in the front row at their gigs in New York. Ari says:

> It's really annoying when someone like Madonna watches our gigs and then the next day she comes and looks like Viv! She won't even wear a Slits T-shirt as a tribute, and no one knows where these things come from![93]

But Madonna reverted The Slits' dramatization of the slut image; as Mimi Schippers notes:

> Both race and class privilege buffer Madonna from simply reproducing hegemonic constructions of femininity by doing slut...when we introduce these multiple levels of social organization and multiple systems of inequality, it becomes difficult to distill which sorts of cultural practices and interactions challenge relations of domination, and which ones reinscribe them.[94]

With Madonna's conventional use of her sexuality to sell music, I would argue that she recuperated The Slits' subversion with great skill by turning their defiant style of dress into part of her commercial pop package. By not acknowledging the source of this look, she contributes to the forgetting of their influence at the time, in a parallel to her plundering of gay music styles. Robin Roberts criticizes Kaplan's comments about Madonna, claiming that "her pessimism is part of a postmodern cynicism about resistance."[95] However, Roberts works on McRobbie's assumption that "postmodernism helpfully diverts us away from canons,"[96] and continues, "Herbert Marcuse's notion of recuperation simply does not apply to a self-reflexive fluid postmodern text like a music video."[97] She ignores the fact that the music reflected in pop videos of the early 1980s had already been recuperated through the gatekeeping process described earlier. Those more feminist in appearance (she cites "Sisters are Doing It for Themselves," which features Annie Lennox and Aretha Franklin and was made exclusively for MTV in 1985) merely fit into the small allotted space given to strong female acts as part of the recuperative act. Pop video recuperation presents the glamour of "women in rock" minus the politics – the gimmick minus the commitment to change practised by the female instrumentalists of the period I have been writing about.

Ari defined the end point of punk quite clearly by the way the record companies fell on MTV with relief as something they could understand, manipulate and capitalize upon, and the way in which the music that filtered through onto MTV was re-branded for mass consumption:

> That was all cut by MTV; suddenly MTV came on and it was all, "New Wave! New Wave! New Wave! New Wave!," never mind what the real people were doing. "We just wanna cash in on what's commercially accepted and label it as something that's commercially accessible. Oh, we could go with New Wave, we could go with that, that's not too threatening, and let's work on the *image*..."[98]

The image has become all-important for women artists, and the image of an artist with a non-ideal body shape, playing a rock instrument, is all too rare. An ex-punk remarks about the punk subculture, "If you see the girls in the pictures, they were all tremendously ugly; it was a great refuge for the plain girl. That's what was so good about it."[99] While his bluntness is insulting, there is truth in the fact that punk was not a subculture that prioritized standardized "good looks" over "be-ing." The effects of the re-glamorization of pop and rock and the shift in focus of the music media towards this and away from "authentic" music-making led to the reintroduction of a "service-with-a-smile" ethos to music for female artists. Pop and rock, in common with other industries, follow the dictum that "the more a woman is perceived as entering male space, in fact, the more she has to conform to standards of dress that enforce gender difference."[100] Surely it is not too ironic to sum this up with a parallel from the world of the office, from Christine Griffin's study:

The non-technical aspects of office work are concerned with women's appearance and manner, and with their servicing role, and they are not confined to office jobs. Waitresses, air stewardesses, hairdressers, prostitutes and some shop assistants are all required to develop particular styles of "service with a smile" as part of their jobs. This non-technical side of women's office work was important to many male managers, and it influenced their criteria for selecting female office staff.[101]

6 The Social Context: Academic Writing on Subcultures, the Rock Press and "Women in Music"

I will start this chapter with an exploration of attitudes expressed by writers in various relevant fields who explore youth subcultures, deviance and moral panics – the rules and actions of young people that differentiate them from their elders, and the attempts by their elders to define, control and assimilate these differences, generation upon generation; these studies focus almost completely on the activities of young men, probably because the writers, as men, can identify with the rites of passage they are documenting.

Academic Gatekeeping: Issues of Gender

Because punk was notable for a distinct difference that marked it from previous identified subcultures, with the involvement of women not just as observers or consumers, but as *visibly* active protagonists in production, Stanley Cohen's sweeping comment, in the Introduction to the 1993 edition of his much-respected work, *Folk Devils and Moral Panics*, needs to be addressed at the outset:

> To re-examine the subject of post-war British youth subcultures is not quite the same as constructing, say, a revised historiography of World War II: there are no new archives to be opened, no secret documents to be discovered, no pacts of silence to be broken. There are just the same (rather poor) sources of information from the same (often inarticulate) informants. The question is what new sense can be made out of this same data.[1]

This regrettable comment has probably returned to haunt Cohen on many occasions, and will return again, I hope, as I have opened new archives, discovered previously hidden documents and allowed suppressed voices to speak.[2]

Any exploration of women's contribution to (what are, by default) men's discourses involves disentangling men's attempts to rationalize suppression (and occasionally oppression[3]) from their empirical observations, and a discussion of the nature of supposedly objective viewpoints. In 1990, Angela McRobbie had made an observation which was effectively ignored until much later on[4] – an observation that now seems obvious but had never been said before:

> Although few radical (male) sociologists would deny the importance of the personal in precipitating social and political awareness, to admit how their own experience has influenced their choice of subject matter (the politics of selection) seems more or less taboo... The point is that this absence of self (this is quite different from the authorial "I" or "we") and the invalidating of personal experience in the name of the more objective social sciences goes hand in hand with the silencing of other areas, which are for feminists of the greatest importance.[5]

Statements of the obvious made by McRobbie (and reiterated by others such as Walkerdine[6]) have prompted even some male writers (for instance Nehring[7] in his study of the Riot Grrrl phenomenon) to acknowledge that the notion of objectivity is, itself, subjective. McRobbie started her academic life living in a house in Birmingham with members of mixed-gender band The Au Pairs, and I think this is significant; she was not content, as a writer, to accept the status quo in terms of what she noticed about the social environment in the late 1970s and women's and girls' places in it. The politicized community of Birmingham bands must have affected her attitude; there is nothing like the lived experience of a "moment" to readjust one's feelings about how history is documented. Although some find great difficulty in adapting what they regard as men's revolution to the feminist discourse,[8] this has been a problem at every stage of the women's movement as women contextualize their attitudes and experiences.[9]

The texts examined in this chapter are relevant for two reasons, in spite of the fact that so many of them speak so little of women. First, the aspects of "being apart from society" that they describe apply as much to the women that I have interviewed as they do to the young men that form their focus. Second, by giving the reader an impression of the volume and variety of these texts, the wide scope of the "silencing of other areas" as described by McRobbie will, I hope, become more apparent.[10]

The relative isolation of *women's* writing on women in subcultures, women in employment and women in rock (women in anything, in fact) is inevitable, since previous historical studies (pre-1980s) have not only referred just to men, but also to a male environment in which women were a mere side issue – at most facilitators, occasionally agitators and at least a hindrance to male advancement. Rosalind Miles reminds us that, even in the developed western world:

> Traditionalist arguments of masculine supremacy have been remark-
> ably resilient over time – all democratic experiments, all revolutions,
> all demands for equality have so far stopped short of sexual equality
> – and women, seen as biologically determined, continue to be denied
> the human right of full self-determination.[11]

Women's writing therefore has to provide a sort of potted context for itself whatever its focus, given the fact that the hegemonic historical context is male.[12] Because the writer is "assumed to be a feminist,"[13] the target audience is also assumed to be female/feminist, by inference. The excitement for male academicians surrounding postmodernism as a social and design phenomenon must have provided a welcome diversion from feminism during the 1980s and 1990s.[14] However, for some female writers it tempered one of the acknowledged drawbacks of the feminist movement in the 1970s; as Barbara Bradby remarks: "Postmodernist theorising has certainly sharpened awareness of the need to…avoid 'speaking for' other groups of women, and to be aware that one's analysis is only ever partial."[15] Bradby thus not only builds upon McRobbie's remark about male writers, but also reminds us that any analysis must always acknowledge the drawbacks of personal bias; this established, the academic context follows.

Interest in the Power of the Adolescent Male

The first major post-war study of teenagers and their habits was *The Teenage Consumer*, written by Mark Abrams in 1959.[16] This heralded the concept of the teenager as an independent entity, with their own income, making decisions about what they spent this income on during their leisure time. Since then, studies on young people's leisure activities have generally swung between market-research-oriented cultural studies (for example, Abrams through Lewis to Thornton) and left-leaning sociology (for example, Becker through Hebdige to Walkerdine), and conclusions have inevitably been drawn about what young people think, and their social groupings, according to the agendas of those who are making the study. There have also been changes in what society accepts as normal behaviour, and this too will be discussed in this section.

Becker's research in 1963 unearthed a degree of fatalism in those involved in the jazz community. In Becker's analysis, subcultures are formed when groups of potentially lone deviants find each other, and redefine themselves according to what they have in common – this is as likely to be an inability to relate to the hegemonic culture as a desire to disrupt it:

> Many people have suggested that culture arises essentially in response to a problem faced in common by a group of people, insofar as they are able to interact and communicate with each other effectively. People who engage in activities regarded as deviant typically have the problem that their view of what they do is not shared by other members of the society... Where people who engage in deviant activities have the opportunity to interact with one another they are likely to develop a culture built around the problems rising out of the differences between their definition of what they do and the definition held by other members of the society. They develop perspectives on themselves and their deviant activities and on their relations with other members of the society.[17]

Becker's study was, of course, made in the US, but it is interesting to note that at the time of Cohen's work on the Mods in the 1960s, the British tabloid press were beginning to feel the effects of television news on their circulation, and sensationalist headlines were seen to be an antidote to this problem. This, twinned with the social visibility of the Mods (like their predecessors the Teddy Boys they were readily identifiable by uniform, albeit different, garb), led to the "moral panic" that Cohen identified.[18] By the time punk came around, the British tabloids were ready for a new moral panic, and relished the pseudo-sexual dress of the punks, while bypassing the political and social aspects of the group. For the punk subculture was about more than just bricolage in dress; it also incorporated idealism, anarchy, gender and race politics, and the creation of art, music and alternative media. The unemployment in the late 1970s and early 1980s that straddled gender divides also dissolved boundaries between classes. One of the most influential studies of post-war youth was made by members of the Birmingham CCCS and published as *Resistance through Rituals* in 1975.[19] Included in their discourse on subcultures, Hall, Jefferson *et al.* had discussed the lack of faith working-class youth had in what they perceived to be the "thinly-disguised middle-class elitism"[20] in ideas of cultural revolution; the luxury of the middle classes taking this attitude was dependent on the security of access to paid work and spending power for the working-class youth. The lack of work in the late 1970s had a profound influence on the DIY culture of punk, and also to attitudes to gender differences within the subculture; unemployment was a levelling force and the predicament of being workless often led to greater communication between young people.

Becker's definition of a deviant subculture can be applied to the simultaneous desire by certain young women all over Britain to assume their right to participate in activities in a way that was normally associated with a world of maleness. With no precedent to follow, the rules of both fashion and music were bent and broken in order to defy classification. This, added to the outlaw nature of punk itself, meant that the "perspectives" of the women interviewed here were well outside those defined as normal. There was not a master plan; as Willis explains:

> Cultural expressions are...likely to be displaced, distorted or con-
> densed reflections of barely understood, or "misunderstood," knots
> of feeling, contradiction and frustration – as well as forms of action
> on these things...we learn from the culture, not from its explicit con-
> sciousness.[21]

The "explicit consciousness" is a composite of the various "deviant" participants in the subculture, here processed by the subjective author; for this reason, I urge the reader to value the oral contributions to this book and to understand the fluid nature of perceptions of history.

Many factors other than unemployment fed into a massive cultural shift in the attitudes of young people in the UK towards the end of the 1970s. For women, there was no doubt that the 1975 Sex Discrimination Act made them understand that they had statutory rights in the workplace, whereas before this they had been merely tolerated. This, combined with the unprecedented increase in unemployment among school- and college-leavers of both genders at this point, resulted in a shift in attitudes "on the ground" or "on the street," which according to some of my informants resulted in a reassessment of women's and men's roles in society. Without jobs (that were still largely gendered), both sexes experienced the same feelings of exclusion and the same freedom from routine. The rearticulation of women's rights undoubtedly affected the expectations of both young men and young women. This introduced a tension into the phenomenon of "girl" instrumentalists, who sometimes found themselves to be unwilling spokespeople for the phenomenon itself, when they aspired to no more than participation or, at most, a role as non-confrontational pioneer.

It was suggested by Abrams *et al.* when analysing data collected in 1981, that the word "deviant" should now be applied to those who had traditional values; the word now applied to the *opposite* attitude to Becker's original study of jazz musicians:

> The "conformists" (those holding anti-traditional values) were more
> prone than the deviant, traditionalist minority of younger people
> to question authority; to approve of cheating and lying when these

served their own self-interest; to denigrate respect for parents; to dis-
avow any pride in being British; to regard the maintenance of public
order as of little consequence; to refuse to accept the idea that there
is a clear-cut difference between what is good and what is evil, and to
have very little contact with organised religion.[22]

This is quoted here for two reasons: partly to show how "rock'n'roll" attitudes had now become hegemonic and partly to reiterate the subjectivity and
transience of works like this, reminding the reader that many of the theories
explored here have been written in different socio-political environments,
sometimes with hindsight gained from previous studies of subcultures. Becker,
Cohen and Willis were observing phenomena in new ways in their own contexts, and although they are criticized here for aspects of their research, it
has to be acknowledged that had their respective studies not existed, several
histories of marginalized groups would not have been recorded and analysed, and their lives and lifestyles may well have disappeared in the meta-
narrative of twentieth-century war/peace/industry/high culture. There are
different understandings of "the purpose" (or lack thereof) of a subculture;
for instance, for Stan Cohen, Hebdige[23] and, later, Thornton,[24] the purpose of
participants in a subculture appears to be to draw attention to themselves and
their activities, while Becker describes his subjects as marginalized by their
differences. To summarize, there are two different definitions of what subcultures are – roughly, they divide into studies of social deviance, and studies
of style statements (leading to media interest and possible money-making
opportunities).[25]

It must not be forgotten that stereotypes are tempting to scholars. Muggleton[26] has pointed out that young people often belong to more than one
subcultural group, and while I do not subscribe to everything he reports (I
found a degree of commitment to punk that is not acknowledged by Muggleton, for instance), any group of people consists of individuals with their
own histories and aspirations, no matter how uniform they appear from the
outside.

Changes in the Definition of "Subcultures"

I believe changes in the way in which subcultures are defined have affected
historical perspectives and have led commentators to believe in a "one size
fits all" definition of what a subculture is and what it means to its participants.
Any person or group of people not fitting this definition is ignored, and their
significance within the group disappears. Hebdige's *Subculture, the Meaning
of Style* had been a groundbreaking attempt to examine subcultures through

semiotics and literary theory. Although there are many interesting observations in his work, women and girls are barely mentioned or acknowledged throughout. It is very much an outsider's study, and indeed he is wont to sound positively paternal in places ("after all, we, the sociologists and interested straights, threaten to kill with kindness the forms which we seek to elucidate"[27]). There is also a problem with his interpretation of the *motivation* of his subjects through their surface appearance. These shortcomings are all the more disappointing because of his skill in acknowledging the purpose of subcultures in relation to society, and the function of the media in mythologizing them through their

> ... continual process of recuperation...[in which] the fractured order is repaired and the subculture incorporated as a diverting spectacle within the dominant mythology from which it in part emanates: as "folk devil," as Other, as Enemy. The process of recuperation takes two characteristic forms: (1) the conversion of subcultural signs (dress, music, etc.) into mass-produced objects (i.e. the commodity form) (2) the "labelling" and redefinition of deviant behaviour by dominant groups – the police, the media, the judiciary (i.e. the ideological form).[28]

Thornton takes Hebdige's ideas further when she describes "The Media Development of Subcultures" thus:

> Youth resent approving mass mediation of their culture but relish the attention conferred by media condemnation. How else might one turn difference into defiance, lifestyle into social upheaval, leisure into revolt? "Moral panics" can now with retrospect, all be seen as a culmination and fulfilment of youth cultural agendas in so far as negative newspaper and broadcast news coverage baptise transgression.[29]

To Thornton, the "labelling" described by Hebdige provides a handy trademark for the attention-seeking youth generation, perhaps so they can take control of the "subcultural signs" described by Hebdige, and capitalize on them.[30] By the end of this book, I hope the reader will conclude that the punk subculture and the music that it produced were not superficial; the most influential and retrospectively respected of the female punk bands, The Slits and The Raincoats, believed utterly in the revolution they felt themselves to be part of – indeed, both bands had personnel that had come to England from countries in which fascism had been a reality. Palmolive, drummer with The Slits, had come to England as a child from Franco's Spain, and Ana Da Silva, singer and guitarist with The Raincoats, had come from authoritarian, dictator-led Portugal. Even the less "aware" bands acknowledge today the pioneering attitudes they had at the time, which were far from attention-seeking, as we saw in the chapter on Brighton. Although Thornton is writing about a later visible youth subculture, one must not be tempted to apply her interpretations across the board. The impression of superficiality can be contrasted with what Willis (the "ideological form") said about the hippies:

> The sense of community was the sense of others being engaged in a similar experiment, enjoying similar insights, sharing common, though often unexpressed, views on the nature of interaction. Only with people who shared the same symbolic atmosphere could there be meaningful interaction. Only with the *sharing* of assumptions could those assumptions be exquisitely shaped and presented as style.[31]

Contrasting attitudes to the definition of subcultures imply that the *meaning* of the word subculture has changed over time, just as much as the *meaning* of the word deviance: perhaps in the almost twenty-year gap between these two studies, a "knowing," self-conscious (therefore postmodern) participation in subcultural activity has developed – the young person has a relationship to the subculture, rather than "living" it; the idea of subcultures being worked up from the street has increasingly been sidelined in favour of a bias towards *lifestyle*.[32]

Hebdige wrote that subcultures develop as a result of "the twin concepts of conjuncture and specificity (each subculture representing a distinctive 'moment' – a particular response to a particular set of circumstances),"[33] and understood that "different youths bring different degrees of commitment to a subculture."[34] This point is constantly explored in writing about rock music too: Frith asks, "What is the relationship between rock as a style and rock as an activity?"[35] He reiterates the observations made by Muggleton and Hebdige as he continues, "For every youth 'stylist' committed to a cult as a full-time creative task, there are hundreds of working-class kids who grow up in loose membership of several groups and run with a variety of gangs."[36] And, of course, many of the women who were part of the punk subculture didn't "look like" the tabloid photographs of "punkettes," but were pivotal to the subculture. Even in London, acknowledged as the epicentre of punk, the audience for punk gigs was not, as media reports would have it, made up exclusively of young men with mohawks and safety pins through their faces; the film *The Filth and the Fury*[37] shows that this was not the case; and for every report such as Charles Shaar Murray's of a young girl piercing her cheek at a Sex Pistols gig in Sweden,[38] there is photographic evidence that punk gigs belonged to variously dressed performers and audiences from different ethnic, cultural and demographic backgrounds. The London punk scene is fairly well documented,[39] and most of these writers acknowledge that, at the beginning, members of the punk subculture were autonomous in their attitudes and dress. Thus we have to acknowledge a large and marginal subcultural "grey area" that applies to every subculture, even the most intense and visually and musically recognizable, which is especially noticeable at related musical events because of the part-time nature of some participants.

Although Street[40] claims that all punks really wanted was to have a good time, I would argue that, for most, their situation was too bleak to be hedonistic: in reality, it was often a time of violence and personal difficulty; although there was pleasure to be gained from creativity, it was also a necessity in the face of a confusing and depressing future. As Liz Naylor told me, 1970s Manchester was a dismal place:

> It felt very bleak; it didn't feel like an optimistic time. I think the 1970s were really grim...my memories are in black and white almost. If you see footage of Britain in 1975, it looks like the war's just finished.[41]

She went on to tell me that punk gave her an identity that protected her and gave her self-respect in an atmosphere of rejection, and her description of her circumstances shows how punk had a positive effect on those who had been defined as deviant by their behaviour and attitudes:

> I got expelled when I was fifteen... I was committed to a secure unit in Macclesfield and I think people were really scared of me, as a punk, and I remember being interviewed and I was wearing a man's suit, albeit fucked up, and I had this spiky hair; I cut it myself with bald patches. And the people who interviewed me saw my behaviour and dress as deeply sociopathic, and dwelt a lot upon it. And I thought, "Well, I'm a punk." I was an Other. I think it was a big gathering-together of people who regarded themselves as freaks.[42]

The fake cheeriness surrounding the Queen's Silver Jubilee in 1977 had an odd effect; there was a feeling that she represented a stratum of society that was oblivious to the chaos that the young people of Britain were experiencing. But what all punks had in common was a sense of self-worth, in spite of their lack of faith in what the future would hold for them. As Savage remarks:

> What was "new," in the stifling summer of 1976, was Rotten's moral authority...the extraordinary behaviour, the splendour of their small group of dedicated followers, and the collective depth of information that went into their creation.[43]

There was indeed a feeling of almost Presbyterian *duty* within some of the punk communities; Frith's and Home's observations about the "art school experience" not only give an insight into the way punk worked, but also, I believe, show how much the art-school ethos fed into punk: "The art school experience is about commitment to a working practice, to a mode of learning which assumes the status of a lifestyle."[44] And Hebdige concludes:

> Punks were not only directly *responding* to increasing joblessness, changing moral standards, the rediscovery of poverty, the Depression, etc., they were *dramatizing* what had come to be called "Britain's decline" by constructing a language which was, in contrast to the prevailing rhetoric of the Rock Establishment, unmistakably relevant and down to earth... The punks appropriated the rhetoric of crisis which had filled the airwaves and the editorials throughout the period and translated it into tangible (and visible) terms.[45]

Tony Parsons's review of The Slits underlines the way this translated into a live experience, with their "bad girl" performance style:

> These four girls make The Runaways look like Girl Guides. I mean, who cares about such trivialities as staying in tune, playing together or striking the right chords when one possesses such a sense of *theatrics?*[46]

I have concluded that the "moment" overarched the variety of different ways in which people defined themselves and were defined by others. The end result, women playing instruments in a previously completely male world, is no less of an unusual phenomenon, whatever the retrospective arguments about punk and feminism tell us. Indeed, the attitudes of my interviewees towards their music-making, both towards their position in the subculture and their transition (or not) from amateur to professional, could change greatly during their period of involvement with their bands.

Authenticity

By far the most challenging debate for rock critics and fans alike is the question of musical authenticity,[47] because it is very rare for authenticity to be ascribed to a female rock artist. This is probably because, as Angela McRobbie points out, male subculture writers see *themselves* as escaping from families and the "trap" of romance (both feminine-identified arenas), thus over-romanticizing the male resistance and escape element of the subcultures they study,[48] although female musicians such as Joni Mitchell and Joan Armatrading who utilized their lyrics to express personal desires that would liberate them from the humdrum, were respected as the female equivalent to male rock artists.[49]

Perhaps the inherent misogyny in all of these studies is not surprising; as Bradley points out, "the standard notion of 'the teenager' is usually of a boy, not a girl, and...the 'threat' of sex is a threat of boys against girls, as seen by parents, teachers etc." He acknowledges that this is never mentioned in rock histories.[50] *Pop* belongs to girls and gay men; it is assumed to be passively consumed, in spite of McRobbie's own recuperation of the word "teenybopper," previously an insulting term. Rock is lived by its male (or honorary male) audience, to the exclusion of girls and women. Within these parameters, the authenticity debate centres on the contrasts between song-writing as a craft (for instance, the Tin Pan Alley manufacture of popular songs for all occasions) and song-writing as self-expression – in other words art (and, implied, expressive of adolescent male dissatisfaction with their lot).

Hidden beneath this debate is another consideration, that of song-writing as a political activity. Folk music is often categorized as political music, but in actual fact politics, and particularly gender politics, underlies all forms of music.[51] For instance, the self-expression of rock must articulate the emotions of its (male) audience, with a strong feeling for the *Zeitgeist*. Lawrence Grossberg identified the necessity of rock culture to the "meaning of life" for young males in the US, and the way its authenticity

> ... was defined by rock's ability to articulate the historical condition to the experience of post-war youth. Only by making youth belong somewhere could it speak to both the identity and the difference of its audience. Because it mattered, rock constituted a generational identity and empowered that generation to define its own ways of articulating meaning into its mattering maps. A differentiating machine is deployed in the service of rock's territorializing work.[52]

Grossberg's description of generational identity and empowerment defines the nature of the politics of traditional rock music. American youth had needed the frisson of identifying and defending territory that being at war had provided. As Attali has pointed out, all music reflects the rules of society, so when the rules of society are redefined, new music is created as part of that redefinition; if music is created in an oppositional environment, its aesthetic rules will run counter to those of the mainstream: "Its order simulates the social order, and its dissonances express marginalities. *The code of music simulates the accepted rules of society.*"[53] Thus rock breaks the aesthetic rules of mainstream art music to the extent that, as Foucault says:

> Rock offers the possibility of a relation which is intense, strong, alive, "dramatic" (in that rock presents itself as a spectacle, that listening to it is an event and that it produces itself on stage), with a music that is itself impoverished, but through which the listener affirms himself; and with the other music, one has a frail, faraway, hothouse, problematical relation with an erudite music from which the cultivated public feels excluded.[54]

Here we see debate in which the hegemonic music is assumed to be conformist (that is, classical) and the oppositional music, nonconformist (that is, rock) that runs parallel to the findings of Abrams *et al.* (mentioned earlier). But rock has become the most popular as well as the most conservative force in western society, particularly, but not exclusively, in terms of gender politics. As I have shown, there is enormous resistance to change in the consolidated world of authentic male rock anger.

The foremost British voice in the "authenticity debate" is that of Simon Frith, because he is a rock fan who progressed to journalism, and from there to academic research. He therefore can claim a sort of "rock writer authenticity" for himself, and hence becomes a gatekeeper of rock history, analysis and sociology in exactly the same way that a record business representative, say an A&R man, is a gatekeeper for the band or artist themselves. Frith, too, had displayed a veiled contempt for young women who began to approach guitar-playing, as this remark about young female musicians in Keighley in 1972 suggests:

> Alison and her friends were a group of sixth formers and college students who had a busy and self-contained social life, meeting weekly at the folk club (most of them picked at guitars themselves)...[55]

Subsequently, however, he teamed up with McRobbie and began to analyse what was actually happening in the world of rock.[56] He points out that "rock operates as counterculture only at moments. There are creative breakthroughs, when the music does express the needs of real communities, but it never takes the industry long to corrupt the results."[57]

Industrialization has had a constantly rocky relationship with art, music and the written word; Adorno pre-mourned the effect of the industrialization of music production on the audience:

> In the sphere of luxury production, to which popular music belongs and in which no necessities of life are immediately involved... [p]seudo-individualisation ... keeps them in line by making them forget what they listen to is already listened to for them, or "pre-digested."[58]

In other words, once music becomes a commodity by becoming a desirable vinyl object, he believes that the fetishization of the commodity itself becomes more important than its content. He also discusses the "handicraft" nature of early recordings, predicting the transformation of listeners from audience to consumer.

Adorno's despair can be applied in many different contexts: the reality for artists is that the element of communication in their artefact, whether visual, conceptual or sonic, communicates marketability to those willing and able to exploit it. I doubt, however, that Adorno would have been cheered by the aural assault of much of punk's "product"; he pursued what he regarded as aesthetic beauty, and there was little romance in the sounds of punk for anybody but its live audience until the public at large had been sold a mediated form which, it had been taught, was the Next Big Thing.

A wide-ranging account of the predicaments and resolutions of artistic practice and its dissemination is given in Becker's *Art Worlds*; although he discusses mainly the visual arts, several of his observations apply to the professional choices made by the previously amateur musicians involved with punk,[59] and the aesthetic judgement of their work. Punk was a live and erratic spectacle, celebrating randomness and chance, which made it difficult for an industry with a production-line mentality to capitalize on – doubly difficult given its implications for women musicians and bands. Punk music and its production and consumption can be thought of as a lived debate about the dilemmas that Adorno analyses, because there is general agreement that a pivotal point in a pop or rock musician's attitude occurs on signing a recording contract (and, indeed, for many of the women I spoke to, this was defined as the moment when everything started to fall apart for them). For instance, Chambers implicates recording itself as the factor that commodifies the experience of the originating community in the creation of new forms in Black music in the US (in the 1950s):

> The resulting music was an expression held together and concretised
> in the shared cultural and social context of audience and performer...
> In other words this music is worked up in a living social and cultural
> context that may later be "captured" on record.[60]

The word "captured" is well chosen, for the mysterious element that guarantees authenticity must be present in the recording in order for it to break commercially; ironically, it is this "capture" of the essence of the music's "worked-upness" that may eventually divorce the music from its original context, leaving behind a dry and indigestible idealism for the original fans to choke upon. Whiteley explores the results of the eventual disconnection from the counterculture of the band Pink Floyd:

> Political and social confrontation had become fragmented; subjective experience had degenerated into *play power*, which had little purchase other than an irreverent and often irrelevant questioning of authority, materialism and capitalism.[61]

Psychedelic rock had developed into an alternative form of entertainment rather than an oppositional "weapon." Later, of course, Pink Floyd demonstrated the same overblown attitude to their concerts as that of Rick Wakeman, described earlier; and the countercultural core to their music was lost in the replacement of energy and imagination with Things – staging, gimmicks and other "unique selling points," possibly devised by a marketing team. This breaking-down of a subculture-based music happens all too frequently; in the case of punk, Laing discusses the detachment of the innovative and marketable ideas from the subculture (leaving the politics to a few die-hard fans), commercializing them and selling them not only to the public at large, but also back to the originators, in their now more polished form. A wry comment from June Miles-Kingston sums up what happened: "When you can buy PVC trousers and pinned-up things in Topshop: once it becomes commercial it's got to end."[62] Laing articulates this internal struggle of the punk movement, whose "open membership" embraced diverse individual ethics:

> It is important to distinguish the tendency towards independence in punk rock from that towards separation from the mainstream. The distinction is that while "independence" (expressed mainly in the production and distribution of records) may be concerned to reach the same people as are reached by the musical mainstream, but by a different route, "separation" is concerned with consolidating a special community of punks, to whom punk rock will have special meanings.[63]

The implication of this is that however much political change is intended or desired by rock bands and their followers at the moment of creation, eventually the different intentions of those involved, combined with external interest and exploitation, will divert the energies of those people into diverse goals at odds with their original intentions.[64] This I found to be particularly pertinent to the women I interviewed; often, they had come to the point of signing a recording contract and discovered a discrepancy between what they wanted in terms of access to a larger audience and the compromises they would have to make in terms of the traditional gender presentation required by their record companies – this could result in the destruction of bands that had been in operation for as long as five years. This problem is a recurring one for "aware" bands, as Schippers discovered in her research of 2002:

> If their desire to eliminate sexism in rock was explicitly attached to the music, once the music lost favour in the mainstream, so would the politics. Rather than making the music a message that would eventually be lost in the heap of past trends, alternative hard rockers have tried to change the rules of the game. And so, alternative hard rockers rarely speak or sing of their feminist politics. They perform and embody them...[65]

Schipper's use of the word "alternative" is pertinent here; British punk was very much oppositional in nature, rather than alternative.[66] An alternative subculture rarely shakes society up, although this is not to say that its ideas do not percolate through to the mainstream.

To return to Laing's statement, the process of alienation from the safe, local environment is part of the rock band experience; punk bands moving out of their punk community were all too often just as isolated from their audience's support as their audience felt disconnected from the bands themselves. The relevance to my study here is that this factor worked to the disadvantage of many of the women I have interviewed; the recuperation of the female punk protagonist was complex. For example, in her study of a male band in the music scene in Liverpool in the 1980s, Cohen found that:

> Each move away from the band's original locality marked another rung on the ladder: from music-making within a close circle of friends and relatives; to performing in front of strangers outside the local-ity: to London, the record industry, and contact, through the media, with a nation-wide audience... Each stage or rung might also involve a change in attitude of bands' members towards music and music-making, representing a gradual transition from music performed largely for self-indulgence in a live, social context, to music and band as commodities to be bartered over and sold to a mass audience.[67]

Accusations of "selling out" are something many male rock bands have to deal with; for girls in mixed bands or all-women bands, there was/is the additional responsibility of being regarded as a pioneering female role model in a small locality, and carrying the expectations of those who have invested time and energy into your career with you as your career progresses into and through a much more traditionally male rock trajectory. Later, we will see what a burden this was to some of the women I spoke to, as they carried not only a responsibility to their local fans, but also to others of their gender.

It must also be noted that the effects of the recuperation of psychedelic music had been observed by Malcolm McLaren, for according to Sadie Plant:

> There is also a sense in which McLaren's tactics can be read as a rather more astute response. Aware that punk would be in any case recuperated, his own anticipation of its commodification did at least ensure that punk had some control over its own recuperation. By the time the dissatisfaction it expressed had grown into a marketable force, it had already been marketed. And if punk did recuperate anything, it was not situationist theory, but the possibility of effective dissent, a danger which, as "The End of Music" points out, punk shares with the spectacle of revolution presented in reggae and any other rebel music.[68]

Plant remarks that although entrepreneurs such as Richard Branson[69] and Manchester's Tony Wilson made relatively large amounts of money by exploiting punk music,

> ... punk's do-it-yourself ethic also produced a host of self-published fanzines and autonomous organisations, and the observation that fortunes were made cannot belittle the sincerity, anger, and achievements of those involved in punk and its later manifestations.[70]

With all forms of new music, the point at which the music becomes commodified is always distressing for its primary audience; for punks at least, the delays and obstructions put in place by the bands along this route to commodification were greatly appreciated by their audiences.

Peter York, who documented London punk sardonically and perceptively from its inception to its premature death-by-media, identified the retail outlet Rough Trade (which was based in Ladbroke Grove) as an important exponent in the lived debate about commercialization of the phenomenon:

> Rough Trade has the look of a head shop – which indeed it once was. The more *oppositional* sixties type, but a head shop nonetheless. You feel there could be discussions on elitism in the new wave and how the groups should relate to the record companies: the whole issue of *selling out...* It is here you begin to think the *politics* could be for real.[71]

In spite of McLaren's ability to profit personally from the spectacle of the selling(-out) of The Sex Pistols, Paul Taylor reports him as saying:

> Punk rock couldn't be sold... It was too much to do with Do-It-Yourself. As soon as you get a Do-It-Yourself force out there, you spawn 5,000 other groups. The record industry never wanted 5,000 groups. They only want one group. One group is more manageable. It's one dictator telling you what the culture is all about rather than 5,000. They don't like the socialist idea that everyone can do it.[72]

Some commentators interpreted this resurgence in political debate about commercialism as part of a "last post-materialist thrust"[73] before Thatcher's materialist influence took effect:

> The unexpected re-emergence of the Campaign for Nuclear Disarmament, the growth of the environmental movement and the more general adoption of conservationist goals may indeed point to an underlying shift in the focus of political values. The change is not dramatic or universal and whether one regards it as a move away from materialist, economic preoccupations towards post-materialist concerns, or as some broader change in values is open to debate.[74]

Even if the challenge to established means and structures of music production and distribution methods was momentary, the "product," too, was challenged – and this is what opened a door for women artists. All of the rock rules were ridiculed, as Street notes:

> The proliferation of independent labels, inspired by the DIY ethos, disrupted the complacency of the majors who had got rich on glam-rock and superstardom. Less tangibly, punk exposed rock's rules. It poked fun at ideas of romantic love; it celebrated boredom and mocked the idea that being a teenager meant perpetual pleasure; it forced the pop business, its controllers and its motives, into the limelight.[75]

Frith seems to have regarded punk rock as a welcome return to something the (male) rock fan could believe in:

> From the progressive point of view, the point of punk was its threat to established means of consumption. Traditionally, "accessible" pop gave access only to a void, to social habits that made no sense of people's needs at all.[76] *Really* accessible music reaches the parts that other musics can't.[77]

However, Street goes on to claim that there was no real political motivation behind the punks:

> The point was to have a good time. This meant causing havoc, not reading Marx; it meant celebrating the moment, not the future; it meant mocking the established order, not working for a new one.[78]

Both Frith and Street display a sort of old-school critical thinking; it is hard for an outsider to understand the way punk worked for its protagonists, the strong link between being and doing punk, the process of creation being part of the product created and the creators being part of a greater community of misfits. For the people I interviewed, it meant *making a* new order, not merely mocking the established one or working for a new one.

It has already been established that subcultures rarely consist of identikit members who all subscribe to the same ideology, wear identical clothing and are all aged seventeen years old. The small Brighton punk subculture used in this book as a case study was vociferously oppositional in nature: there was much discussion and argument about the meaning of our lives and what we were doing.[79] And Angela McRobbie herself, in the Introduction to *Feminism and Youth Culture*, describes the empowering environment of a shared house in which she lived in Birmingham with members of the mixed-gender band The Au Pairs, where students mixed with musicians, artists and writers who were all concerned with punk as a political force.[80]

The Rock Press

The rock press had a vital role in the bestowing of authenticity to music, as well as its role in publicizing new musical styles, and as taste-makers. After the *New Musical Express* advertised for new, younger writers, and employed Tony Parsons and Julie Burchill, who both lauded punk and scorned other, older forms of rock through their aggressive writing styles, other music papers followed suit. The principal three papers that wrote about punk music were *Sounds*, *New Musical Express*[81] and *Melody Maker*, and they all had a strong influence in the promotion of punk music as a countercultural force.[82] Helen Davies[83] discusses the male bias of the music weeklies, a discourse that clearly applies to the experiences of my primary sources. A summary of the general feeling, though, was that men who wrote (and write) about rock music are "wannabe" rock stars, secondary to those who do it. How could women (secondary citizens) get up and do what men could not?[84]

As far as the 1960s counterculture was concerned, women had been seen so much as part of the oppression of the free male spirit (after all, all they wanted was to get married and have babies and mortgages!) that their possible contribution to the revolution was all but ignored. However, Elizabeth Nelson's critique of the underground press in the late 1960s and early 1970s highlights a major issue concerning cultural radicalism, and although this refers to hippies, there is enough relevance in her observations to apply them to the assumptions made about punks. In her discussion of the counterculture's attitudes to women, she remarks that the protagonists basically had a lot in common with mainstream culture and thus were not challenging hegemony in a very important area:

> The question of women's liberation was not only grasped too late and inadequately, but more importantly, women were apparently never considered as suitable candidates in the search for allies... Even if the countercultural revolution had been "won," it would, judging from the evidence presented in the underground press, have been a revolution achieved by and on behalf of men.[85]

The most influential underground publication of the time, *Oz* magazine, regularly featured pictures of naked women, alongside, it must be said, articles by feminist radicals like Germaine Greer, who also appeared naked. Whether tokenism in the form of inclusion of feminist articles in a publication later prosecuted for obscenity was of any lasting benefit to the Women's Liberation Movement in the UK is not my remit here; but it may draw an interesting parallel in terms of the anarchic atmosphere at the time and that at the moment of this work. When "anything goes" culturally, there is an opportunity for women to make their voices heard; historically, however, it is not unknown for progress made by women to be entirely reversed.[86] The pioneering work by Sheila Rowbotham[87] has been discussed in relation to this and my primary sources; the problem, also acknowledged by Elizabeth Wilson,[88] is that the rules of Bohemia dictate that women must ultimately suppress their creativity in preference to that of a male partner – a point that will be returned to in my final chapter. This will have some relevance to the fact that punk as a subculture had so many female protagonists, and why their profile diminished later.

Writing on Women in Rock and Pop Music

The marginalization of women's musical activities that occurs in rock literature reflects the debate regarding separatism that is constantly being played out and possibly even starts at gatekeeper level, just as it does in the music business itself, from reviewers in rock magazines being predominantly male, onwards. Just as with an all-female band, a decision has to be made by a female writer as to whether they are writing for a female audience, a mixed audience or a male audience; this in turn will inform the writing style and the facts disseminated about the artists they are writing about. Rumsey and

Little's comment about the minority nature of feminists in the audience for "serious music" (see Chapter 4) is also reflected in rock criticism.

Should the writer "scare away" the male audience by refusing to pander to misogyny, or write like men do and embrace the ethos of rock-writing? Most of these writers adopt a neutral tone, allowing their enthusiasm for their subjects to drive their writing; occasionally, there is a disappointing evasion of issues that arise. For instance, in Charlotte Grieg's well-researched *Will You Still Love Me Tomorrow?*, which details a history of the 1950s girl groups in the US right through until the late 1980s,[89] there is no real analysis of the fact that so many of the lyrics sung by the apparently strong and self-confident women she talks about are attributed to men, or of the implications for women listeners and performers alike, defined only by those lyrics that are "approved" by men, either as gatekeepers or writers.[90] Although these women provided inspiration for a generation of fans,[91] the reality of their lives, dominated by Svengali figures such as Phil Spector, was far from empowered.[92] When women did become involved in song-writing, it was common that their royalties did not get paid to them.[93] Although this undoubtedly happened to men too, there is something particularly poignant about one of the least empowered sections of American society, Black women, singing songs that empower others, while becoming disempowered themselves. This phenomenon of men articulating what they think women (should) feel is a constant feature of pop and rock; when it does not occur directly in "first person" lyric-writing, it occurs in description (for instance in The Rolling Stones' *Some Girls* album, discussed at length by Reynolds and Press[94]). It is this empowering/empowered dichotomy that was breached by the women in my study.

One of the most interesting and unusual studies of women's experience in the British music industry is that of Sue Steward and Sheryl Garratt in 1984.[95] Steward and Garratt talked to women involved in almost every part of the music industry, and in doing so, demystify parts of the process of record-making. Although Negus[96] later explores the way record companies work as vertical organizations, examining women's roles therein, Steward and Garratt[97] go beyond the boundaries of the companies themselves, describing the whole "machine" behind a record release and how women may be involved in this process, and their study provides an interesting complement to this one.[98]

In *The Sex Revolts*, Simon Reynolds and Joy Press explore the history of recent rock music through an exploration of its relationship to aggression, revolt and reaction.[99] Their discussion makes many valid points (many of which have been discussed in earlier chapters), but is often marred by their own anger, in addition to a lack of analysis that makes the text difficult to read. However, it does reinforce the maleness of rock and helps to contextualize punk rock within the rock discourse; both Deena Weinstein's study of heavy metal[100] and Robert Walser's[101] were also very useful in understanding the way a rock subculture with different values is engaged with by its fans.

The two scholarly writers whose work has been of most relevance to this study are Bayton,[102] whose collection of interviews with women instrumentalists spans more than fifteen years, and Green,[103] whose research on the perception of women instrumentalists has been of great use when analysing the data I have collected myself. Again in the interests of context, some studies on women in punk subcultures in the US have been referred to here. These include studies by Roman,[104] Miles[105] and Leblanc,[106] who mainly discuss female *fans* of punk rock. However, their observations on alienation and class difference within the punk subculture have provided interesting reading.

Finally, for all of the women I spoke to, punk was about individual freedom and self-expression above anything else, and it is the importance of this factor that is lost in many of the texts written after the fact. Hindsight shows up many of the flaws in the ideology of punk, but its protagonists were, in the main, sincere in their activities, and no amount of academic misinterpretation can deny them this.

7 Conclusion

When I took up the banjo, d'you know what I was told? "That's a boy's instrument" and that's exactly why I took it up. Because I was a tomboy and I wanted to play it.
Did you wish you were a little boy, like in your song "I'm gonna be an engineer"?
No, I never wished I was a boy. But I wished I had a boy's privileges...[1]

Gradually it became something you can't put your finger on: it's an unnamed source of grief in your life which...becomes too unbearable if you acknowledge it. I don't want to know. Yes, the music industry is like any other industry, like the car industry or whatever...it's ultimately a cynical machine. But most of the people involved in it are totally besotted by music and you get very emotionally involved in the job, so the last thing you want to know is how shitty and sexist it is.[2]

When I began this work, an element of vanity motivated me. How could the music I had been involved with have felt so important and revolutionary at the time, yet have made no impact at all on the history of rock'n'roll? This concluding chapter, as well as attempting to analyse the information presented previously, will refer once again to primary sources in an attempt to show the role of gatekeepers (particularly those of the music press) in the demise of what was to later appear to be merely a fashion for female instrumentalists in bands: when the next fashion, for drag-garbed singers and electronic music, caught the imagination of the music press, all the issues associated with female instrumentalists, such as women's place in the "rock world," ceased to be of interest to papers such as the *New Musical Express*, which had seemed to take a genuine interest in the effects of feminism on rock music during the early 1980s. Because the bands that included, or consisted of, female rock instrumentalists did not establish themselves to any great degree in the mainstream charts, the impression that they were a passing phase was underlined. Some of the points made in this conclusion have already been explored in depth earlier, but their importance will be reiterated where relevant. I have included the commentary of media gatekeepers to emphasize the importance of pleasing these gatekeepers who were, of course, most frequently male and, if they were not, were rare females in a male-centred environment, who were themselves in the position of pleasing males. As Dale Spender observed of women writers:

> Since women have been able to write, women have written; some of them have achieved publication particularly in specific areas...and some who have been published have enjoyed prestige. But this does not constitute a denial that women are a muted group in terms of writing: it may be nothing other than an indication that some women writers have been able to please some influential men.[3]

Practically speaking, a woman gatekeeper also had a double problem: both of asserting her own views and also asserting the right of women to perform at all in the rock environment, let alone as equal instrumentalists. Caroline Coon describes this experience:

> No women were taken seriously in the music press, or a very limited selection of women were even considered worth writing about... The reason that I had difficulty in persuading the *Melody Maker* that what I saw happening in counterculture was important was because as a woman, and the only woman at that meeting, I was having to overcome a huge amount of sexual prejudice to consider myself, my work, as important. So if I would suggest something it would be automatically laughed out of the way. You have to understand that also those environments are very competitive, the men also are competing for space... So it was doubly loaded against what I was saying.[4]

However, in this conclusion I will attempt to explain first the unusual circumstances that led to the refusal of some young women to engage in the "real world" of jobs and homemaking, and then to examine the many different reasons why their progress (and that of other women who followed them) was stopped in its tracks.

Reaching the Limits of Possibility

The glass ceiling my subjects hit came about partly through loss of interest by the media and industry as the novelty of women players in punk wore off; few of them "performed male" like Chrissie Hynde or Suzi Quatro. Those who spoke to females as much as males, who experimented with the form of rock music, became sidelined as "avant-garde"; this is what befell The Raincoats, who had deliberately looked away from rock music in spite of their rock line-up:[5]

> "The basic theme in rock'n'roll is what goes on between men and women," said The Raincoats, each one chipping into the conversation. "Rock'n'roll is based on black music. And it's based *in* the exclusion of women and the ghettoisation of blacks. Which is why we want to put a bit of distance between what we do and the rock'n'roll tradition."[6]

Christine Robertson, manager of The Slits, reveals how, with hindsight, she can understand the way many of the male punk rock bands fitted into the existing rock world[7] in spite of (or even because of) their revolutionary stance, and the importance of their skills in playing music that fitted into an already-established rock style:

> The Slits had an ability to play together, but often it would almost fall apart and then it would come back even better together – but The Clash could play together all the time and I was quite impressed by that. Of course, looking back now I see what they were, they were just a rock band and they are successful like a rock band. So The Clash earn millions of pounds now[8] and The Slits earn a few thousand every year. It's no measure of the quality of the music at all, but they fit into the male rock thing and The Slits didn't fit into anything.[9]

Her description of the practical experience of The Slits' career drawing to a halt as she desperately tried to make them more accepted by mainstream TV and radio channels in the UK rang very true:

> We tried *everything*. A lot of our meetings would be, "What should we do next, who should we try next?" Their greatest desire was to go on *Tiswas*, maybe with a birthday cake, and have a cake fight, you know, the sort of thing they did on *Tiswas* anyway. Could we? No – we couldn't get *near* it![10] No real anarchy on there at all, I'm afraid; they couldn't get near it. There was a block. I don't want to get into a syndrome of "Oh it's all the men's fault, they were threatened by the women," but I'd have to say that all the media industry, apart from record-pluggers, were men. By the time you got to somebody who was gonna make a decision, like a radio producer, it was a man. And I think they threatened men, or their reputation threatened men.[11]

The responsibility to bring about change was left in the hands of women, who seemed to have the choice of either charm or anger to energize men. In spite of and because of "Women's Lib" and the *Spare Rib* ethos, there was, and remains, little will by men to change popular culture at this time. Bayton ruefully observes:

> It is from the start an unequal race, set up in a way that favours men rather than women. Some individual men do nothing to either help or hinder individual women and may think that the whole issue is irrelevant to themselves, but they are (unwitting) beneficiaries of a set-up that is skewed in their favour, in terms of a whole range of material and cultural resources.[12]

Ironically, the unemployment that had equalized some sections of society polarized others; given the collapse of British industry and the sudden increase in unemployment, there was sometimes a feeling that women were not wanted in the workplace, where they were taking employment that was a working man's entitlement.[13] This resentment channelled itself into many areas with a hitherto unfelt female presence, and by default into youth culture. However, opposition by peers, especially men, is not a new concept for female instrumentalists in spite of the fact that, as young women, even those who plan careers of this nature feel free to choose their occupation. Caroline Coon spoke of the naïve optimism of young women who have not yet experienced the realities of competing against men in a world formed for their own convenience:[14]

> It's interesting because when you're in your own skin, you look out-wards, you don't see yourself "as a woman." You see yourself as a *person*, and as a *person* you can do anything. When you're seeing a great rock'n'roll band, you want to be in a great rock'n'roll band. You are unaware at that point of the politics of it. It's not surprising that women want to do anything, because it's there to do. You want to be like the rest of the world. You want to have the same opportunities as the rest of the world. Just because you don't see women guitarists, it doesn't enter your head that the reason you don't see women guitarists is a political issue. You think, oh maybe somebody just didn't have that idea, but I have that idea, [and] I want to do it.[15]

It must be noted here that even in the past, women with a musical "call-ing" encountered obstruction from their male peers; Carol Kaye, who played bass on many of the Motown hits and was described as the "chick with a pick," had to develop a strategy to deal with male musicians who opposed her. Like many "pre-feminist" female instrumentalists, she is vague about the nature of this opposition:[16]

> They [the male players] did their best to break me, because they don't believe in women, but I proved to them that I could play my instrument. I stuck up for myself, but in a nice way, without destroying the man's ego. Once I established my playing abilities, it was easy. I was no longer a female oddity. I was a musician, commanding $70,000 a year.[17]

Responsibility for Change: A Poisoned Chalice

There was a political burden carried by female band-members, regardless of whether (as did The Au Pairs or Delta 5) they wanted to acknowledge this. The argument about the right of women to be performing in traditionally male territory was (and still is) debated from many different standpoints. It is as difficult to describe the "cutting edge" of the debate, as it applied to rock music at the time, as it is easy for the women involved to explain with hindsight what was actually going on. It is important to remember that there were two general types of musical ethic that most women players subscribed to: broadly, the competent and equal (as personified by Lesley Woods of The Au Pairs, perhaps), and the incompetent and feisty (as personified by many of the local female musicians I interviewed). Both types, however, were perceived to have the same responsibilities *to* their gender and problems *because of* their gender, and in this section I shall summarize what these were. It will help the understanding of the former to describe the experience of the iconic US female performer Joni Mitchell. Lisa Kennedy here explains the projection of male desires onto Mitchell:

> Far too often, Mitchell's critics had located her gift (her peers were better at recognising her discipline) in the deep recesses of feminine power. In fact, in promoting Mitchell as the quintessential feminine poet in the wilderness of a vigorous seventies feminism, her astounding craftsmanship and musical ambition were side-stepped. One writer put it this way in 1974: "Her disarming intelligence had special appeal for men bored by the dull polarity of beach bunnies and hardline feminists."[18]

There was a stigma attached to being a feminist and a musician, and especially, a feminist musician (let alone a lesbian musician, whether feminist or not). The idea of banding together for solidarity that had been so empowering for Mavis Bayton's band The Mistakes, for instance, was deeply unappealing to the women in some other bands, and was seen as commercial suicide; often band-members within the same band would have differing views about this issue. Here is an example, from an interview that feminist band Jam Today gave to *Spare Rib:*

> Deirdre: ... Look at the impact Fanny[19] had though they weren't feminists – they reached thousands of women, which Jam Today can't, by being commercial and getting publicity.
> Terry: How have Fanny reached more women – by saying "you too can be a superstar"? Most women who started playing an instrument as a result of seeing Fanny will have ended up being exploited and demor-

alised by the commercial music business... Angele: But Fanny actually showed the record buying public, who'd only seen male bands before, that there were women who could "do it" – by going commercial. Jam Today, by not doing so, runs the risk of providing an "in-service" for feminists and the converted left.[20]

Jam Today were a band of older women who were technically very competent as instrumentalists;[21] in contrast, Poly Styrene displays an attitude that was very common among younger female band-members:

> You'd rather have a mixed band?
> Yea, 'cos if you think you're as good as guys, then you should be able to work with them on an equal level. Sex isn't an issue, maybe it has been in the past but there should be a new approach. Forget you're a girl, just think of it from a music point of view. I think all girl bands are sort of woman chauvinist, bit women's lib. Women's lib is changed now, it was necessary before, but I feel equal now.[22]

Even at this time, feminism was regarded by both men and some women, like Poly, as no longer necessary. If you "feel equal now" as an individual, then surely women's liberation has succeeded! Caroline Coon was frustrated by the lack of awareness of these younger women; she told me:

> Sitting here interviewing The Slits...having them say, "We have nothing to do with Women's Liberation," I have to just take a deep breath and say, "I'm not going to challenge that," because that's just a normal part of the process of consciousness-raising. There's nothing you can say to young women at that point. I understood it, because the way feminism was presenting itself was, even to me, pretty horrendous. I remember going with a girlfriend of mine who was in a band to a feminist benefit, and they weren't allowed in because they were wearing dresses and lipstick. So there was all that going on. So this was a group of young women, who wanted to be sexually attractive, assertive...naming yourself as a feminist would be a very brave and difficult thing to do.[23]

Steve Beresford has another perspective on their attitude:

> There were ironies, like there was a kind of absolute clichéd feminist who showed up from the *Morning Star*; they were deeply insulted that she was only interested in them because they were women. They said, "We're not interested in talking to you, 'cos you just want to talk to us because we're women. We want you to talk to us because you like the music." I was much more sympathetic to her; all the women I

went out with at that time were pretty hardline feminists to the point where some of them stopped going out with me 'cos they weren't supposed to go out with men... I knew this thing backwards, I'd read all the books, I knew this stuff, and of course The Slits hated feminists. They felt it was patronizing. The whole contradiction of the British Left is that it constantly acts like a colonizing power.[24]

Ari summed up the attitude of the band at the time when I interviewed her, and her attitude could, I think, be applied to everybody I spoke to and, in particular, provide a different perspective to Bayton's point. In a situation with a supportive male community, women can achieve as much as their male counterparts:

There was a big window open for women at the time to take part in this explosion of music and culture – and I don't want to say politics, because that's the whole point; we weren't political, we were just humanly outspoken – so we weren't aware of "Oh, we're women so we've got to defend women's lib and women's rights and we're women-political." It was more like, we all had friends and peers that were mostly boys, and those boys happened to leave a very open window for women to express themselves just as much as they did, because they were not offended by us being women.[25]

This has a parallel with the observations made above by Lisa Kennedy; in spite of the importance of the music to the band (and regardless of their alleged competence/incompetence instrumentally), they are still perceived by elements of the media as protagonists in the "sex war" – this time, ironically, by a publication that should have given the band more respect for their musical achievements. Some bands deliberately tried to identify with the promotion of women artists and the creation of a "space" for them on the rock circuit; but women's bands who were involved with Rock Against Sexism (formed as an offshoot of Rock Against Racism in 1979) got short shrift from rock journalists, who could easily identify the futility of the exercise:

Taken on the most fundamental level, to completely eradicate sexism would mean tampering with the whole structure of modern day music. Certainly the most uneasy implication lies in RAS's hope of getting participating bands to sign an "anti-sexist" contract clause before each gig. Whatever that might mean, its inherent censorship is a frightening thought. Big Sister is watching, and wearing no dancing shoes – otherwise she'd know rock music is all about outrage, and outrageousness. No way can you kick ass with a contract clause, however well intentioned.[26]

It was rare for female rock and pop acts to speak out in favour of other female artists;[27] in this, they echoed what many felt was a *special* woman" syndrome much practised by Thatcher. There was an implied "I am as good as a man" thought behind this. This is demonstrated best by this exchange between Chrissie Hynde and interviewer Andrea Juno:

> AJ: Did you have a support system with other women in the London scene?
> CH: No, there wasn't a support system... But I never thought there was anything to distinguish a female guitar player or a male guitar player any more than you can distinguish a male cellist or a female cellist. Other than the fact that chicks never seemed to be nearly as good at guitar.
> AJ: Why do you think that is?
> CH: I think that, inherently, they don't have the aptitude for it, like men do.
> AJ: Do you think that inability might be self-imposed – that women just think they can't do it?
> CH: Yeah, I think it's self-imposed. When I say aptitude, I don't know if it's the way our brains are wired up, if it's biological, or what it is. All I know is that since I got interested in rock'n'roll music, and up to this present day, I've never heard a woman be an innovator on the guitar, like Jimi Hendrix, Jeff Beck, or any of the great guitar players. I'm not concluding anything from that other than what's obvious: they're not as good at it. I'm not saying why, or for what reason. It's just that so far, no girls have done it.[28]

Perhaps the fact that Hynde was supported largely by male musicians leads her to subscribe to the idea that women "don't have the aptitude" to play guitar.[29] Hynde ignores Maybelle Carter's famous "Carter Scratch," an innovative guitar-picking style, among other respected female guitar innovators:

> Perhaps the most remarkable of Maybelle's many talents was her skill as a guitarist. She revolutionized the instrument's role by developing a style in which she played melody lines on the bass strings with her thumb while rhythmically strumming with her fingers. Her innovative technique, to this day known as the Carter Scratch, influenced the guitar's shift from rhythm to lead instrument.[30]

For Hynde, possibly, it may have been more important to have the self-image of a maverick, rather than as a woman involved in a macho culture, tolerated or celebrated as a token.[31] She had, after all, encountered personal opposition from Vivienne Westwood when she first arrived in London from

America, and this may have led her to withdraw from participating in a female music ethos; about McLaren and Westwood she remarked:

> I always admired and looked up to Malcolm and Vivienne – to the point where I thought, Why should they like me? Maybe I am a despicable piece of shit.[32] Look at my clothes. I've got no style. On the other hand, I was the girl who was musical. Vivienne was shocked when she saw me play a guitar. "You really can squeeze some chords out of that thing, can't you, Chrissie?" They were all surprised that a low-life like me could actually do something.[33]

Hynde's remarks about the reaction, even by supposedly avant-garde colleagues, reflect the "front-line"; her experience was, probably voluntarily, solitary. Although she claims there was not a supportive "movement" of women in London's punk scene to compare with the local situation in Oxford, experienced by Mavis Bayton,[34] or with the later Riot Grrrl phenomenon, Ari cited Hynde in particular as a beneficiary of a support network, simply in terms of the general change in the awareness of female instrumental participation in rock:

> If we weren't supported by our peers and our colleagues who were like brothers to us, we wouldn't have been able to express what we could. This is why people like Chrissie Hynde got their break, because there was all this female support. It wasn't like switching on a button of saying "Let's help girls," it was about being in a revolution and when you're in that type of constant adrenaline, of changing the world every day that you're doing it, and you're so young, they're not busy thinking, "Oh, the women that we've got to compete against, that's a threat," because they can see the rest of the world is reacting really violently towards us, just as they are to the boys, but even more.[35]

But even Gina Birch articulated the frustration she felt at being lumped together with others as a sort of "female band" paradigm:

> When you compare the Riot Grrrl movement to seventies punk, I don't remember us being very supportive of each other. I adored The Slits but didn't take much interest in some of the other groups that were going around like The Mo-dettes, The Delta 5, The Au Pairs... I liked them, but I didn't go crazy about them. We were constantly being thrown together in articles and compared to the point at which it divides you. We never went out with a sense of sisterhood, we never toured together. The idea never entered our heads. We were as supportive of male groups that we liked as female groups. Gender wasn't an issue for us, which perhaps it should have been.[36]

Gina describes almost being defeated by the pressure to "come out" as a feminist, in spite of the stigma attached to the term:

> We finally decided it was important to have a positive attitude towards women – although the word feminism seemed to inspire fear and loathing in people. I mean, I didn't want to be associated with some of the people who claimed to be feminists, but at the same time it began to appear to be cowardly not to. In the end we used to spend most of our interviews discussing feminism.[37]

In contrast, keyboard-player Liz Naylor felt that feminists were a middle-class confection, although her attitude has since changed:

> We hated women musicians. I remember going to see The Raincoats and The Au Pairs at the Polytechnic and me and Cath were at the back going, "Pah, pah, these feminists"; there was a real tension between myself and feminism at the time. In Manchester, Whalley Range and Charlton and Didsbury, where all the feminists lived, that was everything punk *wasn't*.[38]

In print, The Mo-dettes prided themselves on their femininity because they considered their deliberately sexualized, feminine visual image as a reaction to the low-key presentation of The Raincoats, attempting to reclaim the "girly" pop image for themselves, while simultaneously playing "male" instruments onstage:

> Jane: We just go out as ourselves; we're all pretty, vain girls.
> Kate: There's a bit of a reaction against girls like The Raincoats, who try to cover it up...even though that's part of their lifestyles and they don't really go out of their way to dress like *that*, it's just a way of saying: just because I'm a girl, don't *expect* me to do anything.[39]

However, this did not prevent them, also, from hitting the glass ceiling patrolled by record companies. It seems that whatever tactics the bands with a strong female presence employed, they were still not able to attain long-term success of the type that male bands had. The sophisticated tensions between representing womankind, the realities of press hostility, and the exaggerated focus of being a novelty female drummer proved almost too much for Hester Smith:

> That sort of thing was a real burden actually. That's why I think it would be different now, I don't think there would be that kind of political consciousness...having to represent the vanguard of females

in music. I really felt that strongly at the time, that we weren't political enough, or that we were kind of letting the side down by not being like The Slits or something...[40]

Gina describes her practical experience of the situation noted by Sally Potter[41] in which "as more women achieve in a given area they are forced to compete with each other for the same space rather than the space itself expanding":

> There was a kind of competition and a kind of war between each other [The Mo-dettes, Delta 5], and we were pitted against each other, by the press and also a bit probably by ourselves. I remember when I was doing *Dorothy* with Vicky [Aspinall] ...there was this group, a model and a make-up artist or something, and I remember feeling very competitive with them. There wasn't room for both of us; it wasn't like, well, they're doing it, therefore if people like them they will like us. I used to think, well, if they're being successful, somehow it's to our detriment.[42]

Gaar has a more positive view, talking about a "specific realm in which to create their opportunities";[43] however, in light of the constant "forgetting" of women's inroads into rock musicianship by rock historians, this seems a romanticized evasion of reality.

Finally, male journalists of course were only too delighted if they could deny the necessity for further debate. The following review sums up an attitude that started to become more common towards the end of the 1970s. Admittedly, the musicians reviewed here were older and perhaps rather simplistic in their rejection of the approach of male bands, but there is a hint of triumph in the reviewer's delight in giving them a bad review:

> They seem too conscious of competing in what they evidently regard as a male-dominated system. It's a redundant attitude given that we are beyond the stage of regarding women rockers solely as jail-bait or white-garbed fantasy princesses... It's because I believe that the female group is on the verge of becoming more substantial that I refuse to patronise a rock band purely because of its feminine content. Actually, I didn't like Tour De Force.[44]

How easy for a male reviewer to reject the fact that some groups (particularly the previously established ones) still perceived a gender bias in the music business and still wanted to critique the stereotypes so beloved of the rock press! Meanwhile, at the more academic end of the spectrum, Kaplan perceives a strategic move by scholars to avoid engagement with feminism:

> Is it possible that the postmodernist discourse has been constructed by male theorists partly to mitigate the increasing dominance of feminist theory in intellectual discourse?... I am suggesting that certain theorists are drawn to postmodernism (rather than struggling against it) precisely because it seems to render feminism obsolete – because it offers a relief from the recent concentration on feminist discourse.[45]

Collusion by women in this process (and arguably Madonna is the arch-colluder!) meant that any sort of solidarity could be perceived from the women's point of view as weakness, according to Caroline Coon:

> It's also in art that that happened too, because many women artists didn't want to be grouped together as women because "women are second rate." "I don't want to define myself in a group show of women artists because they think we're all second rate, so I'm not going to be anything to do with women's liberation, or feminist." But the way I see it is that actually where women are is the avant-garde.[46]

Green writes that collusion happens "through willingness to conform, through reluctance to deviate, through embarrassment and, extremely, fear";[47] the attitudes of bands like The Mo-dettes and Chrissie Hynde in the interviews with the rock press quoted earlier very probably reflect this.[48]

To conclude this section, it is worth noting that this problem also is not completely genre-related, nor new, as Leslie Gourse discovered in her research on female jazz instrumentalists:

> Some women never agree to play in all-women's groups or all-women's festivals out of an unwillingness to be ghettoised. For that reason, several musicians, primarily those who play in pop groups and studios and occasionally play jazz too, have taken a firm anti-women's group stand. If a forum has sexism and not music as its raison d'etre, all women jazz musicians like to avoid it.[49]

The Gimmick

As the conference delegate cited at the very beginning of this work commented, women instrumentalists have a great "novelty" appeal, but as with anything concerned with "difference," the debate engendered by this novelty was a mixed blessing. Linda Dahl's interview with jazz drummer Dottie Dodgion illustrates not only a reluctance to playing with other women ascribed to the novelty factor, but also a wry stoicism in her awareness of her position:

> Women are still in the minority in the music business. I think you'll
> find there are a lot of lady musicians who never wanted to work with
> other women because you just didn't feel they were serious enough
> about it. They were sold like they were a bag of meat and potatoes,
> strictly because they were women... It's just a natural selling point. Of
> course, we women never make any money off it, only the promoters.
> And nobody likes to be sold because of their gender. It's an under-
> standable tendency and you can't help it, but you don't have to go
> along with it.[50]

Enid Williams brings the situation up to date, explaining the balance Girlschool had to negotiate in order to rationalize their existence:

> It was a big help being female in the sense of getting gigs, because it
> was like, great! women on stage, or girls on stage as they would see
> it; we'll pull the punters in, you know, it was a little bit of a novelty; it
> made us stand out. It was definitely a help in terms of getting work
> and in terms of getting publicity in the music press. But it was a hin-
> drance in terms of being taken seriously.[51]

Ironically, perhaps, the "easy" access to certain aspects of the business for
certain women at certain times could be touted as proof that women were
now equal in rock music, for as Griffin says:

> Debates about women's position in non-traditional jobs have been
> dominated by the ideology of equal opportunities, particularly since
> the sex discrimination legislation was passed in 1975. In these terms,
> both women and men can be discriminated against on the grounds
> of sex, since there is no concept of differential power. Lone "token"
> women (and men) in non-traditional occupations can then be pre-
> sented as evidence that particular jobs are equally open to women
> and men.[52]

Julie Burchill twisted the "token" achievement of Gaye Black into an overt
criticism of her band, implying that not only does she fulfil this role, but that
she provides a novelty aspect for The Adverts that they could not survive without: "without little Gaye's wide, frightened eyes, luscious lips and batman ring,
what are The Adverts but a gaggle of noise-merchants, no worse, no better
than all the others?"[53] This serves to reiterate the divisive nature of journalism,
from the addition of the diminutive "-ette" to female punks by the tabloids
mentioned by Zillah Ashworth earlier, to the attempts to engender jealousy
not only among those of the same gender, but also between male and female
musicians, in the rock press.

The Shelf-life Question: The Duration of the Pop/Rock Career

Simon Frith has rightly pointed out that:

> Pop music is created, however successfully, for a large audience and is marketed accordingly by the record industry... The record industry depends on constant consumer turnover and therefore exploits notions of fashion and obsolescence to keep people buying.[54]

Given that many of the artists in my study entered the arena of rock and pop along the lines of "art as free practice versus art as a response to an external demand,"[55] it is perhaps not surprising that they did not sustain the interest of the music press. The professional life span of a female artist in the UK roughly corresponds to (passing for) the ages seventeen to twenty-three. After the five-year shelf-life, the business wants a new gimmick; in this case, new technology and new "women" – pantomime dames (otherwise known as androgynous male performers) and female-male impersonators, that is, "male" heads in female bodies, for example Annie Lennox, Grace Jones, Tracey Ullman, Toni Basil, Madonna. Women instrumentalists returned to the keyboards and piano; this, after all, was an instrument that they were more likely to have spent their adolescence playing, and did not threaten male space in the way that the playing of traditional rock instruments had done.

Mary Ann Clawson offers an argument that, coupled with the short attention span of the British record industry, shows that it remains unlikely that female guitarists and bass-players will have an impact on British rock music; she discovered that for the young women in her study, "rock musicianship was more frequently a phenomenon of young adulthood than a product of early adolescence. Aspiring women rock musicians are thus often denied the years of teenage apprenticeship and skill acquisition experienced by male counterparts."[56] Although some of the respondents to my study did start learning to play their instruments at school, and some, such as Sue Bradley, had their choice of instrument dictated by this circumstance, others had to wait until the enabling factor of punk started their music-making. Ironically, it was one of the school band guitarists, still trying to continue her career, who told me at the time of interview that although record companies still liked her music, once they discovered her age (late thirties) they were not interested; indeed, one A&R man told her, "We never sign girls over the age of twenty-three."[57] Given the fact that young women have not tended to spend their adolescence in bands working on their guitar-playing skills, and by the time they have acquired such skills, if Clawson is correct, they are likely to be in their early twenties, the ageism/sexism of the British music industry will constantly close the gates of access to any sort of long-term rock music career to young women. It is also interesting to note the results of research by Michael Fogarty, carried out in the late 1970s:

> At a number of points the Study suggests that hard-edged attitudes on work or work-related issues develop later among women than among men, so that women are at a disadvantage where career opportunities and patterns tend to be determined early in life. At age 18-24 women express much less interest than men in a job with opportunity for initiative and one which fully uses their abilities, but at age 25-34 their interest in these features of a job rises sharply and catches up with men's.[58]

In other words, by the time a woman realizes that she has potential, and wants to use this in her work, it may be too late for her, should her interests lie in the direction of becoming a rock or pop performer.

Musical Confidence and Competence: A Chance for Longevity?[59]

When featured on Radio 4's *You and Yours*,[60] Suzi Quatro cited lack of musicianship as the major reason for the short-lived careers of many of the musicians I have discussed in this work. But sometimes, it was the *male* members of the band who were less skilled at playing their instruments;[61] earlier, we saw how Gaye Black was finally acknowledged as a competent bass-player. Her own description of a recording session shows that musical problems in the band came from elsewhere:

> I remember when we were recording, there was this song that we'd do that started with a big, long slide. It starts off on the bass, and the drummer got it wrong every single time and I think we did twenty-three takes; my fingers were bleeding at the end.[62]

Lucy Green points out that there is much admiration for professed incompetence in young men's musicianship (especially in Britain, I believe), and that they use rock music as an escape from traditional musical skills, and amateurism as justification for their involvement in pop or rock instead of classical music. It seems rather unfair that we apply one set of critical criteria to young men and another to young women.

Although many of the women involved in bands as instrumentalists at this time became skilled as time went on, they'd simply not had time to plan careers as musicians, and the very ordinariness that made their activities so appealing in the first place became a burden to them as the opposing poles of business and political concerns removed them from the environments that had "grown" them.[63] Nothing illustrates this better than Naylor's recollection of a typical gig:

> We lived in a high-rise block in Harperhay, one of the grimmest places in the world. I had this enormous keyboard, and Cath had a cheap guitar and a Vox AC30. We needed a team of young men but we didn't have one of those – we had a wheely thing for suitcases which we bungied them on. We had no money; we were pitifully poor. We'd play the Mayfair, a ballroom at Bellevue. We'd catch the bus to be there at 5 o'clock when the PA got there, to see the blokes assembling it. We didn't know anything about soundchecks – we never really learned; we didn't think we had the right...we'd sit in this horrible damp hall, but we didn't mind, it would be part of it...we'd just hang around. Soundchecks seemed really mysterious; I didn't really understand how instruments worked. I'd think, Well, they've assembled the drums, they're up, why does this carry on, why are we last?, and then at about 8.30, somebody would shout at us to go on after being there all day. And always, our instruments were kind of propped up on top of things, so I couldn't see the stickers on my keys. And we'd just kind of plug in and make some noise and somebody would go "Fine," and that was it. I don't even remember being nervous. I don't think there was ever any line about our performing – I don't think I ever stepped across it and thought, I'm a performer and in half an hour's time I shall be performing to about twenty people. I'd just get drunk and hang out – that's what we did.[64]

They had not all intended to become "stars," although some women did come to experience the trappings of stardom; the whole tradition of "genius" musician was an alien concept, even to a respected guitarist like Chrissie Hynde. Added to this was the fact that so many musicians actively wanted *not* to be like rock stars – Reynolds quotes Dennis Bovell, the producer of The Slits' album, *Cut*, talking about their guitarist Viv Albertine, who

> ... was no Jimi Hendrixette... She'd do the occasional bit of single-note lead guitar, but mostly she was more like a female Steve Cropper from Booker T and the MGs, doing all these great rhythm things. She was always very conscious of not wanting to play the guitar like a man, but actually trying to create a style of her own.[65]

Viv adds to this, describing the deliberate minimalism she used as a guitarist:

> We were utterly anti wanky guitar solos, which were just someone showing how fast their fingers moved going up and down some blues scale, and everyone going "wow."

> Unless a note had to be there we wouldn't play it; so it's not that I was happy to be a rhythm guitarist. I love rhythm and I love rhythm for its own sake. Someone like Steve Cropper, I'd much prefer to play like him than Jimi Hendrix. I did play little breaks but they were utterly to undermine guitar solos. They were thought about, and not an indulgent thing to show off.[66]

What happened at this time was an odd sort of accident, a type of "action research" that was unsophisticated, often maverick, occasionally corruptible, and constantly debatable.[67] Sometimes, the practitioners had no empathy with, or support from, their female "fellow travellers" in this experience, like Liz, who found a class issue difficult to empathize with, or Karen from The Gymslips, who said:

> The band I really liked was The Mo-dettes. There were a lot of others that I thought, What the fuck is going on? Like The Raincoats and The Slits, that were very popular, and I couldn't see why because to me it seemed that they couldn't really play at all.[68]

Strangely, women who *were* competent were criticized for this, too:

> Frankie: We have been criticised for being too professional.
> Alison: Yes, it's absurd when women are taking something seriously. This criticism is directed at the arts more than at mechanical things. Why are all male professional standards supposed to be completely thrown out for music and not for, say, plumbing?[69]

In contrast, Hester felt that her skills were never going to improve enough to compete with the better drummers of her gender, and told me that she felt that she had not been assigned the right instrument in the first place by her band:

> If I felt like I'd had a calling to play the drums then it would have been different. I got more embarrassed about that as time went on; I went to have drum lessons...and desperately doing these drum exercises every day. Particularly when I felt I had to be representing female drummers, and I knew how people would be taking the piss anyway before I even started. And I knew there were some really, really good female drummers around and I didn't want them to think that I represented them.[70]

June Miles-Kingston, however, really did learn to play, although she had to "earn her stripes":

> We did a tour with Spizz Energi. Spizz was great 'cos he's really good fun, but the band were like, "An all-girl band, supporting us? They're gonna be crap," especially the drummer, who was like, "I'm the best drummer." By the end of the tour, we were playing two drums together on stage and we were all best mates. You've only got to prove yourself once. Most guys, especially in music, they're gonna be open, aren't they? They're not like the normal guy in the street that reads the *Daily Mail* and won't think about a woman doing any kind of important job. They're musicians – you've only got to prove yourself, I can play.[71]

Eventually, respect came to June automatically:

> I remember in our third year we played in LA at the Whisky, and it was all really exciting, you know, "The Whisky-a-Go-Go, you know." Blondie came to our gig and came backstage afterwards (I loved Blondie and used to listen to her all the time), and her and her drummer Clem Burke came backstage afterwards and said to me, "Hey, you're a really cool drummer."[72]

Notwithstanding obviously skilled musicians, there was a subtext to many of the gig reviews, even those which superficially celebrated the influx of women into bands, that was patronizing and paternalistic. This could appear whether or not a band was "angry" or "decorative." The Slits, in particular, suffered from this; their actual discipline and determination offstage were far removed from the disorganized appearance in their first few gigs documented by punters and journalists alike. Ari described it thus:

> I can't forget us every day walking round, trying to hustle, trying to get better in the rehearsal room, rehearsing every day. Army life, like a fucking army, very disciplined, walking around trying to get into the business, trying to organize gigs, trying to get a record deal, trying to do interviews, trying to rehearse. And there was people saying, "Aow, they're not a serious band, they can't play, they can't play music, they're like a whatever – they're girls." We were incredible for our age; we were all teenagers. I wanna see any girls getting up doing what we did back then! I dare them! We were amazing![73]

A performance by a band with female instrumentalists could be read entirely differently according to the tastes and age of the audience member, regardless of their sex. The Slits, for instance, were "dramatizing" female concerns, in a reflection of the punks' dramatization of Britain's decline.[74] So, while Karen believed that bands like The Raincoats "couldn't play at all," Paul Morley praised their EP *Fairy Tale in the Supermarket* under the title, "Singles of the Week: Exhilarating,"[75] continuing: "The two barbed ballads *In Love* and

Adventure Close to Home are not normal, and expose a new kind of gentleness. They will not remind you of anything." Other reviewers would cover themselves, such as in this review of Essential Logic by Paul du Noyer:

> They're fooling around with the boundaries of rock music dancing on a tightrope. If they ever fell off I'd hate to be there, because the mess could sound so unpleasant. But right now they're walking the line stylishly.[76]

Many other reviews of female bands by male journalists displayed a voyeuristic thrill in waiting for things to go wrong; women felt differently, as they often related to the performers. Eventually, some reviewers "came round" to the idea that they were actually hearing a new type of music being made, as Richard Grabel's 1980 review "The Slits, New York" testifies:

> It works very well live, where the convictions they carry in their persons translates the recorded and fixed sentiments of the songs into comments on the instant, inviting reflection and dialogue. They prove too that the distinctiveness of their recorded sound can't just be credited to Dennis Bovell's production. This was a fortuitous intersection of a producer's proclivities with an artist's intentions. The sound grows from the material.[77]

The reputation of The Raincoats as an avant-garde group was vindicated when Kurt Cobain invited the group to tour with Nirvana, one of the most influential US alternative groups of the 1980s, in 1994. This would have raised their profile in rock histories without a doubt; the unfortunate suicide of Cobain before the tour took place resulted in a return to the margins for the band and their reputation. Susan Suleiman identifies the margins as a place of relegation for women artists, regardless of whether or not they have chosen to belong to the avant-garde:

> Avant-garde movements have wilfully chosen their marginal position, the better to launch attacks at the center, whereas women have more often than not been relegated to the margins: far from the altar as from the marketplace, those centers where cultural subjects invent and enact their symbolic and material rites.[78]

In spite of Sara Cohen's observations about the value attributed by young male rock musicians to *not* having musical skills, and Green's comments about the alternative values about musicianship that they posit in their own rock world, we have seen that lack of skill was assumed to be a major reason for the demise of female rock musicians at the end of this moment. I believe this to be in part due to the redefinition of skill in relation to rock musicianship, and that this is in part to do with the necessity by young males to reassert the male identification of their music.[79] Clawson cites skill shortages as a reason for the incorporation of women into rock bands as bass-players, and remarks that generally both male and female rock musicians regard bass-playing as a lesser skill once it is perceived as a "female instrument."[80] Hartmann (paraphrased here by Phillips and Taylor) remarked that:

> Capitalism in its historical development encounters individuals who are already sex-stratified, and this pre-existing sexual stratification – patriarchy – then becomes harnessed to capital's need for different types of labour.[81]

Women instrumentalists are acceptable in an emergency, whether the social emergency of punk or the political emergency of the First World War, but once they seem to become established, they become a threat. If they become skilled, they become permanent, and the flexibility that led to their acceptance suddenly disappears. The happy amateurs who took to the stage for fun or political expression were not so welcome if and when they began to take themselves more seriously. McRobbie points out that: "as unskilled rock workers women are a source of cheap labour, a pool of talent from which the successes are chosen more for their appropriate appearance than for their musical talents."[82]

Skilled rock workers are instrumentalists; for many skilled male rock workers, there was a double interest in not promoting skilled women – some men think they will be squeezed out by a combination of both attractive appearance and instrumental skill that they cannot compete with, and are not prepared to suffer the consequences of their gender's emphasis on women's sexuality as a selling-point. In other words, with more women instrumentalists, there is not only more competition in instrumental terms, there is also an unfair advantage in terms of both men and women responding positively to female-friendly rock bands.

However, female audience members could be tough on female players. In an article by Robbi Millar in *Sounds*, a woman audience member at a rock gig is asked about Girlschool, who are playing on an otherwise all-male bill. In an interesting slant on Lucy Green's observation about male musicians "listening out" to see how skilled female instrumentalists were in a band, she says:

> Girlschool are a good band, a good example of the music, but I think for a girl to really prove herself in a band, she needs to be a lead guitarist or a drummer, say, on her own with a bunch of guys. Then the

onus would be on her to prove herself. She'd *have* to be good enough to survive. Girlschool are an all-female band so I don't think they have that pressure to be as good as individually they perhaps could be.[83]

Some, like June Miles-Kingston, developed the skills to work in otherwise all-male bands for many years afterwards, having been in an all-female band previously, but it was shocking to discover just how far some male band-members would go to destroy the career of a competent and attractive female rival. In one incident, two male band-members fabricated a drugs incident in order to prevent a female player from taking part in a tour of the US with a major British female new-wave act:

> The drummer was particularly sexist, and although I tried to keep my head down he was gunning for me from the word go, and towed the bass player along with him. In hindsight, I suspect it was the "I fancy her so I'll be vile to her" routine. Anyway, I became friendly with the guitarist, who was a regular guy, and that fuelled the drummer's fire. Accusations about drug-taking, being a disruptive influence, and so on were made in writing, so I had to fight back – I took the issue to the Musican's [*sic*] Union and won compensation for the US tour.[84]

The problem with challenging, and succeeding in winning in, such a scenario is that the musician then finds it extremely difficult to get further work and is also put in the position of fighting her corner in a situation where she should be making music.

For those women who played in mixed bands, we have seen that there was often a need for band personnel who did not desire traditional male roles such as that of "rock star guitarist," and this explains the tendency of women to play bass guitar. In British punk bands, the sheer speed of creation and quantity of bands had been a factor in the inclusion of women causing the relative ease of access to punk music-making. The next musical trend, towards a respect for electronic technology in music-making and the emphasis on the skills of "the producer" as auteur, should have been no excuse for the exclusion of women. This music was keyboards-based, more conventionally associated with women, and should therefore have encouraged women to participate.[85] However, it was also based on electronic innovation, conventionally associated with male technical mastery. The coincidence with this new music and the repositioning of masculine energy into war "drained" rock music of this energy, and the patriarchal solution was to recruit feminized men as practitioners of the new genre. To us, it seemed as though Thatcher had won and, as Thatcher won, the record industry won, returning the creation of music to the status quo, in which the system ensured that abrasive elements were

The Mo-dettes (Kate, June, Ramona and Jane). Photographer Virginia Turbett, Redferns Collection; © Getty Images

smoothed over or eradicated before they had an impact on the mainstream. Music returned to its polished, produced norm, epitomized by the emollient vocal sounds of Boy George; dissenting females were represented by the fun, raggedy-looking, unthreatening Bananarama or the attention-capitalizing Madonna. Margaret Thatcher represented the victory of greed over creativity, and the rewarding of obedience with material goods. The punks had regarded the establishment, and the Queen, if not with affection, then with a humorous dismissal; for many people, the Queen had been reduced to a heritage figure rather than one of authority in the aftermath of The Sex Pistols' "God Save the Queen" single. She had, in the eyes of many punks, become equivalent to the kitsch sold on stalls to tourists in central London – a bit like a diecast metal Routemaster bus, say, or a plastic bobby-on-the-beat. Thatcher was an utterly different prospect; she was a new version of the Queen of England, with a new, humourless establishment that had co-opted enough of the do-it-yourself mentality of the punk subculture to apparently sneer at its manifestations of more deep political unrest. Whereas many punks had seemingly subverted their parents' suburban DIY environments (dad in the garage mending the lawn mower, mum in the kitchen baking cakes), the suburban mentality they had hated came back with a vengeance. The autonomous punk subculture, with its own clothing, media and music, became a series of cottage industries; all the activity that had created a culture to replace that which rejected the punks was capitalized on; the old order, supported and, some would say, throttled by the Trades Unions, was replaced; in the media, union-free newspapers like *Today* came into being; the large record companies regrouped and created their own "independent" labels to service the post-punk music that was more marketable to a large audience. Any humour there had been in the spectacle and realization of punk was forgotten; the dramatization and self-mockery of the subculture were frequently reduced to ridicule by its spectators, and largely abandoned by its practitioners.

What must be remembered, though, is that success in punk terms did not necessarily mean the same thing as it would for a mainstream artist or musician. Not every band wanted a record deal and not every player wanted to be famous. For many, just having the self-confidence to get up on stage and do something was a challenge that gave them a sense of achievement they had never imagined possible; being part of a social group, "the punks," was something that for a person designated a reject at school or at home could completely change their life. Making money out of the music by competing in the mainstream, or even alternative record business, meant becoming part of an established, competitive hierarchy; the activity itself was enough to counter the social and political negativity of the era. The "I can be in a band" mentality undoubtedly rescued many of our generation, whether or not we left behind anything in terms of a concrete musical or artistic legacy; this personal empowerment stayed with everybody I spoke to, and has informed their lives ever since. As Lucy O'Brien says:

> I just found it such an empowering experience and I'd recommend every teenage girl to be in a band – a band particularly, because it's all about doing something together, launching something together that's your own. It does take quite a bit to get it off the ground, quite a bit of guts. Also, the other thing is just appearing on stage. I remember, it was only about six inches off the ground, but it was so scary standing there looking at this sea of faces looking back at me expectantly and I thought, Shit, I've got to actually do something now. To conquer that fear, it's a bit like going on a big sky-dive; at such a young age, it sets you up somehow. I remember for years afterwards nothing scared me – once you've faced that situation, it gives you a certain fearlessness![86]

The punk battle had been one in which people took clearly defined sides. A phenomenal amount of energy went into preventing it from having any lasting influence; as far as the female band personnel were concerned, with the attempts at the beginning to prevent and discourage women from being involved, but also in retrospect with the attempts to belittle and forget those who were part of it all, institutionalized misogyny is the last taboo.

It is interesting that some of the bands discussed here have re-formed at the time of writing: The Slits introduced "new blood" and were recording and touring again with their new members until Ari's untimely death at the end of 2010; Girlschool have toured recently with their original line-up; and Gina Birch continues to play solo gigs and perform with The Raincoats, notably at MoMA in New York in 2010. Palmolive plays with a church rock band in Cape Cod, changing the songs she wrote with The Slits so the lyrics reflect her Christian beliefs. There is an awareness that their past is valid and can provide a foundation for not only further self-expression but also influence succeeding generations. Web communities such as "Typical Girls"[87] and "Women in 70s Punk"[88] have archived much information and encouraged a revival of interest in the women of this period.

This book has described an important historical moment when women instrumentalists established themselves in an influential new rock music genre, and has examined how they were eventually excluded from participation in male-identified music. It also represents a process of rescuing this moment from the amnesia of conventional popular music historiography in the same way that other "histories from below" have been written about the achievements and experiences of other excluded or marginalized social groups. The mechanism of exclusion is not unique to the early 1980s,[89] and it is likely that it will continue to operate in the future, particularly if such histories as this are not brought to light. We should regard this as cautionary as we congratulate ourselves for progress made in the twentieth century.[90] As Enid Williams said:

> There was a programme on television some years ago, and it was an hour long, and they had all the Zeppelins and Deep Purples, but also lots of really tiny little bands that most people would never have heard of, and they didn't mention Girlschool once! We certainly weren't in the league of Led Zeppelin, although they did come to see us play once, but we were far, far more successful than half the bands on that programme and they didn't even mention our name, because to them we were a female band; we didn't come under the banner of "heavy metal" and somehow we were forgotten about.[91]

Notes

Acknowledgements

1. Susan Acton, Lindsay Aitkenhead, Kirsty Angwin, Miranda Aston, Robina Baines, Sue Ballingall, Maria Biggart, Charmaine Bourton, Cathy Crabtree, Lynn Cunningham, Caroline Davis, Jaki Florek, Lorraine Forbes, Lorraine Hilton, Martine Hilton, Janice Jackman, Caroline Jones, Kit Jordan, Julie [sic], Suzanne Long, Lindsay Marshall, Susan Mirrey, Carol Otter, Gris Sanderson, Eliza Taylor, Suzy Taylor, Heather Thomas, Sian Trehearne.

Introduction

1. Caroline Coon's work, *1988: The New Wave Punk Rock Explosion* (London: Omnibus, 1982), is a rare exception.
2. Jon Savage, *England's Dreaming* (London and Boston: Faber and Faber, 1991).
3. Malcolm McLaren (dir.), *The Great Rock'n'Roll Swindle* (Universal Films, 1982).
4. Conference, "No Future?" University of Wolverhampton, September 2001.
5. It is not the intention to ignore or belittle the contribution of female folk rock singers from the mid-1970s onwards, but rather to describe the atmosphere of maleness in rock music and maleness-of-definition in pop at this time in order to show the extraordinary nature of the phenomenon explored in this book.
6. Ann Oakley, *The Sociology of Housework* (Oxford and Cambridge, MA: Basil Blackwell, 1985 [1974]), 4.
7. Angela McRobbie and Jenny Garber, "Girls and Subcultures," in Angela McRobbie, *Feminism and Youth Culture* (Basingstoke and London: Macmillan, 2000 [1991]), 12–15.
8. Ibid., 19.
9. Barbara Hudson, "Femininity and Adolescence," in Angela McRobbie and Mica Nava (eds), *Gender and Generation* (Basingstoke and London: Macmillan, 1984), 35.
10. Christine Griffin, *Typical Girls? Young Women from School to the Job Market* (London: Routledge, 1985), 15.
11. Simon Frith, *Sound Effects* (New York: Pantheon, 1981), 86.
12. John Berger, *Ways of Seeing* (London: BBC and Pelican Books, 1972), 45, 47.
13. Laura Mulvey, "Visual Pleasure and Narrative Cinema," *Screen* 16.3 (1975): 27.
14. Lucy Green, *Music, Gender, Education* (Cambridge: Cambridge University Press, 1997), 54.
15. Judith Butler, "Performative Arts and Gender Constitution: An Essay in Phenomenology and Feminist Theory," *Theatre Journal* 40.4 (December 1985): 519, italics in original.
16. Frith's *Sound Effects* (op. cit., 1981), has two pages on women, pp. 86 and 87. On p. 162, Frith manages to say this without specifically mentioning women:

"The challenge thrown up by the punk vanguard was to develop a general account of rock's means of signification. Musical effects are not biologically given, even if in a particular culture people communicate through music as naturally as they communicate through language."

17. Pierre Bourdieu, *Masculinities* (Cambridge: Polity, 2001), 8.
18. Margaret Marshment, "Substantial Women," in Lorraine Gamman and Margaret Marshment (eds), *The Female Gaze: Women as Viewers of Popular Culture* (London: The Women's Press, 1988), 27.
19. Griffin, *Typical Girls?*, 5.
20. Ruth Finnegan, *The Hidden Musicians: Music-Making in an English Town* (Cambridge: Cambridge University Press, 1989), 304.
21. For example, see Dave Laing, *One Chord Wonders: Power and Meaning in Punk Rock* (Milton Keynes and Philadelphia: Open University Press, 1985).
22. John Lydon, *Rotten: No Irish, No Blacks, No Dogs* (London: Coronet, 1995), 378.
23. Jean Genet, 1971, quoted in Dick Hebdige, *Subculture, the Meaning of Style* (London: Routledge, 1979), 135.
24. http://news.bbc.co.uk/onthisday/hi/dates/stories/april/5/ (accessed 12 April 2011).
25. Penny Rimbaud, drummer and founder-member of Crass, says that The Sex Pistols were no more than a "blip" in pop music, and claims that punk existed in Britain for years before they appeared on the scene; it has long been accepted that the origins of British punk music may have been CBGBs in New York, but Rimbaud claims the attitudes were here already, having developed from those of the alternative society of the late 1960s. Coon's comments from author's interview, 24 January 2002.
26. Female rock and pop musicians in the US have a much longer "shelf-life" than those in Britain, which tends to be limited to (passing for) age 17–23; this has a strong bearing on the nature of my work.
27. The Centre of Contemporary Cultural Studies, at the University of Birmingham, which was closed in 2002.
28. Michael Bracewell, *England is Mine: Pop Life in Albion from Wilde to Goldie* (London: Flamingo, 1998), 93.
29. It was also accepting of difference: for instance, Helen of Troy, an ex-girlfriend of catalyst Malcolm McLaren, was a dwarf-lady, and one of Brighton's prominent punks had been a thalidomide baby and possessed a pair of Doc Martens boots, part of the punk "uniform" for many) with zips at the back to allow her to remove them without undoing the laces.
30. Mavis Bayton, *Frock Rock* (Oxford: Oxford University Press, 1998).
31. My appeals for interviewees led instrumentalists in jazz, funk and other genres to contact me; a surprising number of these women claimed the attitudes of punk were of importance to them.
32. Letters printed were sent to me via Durrant's Press Cutting Agency. Although Scotland, Wales and Northern Ireland were included in the survey, I received no enquiries from these areas; perhaps if the request for questionnaire subjects had taken the form of an advertisement the exercise would have been more successful – a letter to this effect from the *Yorkshire Evening Post* leads me to believe that this is a possibility. The survey was therefore limited by the interests of the Letters Page Editor in each case.

33. A journalist from the *Daily Mail* refused to print my request for interviewees, after asking me for contact details of those I had spoken to already, because I would not tell her my husband's name and occupation.
34. Laing, *One Chord Wonders*, 97.
35. For example, Barbara O'Dair (ed.), *The Rolling Stone Book of Women in Rock* (New York: Random House, 1997).
36. It is interesting to observe a parallel between this phenomenon and the penchant of male opera-writers to concentrate almost exclusively on tragic female heroines in their storytelling. See Catherine Clement, *Opera or the Undoing of Women* (London: Virago, 1989).
37. Lucy O'Brien, *She-Bop: The Definitive History of Women in Rock, Pop and Soul* (London: Penguin, 1989).
38. Gillian G. Gaar, *She's a Rebel* (London: Blandford, 1993).
39. O'Dair, *Rolling Stone Book*.
40. Susan McClary, *Feminine Endings: Music, Gender and Sexuality* (Minneapolis and Oxford: University of Minnesota Press, 1991), and "Afterword" in Jacques Attali, *Noise: The Political Economy of Music* (Minneapolis and London: University of Minnesota Press, 1985).
41. Carol Neuls-Bates, *Women in Music: An Anthology of Source Readings from the Middle Ages to the Present* (Boston: Northeastern University Press, 1996).
42. Jill Halstead, *The Woman Composer: Creativity and the Gendered Politics of Music* (Aldershot: Ashgate, 1997).
43. Marcia J. Citron, *Gender and the Musical Canon* (Cambridge: Cambridge University Press, 1993).
44. Camille Paglia, "Madonna II: Venus of the Radio Waves?" in C. Paglia, *Sex, Art and American Culture: Essays* (New York: Vintage, 1992).
45. Amy Raphael, *Never Mind the Bollocks* (London: Virago, 1995).
46. Sarah Cooper (ed.), *Girls! Girls! Girls! Essays on Women and Music* (London and New York: Cassell, 1995).
47. David Buckingham, *The Making of Citizens* (London: Routledge, 2000).
48. Joanne Hollows, *Feminism, Femininity and Popular Culture* (Manchester and New York: Manchester University Press, 2000), 174–5.
49. Dick Bradley, *Understanding Rock'n'Roll: Popular Music in Britain 1955–1964* (Buckingham and Philadelphia: Open University Press, 1992), 12.
50. David Sanjek, "Can Fujiyama Mama be the Female Elvis? The Wild, Wild Women of Rockabilly," in Sheila Whiteley (ed.), *Sexing the Groove: Popular Music and Gender* (London: Routledge, 1997).

1. A Ladder Through the Glass Ceiling?

1. Dick Hebdige, *Subculture, the Meaning of Style* (London: Routledge, 1979), 99. The "energy, expansion and upward mobility" aspect was later capitalized upon by Thatcher and presented in its recuperated form as enterprise culture.
2. This will include information from questionnaires that were filled in by women instrumentalists from other areas in the UK.
3. Although The Clash played many reggae-influenced songs, their repertoire became

predominantly rock-influenced, and this assured them a crossover into mainstream audiences.

4. See, for example, Liz Thomson, *New Women in Rock* (London: Omnibus, 1982).

5. Toby Goldstein, "Have You Seen Your Sisters, Baby, Playing in the Shadows?," in *Let It Rock, Women and Rock, a Special Issue* (July 1975): 31.

6. Mina Carson, Tisa Lewis and Susan M. Shaw, *Girls Rock! Fifty Years of Women Making Music* (Kentucky: University Press of Kentucky, 2004).

7. Interview with Ari Up, lead vocalist with The Slits, 21 February 2006.

8. Mavis Bayton, *Frock Rock* (Oxford: Oxford University Press, 1998).

9. Virginia Caputo, "Anthropology's Silent 'Others': A Consideration of Some Conceptual and Methodological Issues for the Study of Youth and Children's Cultures," in Vered Amit-Talai and Helena Wulff (eds), *Youth Cultures: A Cross-Cultural Perspective* (London and New York: Routledge, 1995), 29.

10. Sue Glyptis, *Leisure and Unemployment* (Milton Keynes and Philadelphia: Open University Press, 1989), 21, from the 1983 Department of Education and Science Survey.

11. Caputo, "Anthropology's Silent 'Others'," 37.

12. Stephen Harding, "Values and the Nature of Psychological Wellbeing," in Mark Abrams, David Gerard and Noel Timms (eds), *Values and Social Change in Britain* (Basingstoke and London: Macmillan, 1985), 73.

13. Glyptis, *Leisure and Unemployment*, 77, emphasis added.

14. Ibid.

15. Elizabeth Nelson, *The British Counter-culture 1966–73: A Study of the Underground Press* (Basingstoke and London: Macmillan, 1989), 86.

16. Paul E. Willis, *Profane Culture* (London and Boston: Routledge and Kegan Paul, 1978), 172.

17. Simon Frith, *Sound Effects* (New York: Pantheon, 1981), 266.

18. Elizabeth Wilson, *Bohemians: The Glamorous Outcasts* (London and New York: I.B. Tauris, 2000), 134.

19. For example, Glyptis, *Leisure and Unemployment*, 85, says people are drawn to youth subcultures, or extreme left or right politics, particularly in areas with high unemployment.

20. Valerie Walkerdine, *Counting Girls Out: Girls and Mathematics* (London and Bristol, PA: Falmer Press, 1998), 163.

21. Ibid.

22. Interview with Liz Naylor, 7 September 2000. Liz formed The Gay Animals and played keyboards for them before becoming a fanzine producer/editor.

23. Interview with Mavis Bayton, 14 July 2000. Mavis played guitar for the feminist punk band The Mistakes.

24. Interview, 23 June 2000.

25. Sheila Rowbotham, *Woman's Consciousness, Man's World* (Harmondsworth and New York: Penguin, 1981 [1973]), 13.

26. Valerie Walkerdine, *Daddy's Girl: Young Girls and Popular Culture* (Basingstoke and London: Macmillan Press, 1997), 154.

27. McRobbie criticizes Angela Carter for assuming that only "rich girls" can afford to look poor, noting that many female students were "barely scraping along on their grants with no parental backup," and noting also that "In the 1980s, for old and young

alike, the discipline of the factory clock no longer prevails. The unemployed and the semi-employed have been cast adrift, and for many young men and women their attention has turned inwards towards the body." Angela McRobbie, "Second Hand Dresses and the Ragmarket," in McRobbie (ed.), *Zoot Suits and Second Hand Dresses: An Anthology of Fashion and Music* (London: Macmillan, 1989), 47. See pp. 39–48 for a discussion of androgynous clothing and extended childhood.

28. My findings are supported by research done by Abrams in the late 1970s, which found that "Among those aged 18 to 34 anti-traditionals outnumber traditionals by 5 to 1 in all three social classes – though ambivalents predominate numerically in all but class DE... Looking at all three age groups, what predominates is the fact that in their values, young middle class people have much more in common with young working class people than with their middle class elders." Mark Abrams, "Demographic Cor-relates of Values," in Mark Abrams, David Gerard and Noel Timms (eds), *Values and Social Change in Britain* (Basingstoke and London: Macmillan, 1985), 29.

   It could be argued that eventual employment destiny defines class, but from my sample interviews and questionnaires this also would appear to be untrue; see the Appendix. This was also found by Ruth Finnegan: "the widely assumed national associations of musical with social categories did not always fit in with the Milton Keynes situation. Thus the classification of a performance as say, 'punk' depended as much upon the image developed by a *particular* local band as on nationally detect-able differences in musical style, general behaviour or class background." However, "The predominance of male players was striking: out of 125 players in the 1982–83 survey only 8 were women. In the bands in which women *were* included, however, they mostly took part on equal instrumental terms with the men rather than merely being just the front singer – the 'sex symbol' role so castigated by feminist critics." Ruth Finnegan, *The Hidden Musicians: Music-Making in an English Town* (Cambridge: Cambridge University Press, 1989), 105 and 119. As Iain Chambers rightly says, "it must not be overlooked that, when the accounts are settled, after the negotiations and local victories noted, the wider choices and possibilities – from the macho heavy metal guitar hero through the glitter androgynoid to the gay disco star – stubbornly remained with the boys." Iain Chambers, *Urban Rhythms: Pop Music and Popular Cul-ture* (Basingstoke and London: Macmillan, 1985), 128.

29. Glyptis, *Leisure and Unemployment*, 85.

30. Sara Cohen, *Rock Culture in Liverpool: Popular Music in the Making* (Oxford: Clarendon Press, 1991).

31. Interview/conversation on BBC Radio 4, *You and Yours*, 19 July 2000.

32. I found this interesting, as Malcolm McLaren's version of punk rock music has The New York Dolls, a band he managed for a while, at the epicentre of influence on Brit-ish punk bands' music.

33. John Cale, April 1974, in Dave Thompson, *Beyond the Velvet Underground* (London and New York: Omnibus, 1989), 9.

34. As the driving force behind Rough Trade Records, Geoff Travis was a major interme-diary in the spread of DIY culture in the record industry. Interview, 1 February 2002.

35. Interview, 9 October 2001. Christine managed The Slits during their busiest period, travelling with them on tour to the US and Europe.

36. Walkerdine, *Daddy's Girl*.

37. Iona Opie and Peter Opie, *The Lore and Language of Schoolchildren* (St Albans: Paladin, 1977).

38. Caputo, "Anthropology's Silent 'Others'," 40. This study refers to Canadian children, but I believe there to be a parallel with British children.

39. Jacques Attali, *Noise: The Political Economy of Music* (Minneapolis and London: University of Minnesota Press, 1985), 110.

40. "Letters," *Sounds* (10 July 1976): 42.

41. There were rare instances in the 1970s of women instrumentalists in, for instance, club bands. Kate Stephenson was one such: "It was a working men's club band, and that's when I started to feel that it was a little bit strange: the very middle-class girl from a very stable background starts to enter a world of unreconstituted men. It would be three or four gigs a week: you'd do a gig at lunchtime and then one in the evening. Of a lunchtime there'd also be a stripper on, more than one, as I came into the room humping my drums on to stage. Working on the same bill as a stripper, it was all so new, it was a bit eye-opening. It was so important to me to fit in and not to make it an issue for them that I was a female in the band." Interview, 1 February 2011.

42. "Not being a groupie" was a wonderful side-benefit of playing in a band – you could participate in all the excitement without being scorned as a lesser being by men in rock bands! At an interview by a local paper in Brighton, which a male band tried to hijack by showing off, I was asked by the journalist, in their hearing, if they were my groupies (see Chapter 3).

43. Amy Raphael, "Chrissie Hynde," in Barbara O'Dair (ed.), *The Rolling Stone Book of Women in Rock* (New York: Random House, 1997), 304.

44. Angela McRobbie and Jenny Garber, "Girls and Subcultures," in A. McRobbie (ed.), *Feminism and Youth Culture* (Basingstoke and London: Macmillan, 2000 [1991]), 221.

45. This was also something that male bands did; for a description of imaginary bands in Sheffield, some of which became real bands in time, see Simon Reynolds, *Rip it Up and Start Again: Post-Punk 1978–1984* (London: Faber and Faber, 2005), 154.

46. Interview, 8 September 2000. Zillah is a vocalist with Rubella Ballet, who still perform to this day.

47. *Rock Follies* was an ITV series that followed the career of three female rock singers as they tried to forge careers in the music business; it achieved cult status in 1976/77. Other influences cited include Julie Andrews (Gina Birch).

48. Interview, 26 January 2000. Hester was a founder-member of Dolly Mixture and played drums.

49. Interview, 23 April 2010.

50. Interview, 14 February 2011.

51. Paul Rambali, interview with Talking Heads, *New Musical Express* (4 February 1978): 7.

52. Interview, 6 December 2001.

53. Interview, 13 October 2001.

54. Email from Jane Woodgate, 7 March 2006. Jane played bass for The Mo-dettes.

55. Interview, 2 February 2000. Rachel played guitar for Dolly Mixture.

56. From an interview with Mike Appelstein, via *Caught in Flux* website, http://www.

appelstein.com/, at http://www.nstop.com/paloma/intervw.html (accessed 12 April 2011).

57. Interview, 23 June 2000. Gina played guitar and bass for The Raincoats.
58. Interview, 30 January 2006. Tessa was a founder-member of The Slits and played bass guitar.
59. Interview, 30 November 1999. Enid played bass with Girlschool, a rock band active at this time.
60. Interview, 14 July 2000.
61. Interview, 2 February 2000.
62. Interview, 26 January 2000.
63. Bass guitar is also easier to play if you have small hands; bar chords on six-string guitar are difficult. This may be one reason why it is used so much by women rock musicians. The most comprehensive study on women bass-players is Mary Ann Clawson, "When Women Play the Bass: Instrument Specialization and Gender Interpretation in Alternative Rock Music," *Gender and Society* 13.2 (1999): 192–211.
64. Interview, 20 November 2001. Sue played violin and keyboards with Brighton band The Reward System.
65. Interview, 13 July 2000. Karen played drums for The Gymslips, an all-female band, and, later, Serious Drinking, whose other members were male.
66. Interview, 6 December 2001.
67. Interview, 7 October 1999. The Mockingbirds were an all-female band in Brighton.
68. Interview, 7 September 2001.
69. Interview, 21 February 2006.
70. Interview, 23 June 2000.
71. Interview, 3 February 2006. June was a founder-member of The Mo-dettes, and played drums with them.
72. Paul Cook in interview, 13 August 2010.
73. Interview, 3 March 2006. Rhoda co-formed the seven-piece all-female rocksteady band The Bodysnatchers, and was their vocalist.
74. Deanne Pearson, "Twins: How to Tell Them Apart," *The Face* 11 (March 1981): 54–5.
75. Interview, 7 October 1999.
76. Interview, 6 December 2001.
77. John Hamblett, "*Prag Vec*," *New Musical Express* (16 June 1979): 7–8.
78. Interview, 11 February 2011.
79. Paul E. Willis, *Profane Culture* (London and Boston: Routledge and Kegan Paul, 1978), 6.
80. This will be explored further in the primary research.
81. Interview, 2 February 2000.
82. Interview, 7 October 1999.
83. Unless, like Siouxsie and the Banshees, you played support acts to the same bands all the time; the band are documented as borrowing equipment mainly from New York band Johnny Thunders and the Heartbreakers, until they signed a record contract – for almost two years. See Stephen Colegrave and Chris Sullivan, *Punk: A Life Apart* (London: Cassell, 2001), 332–3.
84. Interview, 13 July 2000.

85. Interview, 18 October 2001. Lora Logic was saxophonist with X-Ray Spex, before leaving to form Essential Logic.
86. Interview, 7 October 1999.
87. Interview, 30 November 1999.
88. Interview, 23 June 2000.
89. Interview, 6 December 2001.
90. Interview, 14 July 2000.
91. Interview, 30 July 2010.
92. This information came from the questionnaires I sent out to female instrumentalists who responded to my letters to local papers in the UK.
93. Stella Clifford, 11 February 2011.
94. Interview, 26 January 2000.
95. "No Future?" conference, University of Wolverhampton, September 2001; reiterated by The Adverts' bass-player Gaye Black, when describing the London venue the Roxy: "You didn't just go when there was a band you wanted to see, you just went there." In Nils Stevenson and Ray Stevenson, *Vacant: A Diary of the Punk Years 1976–79* (London: Thames and Hudson, 1999), 84.
96. Interview, 9 October 2001.
97. Interview, 15 January 2001.
98. Interview, 9 October 2001.
99. Later, bands became much more stereotyped along aesthetic and political lines, resulting in everything from right-wing skinhead involvement to separatist feminist gigs.
100. Interview, 26 January 2000.
101. Interview, 14 July 2000.
102. Interview, 6 December 2001.
103. Ibid.
104. From questionnaire reply.
105. Interview, 7 September 2000.
106. Interview, 18 June 2010. A Polytechnic was a precursor to a new University, a Higher Education establishment that had recently moved from awarding diplomas to awarding degrees.
107. This perhaps contrasts with the punk ethic mentioned earlier.
108. Interview, 30 November 1999.
109. The capacity of the Cambridge Corn Exchange is 2,000 – a relatively large venue.
110. Interview with Hester Smith, 26 January 2000.
111. Interview with Pauline Murray, 5 February 2011.
112. Interview, 30 January 2006.
113. Interview with June Miles-Kingston, 3 February 2006.
114. Interview with Rhoda Dakar, 3 March 2006.
115. By email, 18 January 2006.
116. An early incarnation of male punk band The Clash.
117. Interview with Gina Birch, 23 June 2000.
118. Interview, 15 September 2010.
119. Interview, 26 March 2010.

120. Interview, 8 February 2011.
121. A slang term for the triumvirate of weekly rock newspapers: *Sounds*, *New Musical Express* and *Melody Maker*, all of which targeted the young male rock fan.

2. Media Gatekeepers and Cultural Intermediaries

1. This term was coined by Reynolds and Press to describe the attitude of The Slits; see S. Reynolds and J. Press, *The Sex Revolts: Gender, Rebellion and Rock'n'Roll* (London: Serpent's Tail, 1995), 307–8.
2. Indeed, the American Weymouth had followed the classic British punk trajectory, moving from being a fan to playing in the band and co-wrote their first British hit, "Psycho Killer."
3. Miles, Review of Talking Heads at CBGBs, *New Musical Express* (2 April 1977): 49.
4. Gaye Black talks about the Roxy Club in London: "I wasn't made to feel conscious of the fact that I was female there as I was by the music press – a band full of Martians could have played there and no one would have batted an eyelid." Nils Stevenson and Ray Stevenson, *Vacant: A Diary of the Punk Years 1976–79* (London: Thames and Hudson, 1999), 5.
5. From Chris Salewicz, Review of The Adverts, *New Musical Express* (11 June 1977): 44.
6. Angie Errigo, "I was a Dull Housewife until I Discovered Sadisto-Rock," *New Musical Express* (24 September 1977): 7.
7. Lucy Green, *Music, Gender, Education* (Cambridge: Cambridge University Press, 1997), 76.
8. Green calls this "listening out" for playing skill. Ibid., 55.
9. Interview, 3 February 2006.
10. Interview, 10 February 2006.
11. *New Musical Express*, 27 May 1978, 58. Other examples include *New Musical Express* (16 April 1977): 41, a bad review of The Adverts by Tony Stewart with a sultry photograph of Gaye, described as a "pretty bassetist"; and *New Musical Express* (10 February 1979), 46, a review of The Tourists at the Hope and Anchor, London, by Rick Joseph: "and curvaceous Scotette Ann Lennox on vox, larynx, flute, sax and industrial stoppage whistle" (with a photograph of Annie Lennox playing keyboards at the gig). This trend has continued to this day with the branding of honorary males as "ladettes."
12. Interview, 8 September 2000.
13. Dale Spender, *Man Made Language* (London: Pandora, 1990), 20. This gives an interesting perspective on the girls groups in the US in the 1960s, such as The Ronettes, The Marvelettes, and so on.
14. Helen Davies, "All Rock and Roll is Homosocial: The Representation of Women in the British Rock Music Press," *Popular Music* 20.3 (2001): 295–313.
15. *New Musical Express* (10 September 1977): 46. The lead singer was actually a man.
16. This is a reference to the popular ITV series *Rock Follies*, broadcast in 1976/77. The series followed the careers of four fictional female rock singers and was cited as an inspiration by some of the people I interviewed, although it was heavily criticized by rock bassist Suzi Quatro.
17. *New Musical Express* (10 September 1977), 46.

18. Things have not changed, if the quotation at the beginning of my study is representative of the general view.
19. Dick Hebdige, *Subculture, the Meaning of Style* (London: Routledge, 1979), 54–5.
20. Punk "metamorphosed misogyny into militancy" according to Reynolds and Press, *The Sex Revolts*, 68. This phenomenon will be discussed in a later chapter.
21. Interview, 24 January 2002.
22. *New Musical Express* (16 April 1977): 11. An earlier *NME* interview "with Patti Smith" by Paul Morley had consisted mainly of quotations from Lenny Kaye *about* her, her music and what it's like to be in a band with her. *New Musical Express* (1 April 1977): 7.
23. Sally Potter, "On Shows," in Rozsika Parker and Griselda Pollock (eds), *Framing Feminism: Art and the Women's Movement 1970–85* (London: Pandora, 1987), 30.
24. From Stephen Colegrave and Chris Sullivan, *Punk: A Life Apart* (London: Cassell, 2001), 206.
25. Phil McNeill quotes the *Strangled* magazine review of *Rattus Norvegicus*, "about giving the woman some stick" in his strongly worded critique of their lyrics, but remarks that the group possesses the aggressive stance that is "today's currency." McNeill, "Women are Strange When You're a Strangler," *New Musical Express* (30 April 1977): 35.
26. Lucy Toothpaste interview, 8 August 2010.
27. Interview, 30 November 1999.
28. March 1975, no pagination, in Dave Thompson, *Beyond the Velvet Underground* (London and New York: Omnibus Press, 1989).
29. Kim Davis, *New Musical Express* (27 August 1977): 40.
30. *New Musical Express* (8 April 1978): 48.
31. Interview, 18 October 2001.
32. Sometimes, a band would not possess the financial resources to provide what a potential label required in order to consider signing them. For example, Rubella Ballet's Zillah Ashworth told me, "EMI asked us to send a demo tape and we thought, 'How are we going to record that, then?' I don't know why, but we sent them a really crap recording we'd made at a rehearsal." Interview, 8 September 2000.
33. Interview, 30 November 1999.
34. Interview, 20 October 2001.
35. Ibid.
36. Ibid.
37. Interview, 9 October 2001.
38. Interview, 20 October 2001.
39. Interview, 2 February 2000.
40. Paul Taylor (ed.), *Impresario: Malcolm McLaren and the British New Wave* (Cambridge, MA and London: MIT Press, 1988), 30.
41. From interview with Geoff Travis, 1 February 2002.
42. From interview with John Peel, 20 October 2001.
43. Ibid.
44. Interview, 1 February 2002.
45. One had to employ an "agency" ("Bullet") that charged £5000 in order to get records into chart return shops; without this help, the band's single sales did not appear on the Gallup computer. My band could not afford this.

46. Interview, 13 July 2000.
47. From interview with Tony Fletcher, "Campaign Strategies," *The Face* 21 (January 1982): 44–5.
48. Ibid.
49. Interview with Mavis Bayton, 14 July 2000.
50. Interview with Geoff Travis, 1 February 2002.
51. Ibid.
52. Mavis Bayton, *Frock Rock* (Oxford: Oxford University Press, 1998), 6.
53. Interview, 10 February 2006.
54. Interview, 2 February 2000.
55. Interview, 26 January 2000.
56. Captain Sensible, of punk band The Damned.
57. Interview, 2 February 2000. Pauline Murray (8 February 2011) described an experience where, after two positive experiences recording albums in the studio, a producer hired for her solo work made her feel: "that I had no control over it, I didn't know what was going on, and I sort of I left the business after all of that because I lost all my confidence, you know. I felt like I knew everything then I realised I knew nothing, do you know what I mean?"
58. Interview, 6 December 2001.
59. I worked for a while for the independent PR company that acted as press agents for Siouxsie and the Banshees. Although Polydor were desperate for Siouxsie to grace their premises, she flatly refused, being fully aware of the delicate balance of power between the artist and their record company.
60. Interview with Ari Up, 21 February 2006.
61. Ibid.
62. Zoe Street-Howe, *Typical Girls: The Story of The Slits* (London: Omnibus, 2009), 152. Street-Howe also reports a very funny episode in which Island assumed that the reggae singer Dennis Brown was a producer, and the band themselves, aided by the woman employed to make refreshments, had to mix their track when Brown confessed himself unable to do so (105). This is ironic, given the belief that "men know best" in the studio!
63. Interview with Viv Albertine, 26 March 2010.
64. The author's band The Chefs was helped by Pete in the early stages of their career, and this point was discussed at one of their meetings.
65. In Carol Neuls-Bates, *Women in Music: An Anthology of Source Readings from the Middle Ages to the Present* (Boston: Northeastern University Press, 1996), 330.
66. Deena Weinstein, "Art versus Commerce: Deconstructing a (Useful) Romantic Illusion," in Karen Kelly and Evelyn McDonnell (eds), *Stars Don't Stand Still in the Sky* (London: Routledge, 1999), 61–2.
67. S.T., The Bright Girls, by email, 2 December 2002.
68. *Sounds*, throughout 1976.
69. Unattributed, "Krauts in New Album Sleeve Outrage Horror Shock etc.," *Sounds* (18 December 1976): 7.
70. Hugh Fielder, "Prude or Rude?" *Sounds* (24 January 1976): 8.
71. Unattributed, "Hardware," *Sounds* (26 February 1977): 46.
72. Ibid., 55.

73. *New Musical Express* (16 July 1977) featured a review of the Blonde on Blonde single (p. 23); the same paper on 23 July 1977 featured the official launch of the band by Mick Farren (p. 15).
74. *New Musical Express* (4 February 1978): 25, interview with Blondie by Tony Parsons.
75. Erica Echenberg and Mark Perry, *And God Created Punk* (London: Virgin, 1996), 27.
76. Mark Perry, *Sniffin' Glue: The Essential Punk Accessory* (London: Sanctuary, 2000), no pagination.
77. *New Musical Express* (12 November 1977): 45. In "Orgasmic Review Dept. Runaways: Getting Better all the Time," *Sounds* (27 January 1977): 21, Barry Myers writes: "The cover pics are far more flattering than previously. Cherie, Joan, Sandy, Jackie and Lita are caught by the camera, decked out in black, clinging to long, metallic shafts." One does not have to be a rabid feminist to understand the attempts to appeal to male adolescents by using photographs of young women clinging to long metallic shafts.
78. *New Musical Express* (21 May 1977): Suzi Quatro on *Rock Follies*.
79. *New Musical Express* (18 March 1978), interview with Steve Clarke, p. 16.
80. Errigo, "Dull Housewife."
81. John Ingham, "Rock Special," *Sounds* (2 October 1976): 22.
82. John Lydon, *Rotten: No Irish, No Blacks, No Dogs* (London: Coronet, 1995), 259.
83. See Jon Savage, *England's Dreaming* (London and Boston, MA: Faber and Faber, 1991). He is also reported as "throwing Jordan across the floor" (Jordan was a female shop assistant in the shop Sex) by Nils Stevenson, in ibid., 151.
84. Lydon, *Rotten*, 378.
85. Interview, 20 November 2001.
86. Conversation with author, 2 February 2002.
87. Email, 15 May 2006.
88. Leslie Gourse, *Madame Jazz: Contemporary Women Instrumentalists* (New York and Oxford: Oxford University Press, 1995), 19.
89. Interview, 24 January 2002.
90. Email, 4 January 2006.
91. Interview, 3 March 2006.
92. Email, 18 January 2006.

3. The Brighton Scene

1. The lead singer of my first band (alternatively known as BBC Phil, Joby Visigoth or Joby Jackson) was pictured in the local paper, the *Evening Argus*, captioned a "menace to the homeless." This was one of our first songs, and described what Joby considered the principal elements of the population of Brighton at the time.
2. Andy Bennett, *Popular Music and Youth Culture: Music, Identity and Place* (Basingstoke and London: Macmillan Press, 2000), 67. The punk umbrella covered many different styles of music and political attitudes in Brighton; aurally, in the context of their time, they are all recognizable as punk music.
3. Ruth Finnegan, *The Hidden Musicians: Music-Making in an English Town* (Cambridge: Cambridge University Press, 1989).
4. Sara Cohen, *Rock Culture in Liverpool: Popular Music in the Making* (Oxford: Clarendon Press, 1991).

5. Will Straw, "Systems of Articulation, Logics of Change: Communities and Scenes in Popular Music," *Cultural Studies* 5.3 (1991): 368–88.

6. Thomas Swiss, John Sloop and Andrew Herman, *Mapping the Beat* (Oxford and Cambridge, MA: Blackwell, 1998).

7. Leslie C. Gay Jr., "Rockin' the Imagined Local: New York Rock in a Reterritorialised World," in Will Straw *et al.* (eds), *Popular Music: Style and Identity* (Montreal: The Centre for Research on Canadian Cultural Industries and Institutions, 1993), 123–6.

8. Barry Shank, *Dissonant Identities: The Rock'n'Roll Scene in Austin, Texas* (Hanover and London: Wesleyan University Press, 1994).

9. Ibid., 251.

10. Cohen, *Rock Culture in Liverpool.*

11. Gay, "Rockin' the Imagined Local."

12. Cohen, *Rock Culture in Liverpool*, 81. It is rather sad to see women reduced to nothing more than unusual gimmicks, but there is a rather unfortunate truth in this comment (see the anecdote in the Introduction). Later, the re-relegation of women to backing vocalist roles (albeit prominent ones) will be discussed.

13. Frank Cartledge, "Distress to Impress," in Roger Sabin (ed.), *Punk Rock: So What?* (London and New York: Routledge, 1999).

14. Interview, 9 October 2001.

15. Finnegan, *The Hidden Musicians*, 15.

16. Heavy rock band Tonge changed their name to The Depressions at the onset of punk, and to The Vandells when it seemed that a Mod revival was about to take off in the late 1970s.

17. Email, 16 May 2002.

18. Mufti Berridge, No Man's Band, interview, 15 February 2006.

19. A visitor to our house in Brighton observed, on being told we had a band, "Punk's over in London, you know. I don't know why you're bothering."

20. Stephen Colegrave and Chris Sullivan, *Punk: A Life Apart* (London: Cassell, 2001), 227.

21. George McKay, University of Central Lancashire, quoted in Colegrave and Sullivan, *Punk: A Life Apart* , 227. See also George McKay, "I'm So Bored with the USA," in Roger Sabin (ed.), *Punk Rock: So What?* (London and New York: Routledge, 1999), 58.

22. Finnegan, *The Hidden Musicians*, 13.

23. See D. Hebdige, *Subculture: The Meaning of Style* (London: Routledge, 1979), 85.

24. Sue Glyptis, *Leisure and Unemployment* (Milton Keynes and Philadelphia: Open University Press, 1989), 73.

25. "We were all highly politically motivated, anti-fascist, communist, I was in the Socialist Workers' Party, very involved with Rock Against Racism." Interview with Attila the Stockbroker, 15 January 2001, originally bass-player with Brighton Riot Squad, now an internationally acclaimed punk poet. Later, we will see the variety of attitudes displayed by Brighton bands.

26. Interview, 15 February 2006.

27. The Brighton Punk website, www.punkbrighton.co.uk, is a constantly updated source of contacts and information

28. Michael Brake, *Comparative Youth Culture* (London and New York: Routledge, 1993 [1985]), 177.

29. Dress codes in subcultures and their class and gender implications (particularly in British punk) have been the subject of many studies, for instance Angela McRobbie (ed.), *Zoot Suits and Secondhand Dresses* (London: Macmillan, 1989). See also Joanne Hollows, *Feminism, Femininity and Popular Culture* (Manchester and New York: Manchester University Press, 2000), 174, for a discussion of "dressing down."

30. Angela McRobbie, *Feminism and Youth Culture* (Basingstoke and London: Macmillan, 2000 [1991]), 9.

31. It could be argued that middle-class women were more capable of using the opportunities provided by punk in the fallow unemployment years to build lucrative careers post-punk. This was not always the case.

32. Valerie Walkerdine, *Daddy's Girl: Young Girls and Popular Culture* (Basingstoke and London: Macmillan, 1997).

33. Email, 16 May 2002.

34. Attila the Stockbroker, interview, 15 January 2001. Attila's technique of getting to perform did not just apply to relaxed venues like the Vault. Joby and the Hooligans supported Johnny Thunders and the Heartbreakers at Sussex University; we just went along to the gig with our guitars and begged the manager to let us play. When he said no, we got drunk to drown our sorrows; later, he changed his mind. I remember standing on stage being too drunk to see the strings of my bass guitar, and being vaguely aware of Joby howling wildly off-key even for him: they pulled the plugs on us.

35. From *Spitting Blood* (September 1977), no pagination.

36. Interview, 7 October 1999. Julie was married to Rick Blair, who started the local label Attrix. His band The Parrots played regularly at the Vault in Brighton. Julie was slightly older than some of the punks and seemed responsible as she had two children at this time; however, she was very friendly and knew most of the people in the Brighton punk bands.

37. Interview, 8 June 2002. Kate was a good friend of my brother and we often used to go to see The Objeks play.

38. Interview with Stella Clifford, 11 February 2011.

39. Interview, 20 November 2001. I was aware of the Reward System but did not know Sue to talk to at the time.

40. Jamie Reid was the artist who designed The Sex Pistols' artwork and who popularized the "blackmail writing" style of typography.

41. From *Graffiti*, Depressions interview with Dave Barnard (The Depressions), 1977.

42. Ibid., interview with "Dan Dadandan" (dole evasion name!) from Flesh.

43. "Part (iv) of the Public Health Act (amendment) of 1890 was introduced to allow late-night drinking in some pubs, and the resulting increase in health and safety regulations meant that thirty-two applications by licensed premises for certificates were adjourned by magistrates pending further works in order to comply with the act; local musicians took this to be an attempt to prevent them from playing at their regular venues." *Evening Argus*, 18 January 1979.

44. Andrew Partington, "With this Pin... Punks Wed for Bet," *Evening Argus* (23 February 1979): 1.

45. Peter Archer, "Spin Off: Now Fan Club Play a Four-Way Cut," *Evening Argus* (31 March 1979): 11.

46. One night we had to escape through the toilets because we were wearing plastic sandals, and Teds would sometimes beat punks up for wearing this type of footwear.

47. At http://www.punkbrighton.co.uk/ybmail02.html, email from Carmen, undated (accessed 16 April 2011).

48. This was promoted by Adrian York, who was elected unopposed as social secretary; he booked local bands to support big-name bands, and employed Hell's Angels as bouncers until their alcohol consumption became a problem. Interview with York, 14 March 2002.

49. At http://www.punkbrighton.co.uk/ybmail00.html, email from Russell Pointing, 10 October 2000 (accessed 16 April 2010).

50. Personal letter, 25 February 2001; Vi (real name Frances) was a lynchpin of the early punk scene in Brighton. She was at least forty years old, but was totally at ease with anyone she came into contact with. She encouraged many young people, both male and female, to join bands, even if she did not agree with their personal politics. I regard her in retrospect as a subtle and wise mentor.

51. At http://www.punkbrighton.co.uk/ybmail01.html, email from Chris Nicholls, 7 May 2001 (accessed 16 April 2011).

52. Interview with Attila the Stockbroker (Brighton Riot Squad), 15 January 2001. Attila encouraged local bands to gig further afield, taking some of the Brighton bands to the University of Kent to play Rock Against Racism gigs. Joby and the Hooligans did this on at least one occasion.

53. H. Stith Bennett, *On Becoming a Rock Musician* (Amherst: University of Massachusetts Press, 1980), 59–66, quote on 66.

54. Interview, 7 October 1999.

55. Interview, 23 March 2003.

56. Kate Hayes, interview, 8 June 2002.

57. This argument continues to this day: at the "No Future?" conference in Wolverhampton, author and campaigner Caroline Coon, author Stuart Home, anarchist writer/musician Penny Rimbaud and musician Gary Valentine all mentioned their experience of punk as being the authentic one; Chris Sullivan does this also in Colegrave and Sullivan, *Punk: A Life Apart*.

58. Personal memory of the author.

59. Interview with Attila the Stockbroker, 15 January 2001.

60. N, by email, 14 June 2002. N was originally a guitarist in Joby and the Hooligans, but he left; he did not like our involvement with politics.

61. Conversation with the author, 1979. This wedding was reported on the front page of the Brighton *Evening Argus*; see Partington, "With this Pin...," 1.

62. The Piranhas were one of the first bands to incorporate reggae rhythms into punk music; the band Madness used to attend their gigs in London on a regular basis before they became a performing entity. The Piranhas had chart hits with the singles "Tom Hark" (Sire, 1980) and "Zambezi" (Dakota, 1982) before splitting up.

63. Noted in Cohen, *Rock Culture in Liverpool*, 11; in Brighton, possessiveness began as soon as a band started recording for singles release or sessions.

64. Bennett, *Popular Music and Youth Culture*, 193.

65. Hester Smith, drums, Dolly Mixture, interview, 26 January 2001.

66. Lucy O'Brien, synthesizer, The Catholic Girls, interview, 6 December 2001.

67. Peter Archer (ed.), "Spin-Off: Back on the Road," *Evening Argus* (28 April 1979): 11.
68. Stuart Home, *Cranked Up Really High: Genre Theory and Punk Rock* (Hove: CodeX, 1995), 70.
69. From local fanzine *Graffiti*, Depressions interview with Dave Barnard, 1977.
70. From local fanzine *Spitting Blood*, September 1977, interview with Tom Maltby from Wrist Action, no pagination.
71. Interview, 15 January 2001.
72. Email interview, 16 May 2002.
73. Interview, 8 June 2002.
74. Frith and Home discuss "art-school punks" – see Simon Frith and Howard Home (eds), *Art into Pop* (London and New York: Routledge, 1989), discussed elsewhere. Mark P. writes: "In many ways the punk scene gave kids a chance to realise their dreams without going to college or art school. Those who were or had been at college soon changed their perceptions, and it was their input allied with that of working class kids like myself which made punk so diverse." Erica Echenberg and Mark Perry, *And God Created Punk* (London: Virgin, 1996), 119.
75. Interview, 13 October 2001.
76. From *Rapid Eye Movement*, Winter 1970, published by Rough Trade.
77. The Grunwick dispute happened in the summer of 1977; it centred on the treatment of Asian workers at the Grunwick photographic plant in North London. Various punks and squatters travelled to the picket line, organized by Steve (now Lord) Bassam, who told me, "I've always had this thing of wanting to expand the world of people in left of centre politics. Grunwick was a big issue at the time; it seemed important to me that we all played a part in showing some solidarity. It woke a lot of white middle-class people up to some fairly political issues." Steve Bassam was heavily involved in the squatting community at the time.
78. Personal communication, 14 June 2002.
79. Peter Archer, "Spin Off: What's in a Name," *Evening Argus* (21 July 1979): 11.
80. From *Spitting Blood*, September 1977.
81. Interview, 7 October 1999. This was the first interview I did when I sought out Brighton band personnel, and I had assumed that all of the bands were as involved with direct politics as Joby and the Hooligans. I therefore learned from the start that there were many different experiences of the Brighton punk scene apart from my own.
82. Rick died of a brain haemorrhage in 1999. I am grateful to Julie for her articulation of the ethos of Attrix, and her help in this research.
83. Simon Frith, *Sound Effects* (New York: Pantheon, 1981), 156: "At a time when British rock companies were in trouble, the punk independents, however small, had the authority of their own idealism," with "a concern for music as a mode of survival rather than as a means to profit."
84. At http://punkbrighton.co.uk/sjmemcon1.html; http://www.punkbrighton.co.uk/sjmemcon2.html (accessed on 22 March 2007).
85. Interview, 7 October 1999.
86. Ibid.
87. Simon Reynolds, *Rip it Up and Start Again: Post-Punk 1978–1984* (London: Faber and Faber, 2005), 108–9.
88. Sara Furse, No Man's Band, interview 15 February 2006.

89. Interview, 31 March 2006.

90. Letter to author, 1 December 2001.

91. Ibid.

92. There is a quotation attributed to John Peel in which he is alleged to have praised the music-making opportunities of punk for allowing "fat girls in dungarees" to take to the stage. See Chapter 5.

93. Interview, 20 November 2001.

94. For instance, an elderly man started "hanging out" with my band, and although we did not like him we tolerated his presence until there was a sudden power-cut in the Vault, at which point he took the opportunity to sexually assault me. After that, I chose to wear cheap spray-painted boiler suits instead of short skirts and fishnets.

95. Mavis Bayton, *Frock Rock* (Oxford: Oxford University Press, 1998), 107–22.

96. Steve Beresford played various instruments with The Slits when they toured.

97. Interview, 7 October 1999.

98. Caroline Coon, "Groupies Must Become Musicians," *Sounds* (31 December 1977): 6.

99. From questionnaire reply, Barb Dwyer, 2 January 2003.

100. Interview, 8 June 2002.

101. *Evening Argus* (7 October 1980): 10.

102. John Buss, "Workers See a Dream End," *Evening Argus* (7 October 1980): 10.

103. Interview with Mufti Berridge, drummer, No Man's Band, 15 February 2006.

104. Interview, 15 January 2001.

105. Interview, 8 June 2002.

106. Interview, 20 March 2002. Steve Bassam is now Lord Bassam. He used to drive the squatters and punks to demos such as Grunwick and the Lewisham anti-racist march. He lived in a squat, and was a friend – the squatting community was a close and supportive community in spite of its varied and volatile personnel.

107. There was a definite attempt to "brand" local bands that seems like the eternal quest by the music industry for the elusive second "Mersey Beat"; for instance, Simon Frith asks the question, "What is the Sheffieldness of Sheffield groups?," in "Popular Music and the State," in Tony Bennett *et al.* (eds), *Rock and Popular Music: Politics, Policies, Institutions* (London and New York: Routledge, 1993), 22.

108. Interview, 7 October 1999.

109. Their single "Tom Hark" went to no. 12 in the National Charts in 1980.

110. Paul E. Willis, *Profane Culture* (London and Boston: Routledge and Kegan Paul, 1978), 4.

111. Carola Dibbell, "Inside Was Us: Women and Punk," in Barbara O'Dair (ed.), *The Rolling Stone Book of Women in Rock* (New York: Random House, 1997), 287.

112. Interview by Paul Morley, *New Musical Express* (17 December 1977): 14.

4. Noise, Violence and Femininity

1. Song sung by two little girls draped in Union Jacks, *The Filth and The Fury: A Sex Pistols Film* (dir. Julien Temple, Filmfour, 1999).

2. Dick Hebdige, *Subculture, the Meaning of Style* (London: Routledge, 1979), 90.

3. Holly Kruse, "Abandoning the Absolute: Transcendence and Gender in Popular Music

Discourse," in Steve Jones (ed.), *Pop Music and the Press* (Philadelphia: Temple University Press, 2002), 136.

4. See Chapter 2 for Sue Denom's reviews as an illustration of this tendency.

5. Julie Burchill and Tony Parsons, *The Boy Looked at Johnny: The Obituary of Rock and Roll* (London: Pluto Press, 1978), 86. Burchill retained this attitude; in 1994, she told Amy Raphael: "I know it's a sexist thing to say, but women aren't as good at making music as men – like they're not as good as men at football. A girl in a dress with a guitar looks weird. Like a dog riding a bicycle. Very odd. Hard to get past it. It's OK on the radio, because you can't see them. Chrissie Hynde is an exception. Very few of them are exceptions. And if they don't have a guitar, they become the dumb girl in front of the band. I'm not a great fan of girls in pop." This quotation will be referred to again later, with particular reference to Chrissie Hynde. From Amy Raphael, *Never Mind the Bollocks* (London: Virago, 1995), xi.

6. See Evan Eisenberg, *The Recording Angel: Music, Records and Culture from Aristotle to Zappa* (London and New York: Picador, 1987) for a discussion of The Futurists' love of war and machinery and Sibelius' appreciation of the "crescendo" of guns that "ended in a fortissimo I could never have dreamed of" (194).

7. S. Reynolds and J. Press, *The Sex Revolts: Gender, Rebellion and Rock'n'Roll* (London: Serpent's Tail, 1995), 23.

8. Ibid., 311: "As with a lot of the demystification bands (see also The Au Pairs' Sense and Sensuality), The Raincoats' discovery of desire and the pleasures of the body couldn't escape being rendered dull and worthy by the programmatic nature of their politics."

9. Ibid., 3.

10. Ibid., 71.

11. Ibid., 74 (after Donna Gaines, *Teenage Wasteland: Suburbia's Dead-End Kids* [New York: Pantheon Books, 1990], 168).

12. "A lot of people got into it almost like an equivalent to National Service... Punk as a replacement for National Service! The great things it taught you were petty theft and evasion, so it made you kind of cunning in a way that I'd not been before. I would imagine that being in a band would give you similar skills." John Peel, interview, 20 October 2001. Simon Frith, in *Sound Effects* (New York: Pantheon, 1981), 183, comments that (male) teenagers' lack of obligations increased after the end of National Service. There is much to be said for a theory that rock music replaced it in the national male adolescent psyche, and this factor will be returned to at other points of the thesis.

13. Lawrence Grossberg on Bruce Springsteen: "Rock & Roll in Search of an Audience," in James Lull (ed.), *Popular Music and Communication* (London: Sage, 1992), 172.

14. Reynolds and Press also explore issues surrounding the term "mom-ism" coined by Philip Wylie in 1942. See Wylie, *Generation of Vipers* (New York: Larlin Corporation, 1979).

15. Frith, *Sound Effects*, 241.

16. Ibid., 228. He continues: "It is boys, as we have seen, who are interested in rock as music, want to be musicians, technicians, experts. It is boys who form the core of the rock audience, become rock critics and collectors (girl rock fanatics become, by contrast, photographers)."

17. Arlene Stein describes the dilemma she found herself in as a fan of rock music: "I

didn't necessarily want to be a guy, or even want to date one, but I did fantasize, perhaps unconsciously, about possessing their power. If my embrace of rock was at least partly a revolt against my mother, it was also a revolt against the gender system that trapped her." From "Rock Against Romance: Gender, Rock'n'Roll and Resistance," in Karen Kelly and Evelyn McDonnell (eds), *Stars Don't Stand Still in the Sky* (London: Routledge, 1999), 221.

18. Although Springsteen is not regarded as a punk rocker, he is used here because of his symbolic place as an authentic rock'n'roll male.

19. Gareth Palmer, "Springsteen and Authentic Masculinity," in Sheila Whiteley (ed.), *Sexing the Groove: Popular Music and Gender* (London: Routledge, 1997), 104. Hilariously, Keith Negus provides a coda to the above observations about Springsteen, describing his chat between songs at a live gig: "Springsteen went on to tell his audience about how men are afraid of their mothers, and how this fear informs the relationship between men and women. Exposing his anxieties about his own 'macho posturing' he concluded that he was 'man enough' to sing about his own mother, and then performed the song." "Mrs Springsteen's Boy," in Keith Negus, *Producing Pop: Culture and Conflict in the Popular Music Industry* (London: Edward Arnold, 1992), 75.

20. Deena Weinstein, *Heavy Metal: The Music and its Culture* (Cambridge, MA: Da Capo, 2000), 104–5.

21. Robert Walser, *Running with the Devil: Power, Gender and Madness in Heavy Metal Music* (Middletown, CT: Wesleyan University Press, 1993), 195.

22. For an analysis of "cock-rock" singing styles and their shunning of social relations, see John Shepherd, *Music as Social Text* (Cambridge: Polity, 1991), chapter 8.

23. Jacques Attali, *Noise: The Political Economy of Music* (Minneapolis and London: University of Minnesota Press, 1985), 28.

24. Sheila Rowbotham, *Woman's Consciousness, Man's World* (Harmondsworth: Penguin, 1981 [1973]), 14.

25. Barbara O'Dair (ed.), *The Rolling Stone Book of Women in Rock* (New York: Random House, 1997), xx.

26. Mavis Bayton, interview with the author, 14 July 2000. The Rolling Stones frequently crop up in critiques of rock attitudes, notably in Reynolds and Press, *The Sex Revolts*. It was Dave Laing, however, who underlined the *sincerity*, or authenticity, of their misogyny: Dave Laing, *One Chord Wonders: Power and Meaning in Punk Rock* (Milton Keynes and Philadelphia: Open University Press, 1985), 64.

27. Gina Rumsey and Hilary Little, "Women and Pop: A Series of Lost Encounters," in Angela McRobbie (ed.), *Zoot Suits and Second-hand Dresses: An Anthology of Fashion and Music* (London: Macmillan, 1989), 244.

28. Kembrew McLeod, "Between a Rock and a Hard Place: Gender and Rock Criticism," in Steve Jones (ed.), *Pop Music and the Press* (Philadelphia: Temple University Press, 2002), 93.

29. For a discussion on the inclusive/exclusive nature of "language communities" see Steven Pinker, *The Language Instinct* (London: Penguin, 1995).

30. Susan McClary, "Afterword," in Jacques Attali, *Noise: The Political Economy of Music* (Minneapolis and London: University of Minnesota Press, 1985), 156–7.

31. Mavis Bayton, "Feminist Musical Practice," in Tony Bennett *et al.* (eds), *Rock and Popular Music: Politics, Policies, Institutions* (London and New York: Routledge, 1993), 186.

32. Bayton, "Feminist Musical Practice," 186.
33. Shanne Bradley, interview, 15 September 2010.
34. Ros Allen, interviewed by Mike Applestein, *Caught in Flux* (accessed 28 September 2001).
35. Lucy Green, *Music, Gender, Education* (Cambridge: Cambridge University Press, 1997), 167.
36. Laing, *One Chord Wonders*, 68.
37. Burchill and Parsons, *The Boy Looked at Johnny*, 78.
38. Reynolds and Press, *The Sex Revolts*, 296; quotation from Simon Frith and Angela McRobbie, "Rock and Sexuality," in Angela McRobbie (ed.), *Feminism and Youth Culture* (Basingstoke and London: Macmillan, 2000 [1991]), 385.
39. Underneath the "shouting" text there are interesting observations about, for instance, the chastity of The Clash's lyrics (*The Sex Revolts*, 66). The potential implications of this are not explored in any depth, and this is a wasted opportunity. Perhaps the volume of artists they have chosen to cover prevents them from analysing them in greater depth.
40. One has an amusing visualization of an adolescent's parents looking at their watches and calendars, waiting for the moment of rock rebellion to begin.
41. George Upton, *Woman in Music* (Boston: J. R. Osgood, 1880), 21–8. This is followed up later in this work in a comment by Hugh Cornwell.
42. Barbara Engh, "Adorno and the Sirens: Tele-phonographic Bodies," in Leslie C. Dunn and Nancy A. Jones (eds), *Embodied Voices: Representing Female Vocality in Western Culture* (Cambridge: Cambridge University Press, 1994), 120.
43. Shepherd, *Music as Social Text*, chapter 8: "Music and Male Hegemony," 152–73.
44. Laing, *One Chord Wonders*, 57.
45. The timbres utilized by many female punk singers are close to the "hollerin" practised by early hillbilly singers, who had to make themselves heard over loud bands. It was not until radio became ubiquitous that crooning regained popularity.
46. Jill Nicholls and Lucy Toothpaste, "I Play the Vocals," *Spare Rib* 83 (June 1979): 16.
47. Joy Press, "Shouting Out Loud: Women in UK Punk," in B. O'Dair, *The Rolling Stone Book of Women in Rock* (New York: Random House, 1997), 300.
48. Greil Marcus, *Ranters and Crowd-Pleasers: Punk in Pop Music 1977–92* (New York: Doubleday, 1993), 188–9.
49. Angela McRobbie, *Feminism and Youth Culture* (Basingstoke and London: Macmillan, 2000, 2nd edn), 8.
50. Simon Frith, "What Can a Poor Girl Do?," *Let it Rock: Women and Rock, a Special Issue* (July 1975): 20–21.
51. Stuart Hall and Tony Jefferson (eds), *Resistance through Rituals: Youth Subcultures in Post-War Britain* (London: Hutchinson, 1975), 210.
52. What constitutes sexual titillation, of course, is defined by men, especially in rock: "... The Monster of Sexual Discrimination. Inevitably, in response to this lousy situation, the lady hangs her tits out over the boardroom table, she is accused of using her sexuality instead of her credentials. Of course, the Catch 22 is that it is not woman, but caddish men who have turned her tits into her credentials... We have all been turned into whore by the male's refusal to credit us with any more valid reason for existing than to please him. This sad state of affairs is nowhere more blatant than in the very

place which, as the vanguard of the Bright and Hopeful New Age, should be seen to be setting some kind of enlightened example to the rest of us drogos. Ladies and gentlemen, I give you... Rock'n'Roll." Wendy Hamilton-Des Barres, "The Big Lie," in *Let it Rock: Women and Rock, a Special Issue* (July 1975): 36–7.

53. Caroline Coon, interview with The Slits, in *1988: The New Wave Punk Rock Explosion* (London and New York: Omnibus, 1982).

54. Ian Penman, Review of The Slits, Liverpool "Eric's," *New Musical Express* (13 January 1979): 35.

55. Ibid.

56. This refusal to "be stars" or even to "be seen to be trying" has been described by other reviewers; see, for example, Sue Denom, "Women in Punk," *Spare Rib* 60 (July 1977): 48–9.

57. Penman, Review of The Slits (13 January 1979): 35.

58. *New Musical Express* (27 January 1979): 43.

59. Interview, 23 June 2000.

60. Interview, 24 January 2001. The most desirable women in all forms of music often seem to be dead. See Catherine Clement, *Opera or the Undoing of Women* (London: Virago, 1989) for a critique of the tragic heroines of classical opera.

61. Punk, however, provided a sonic oppositional precedent for the Riot Grrrl movement that appeared around ten years later, but which has also disappeared.

62. Interview, 21 February 2006.

63. Iain Chambers, *Urban Rhythms: Pop Music and Popular Culture* (Basingstoke and London: Macmillan, 1985), 127; italics in original.

64. Barbara Bradby, "Sampling Sexuality, Technology and the Body in Dance Music," *Popular Music* 12.2 (1993): 156.

65. Susan McClary, *Feminine Endings: Music, Gender and Sexuality* (Minneapolis and Oxford: University of Minnesota Press, 1991), 154.

66. Mavis Bayton, *Frock Rock* (Oxford: Oxford University Press, 1998), 107–22.

67. Green, *Music, Gender, Education*, 29.

68. Mica Nava, "Youth Service Provision, Social Order and the Question of Girls," in Angela McRobbie and Nava, *Gender and Generation* (Basingstoke and London: Macmillan, 1984), 25.

69. Ibid.

70. Often, this trouble would be mentioned in passing. For example, in *New Musical Express* on 18 February 1978 there is a review of The Adverts at the Roundhouse by Adrian Thrills. He reports trouble with skinheads at the beginning of the gig, largely because Sham 69 were playing, and they had a large skinhead following (p. 43).

71. Interview with Ari Up and Tessa Pollitt, 21 February 2006.

72. Interview, 6 December 2001.

73. Interview, 3 February 2006.

74. Mo-dettes, Marquee, *New Musical Express* (19 July 1980): 41.

75. Lucy Toothpaste, "Bodysnatchers," *Spare Rib* 100 (November 1980): 13–14. The article continues that a female skinhead climbed up on stage, Sieg-Heiling, until she was pushed off by a band-member: "from then on the band didn't look as if they were enjoying themselves very much, and I didn't feel as if I was."

76. Interview, 3 March 2006.

77. Greil Marcus, "It's Fab, It's Passionate, It's Wild. It's Intelligent! It's the Hot New Sound of England Today!" in Marcus, *Ranters and Crowd-Pleasers*, 156.

78. *New Musical Express* (6 May 1978): 51, review of Nico at the Music Machine, playing between The Killjoys and The Adverts.

79. Interview, 24 January 2002.

80. Lauraine Leblanc, *Pretty in Punk: Girls' Gender Resistance in a Boys' Subculture* (New Brunswick, NJ and London: Rutgers University Press, 2001).

81. Leslie G. Roman, "Double Exposure: The Politics of Feminist Materialist Ethnography," *Educational Theory* 43.3 (1993): 297–308, and "Intimacy, Labor and Class: Ideologies of Feminine Sexuality in the Punk Slam Dance," in Roman and L. K. Christian-Smith (eds), *Becoming Feminine: The Politics of Popular Culture* (London: Falmer Press, 1988), 143–84.

82. From issue no. 7, undated, no pagination.

83. Shanne Bradley, interview, 15 October 2011.

84. For full details of this incident, see Alex Ogg, *No More Heroes: A Complete History of UK Punk from 1976 to 1980* (London: Cherry Red Books, 2006), 13–15.

85. The word used by record companies to describe the areas where they sell their products.

86. Marina Warner, *Monuments and Maidens: The Allegory of the Female Form* (London: Weidenfeld and Nicholson, 1985), 41.

87. Chambers, *Urban Rhythms*, 185.

88. Ibid.

89. Reynolds and Press, *The Sex Revolts*, 73.

90. Jon Savage, *England's Dreaming* (London and Boston: Faber and Faber, 1991), 541.

91. "The party appealed not so much to the rich as to those with little or no capital of their own, and who, therefore, were frightened of losing what little they had. It was the small employers and the self-employed such as the small shopkeepers who saw themselves as the prime victims of Edward Heath's economic policies; and it was this section of society which felt most frightened by the seeming triumph of the trade unions in 1974 and by the *grande peur* of the 1978–79 'Winter of Discontent.' Not belonging to one of the great estates of the realm which the postwar settlement had legitimised, the petty bourgeoisie seemed bereft of any organisation by which to defend its interests. Only a Conservative Party purged of its corporatist heresies could undertake that role." Vernon Bogdanor, "The Fall of Heath and the End of the Postwar Settlement," in Stuart Ball and Anthony Seldon (eds), *The Heath Government 1970–74: A Reappraisal* (London and New York: Longman, 1996), 386.

92. Stan Cohen is acknowledged as the popularizer of this term, after using it as the title of his book *Folk Devils and Moral Panics: The Creation of the Mods and Rockers* (Oxford: Martin Robertson, 1993 [1972]).

93. Paul E. Willis, *Profane Culture* (London and Boston: Routledge and Kegan Paul, 1978), 6.

94. Especially given the equation of rock music to National Service.

95. Christopher Ballantyne, "Music, Masculinity and Migrancy under Apartheid: Gender and Popular Song in Africa c. 1948–1960," in David Hesmondhalgh and Keith Negus (eds), *Popular Music Studies* (London: Arnold, 2002), 24, 30.

96. This has not gone unnoticed; Moe Tucker, drummer with The Velvet Underground,

who influenced many female instrumentalists, has this to say: "Now, there's a thousand times more women musicians than when I was around, but even so, there's very few women *players*. When you think of every culture, when you see a documentary, for instance, on Africa, it's always the men playing the drums and the women dancing. Dancing requires rhythm so why can't they play the drums?" Karen O'Brien, *Hymn to Her: Women Musicians Talk* (London: Virago Press, 1995), 109.

97. Yet another example of "forgetting," described in more detail by Lucy O'Brien, in *She-Bop II: The Definitive History of Women in Rock, Pop and Soul* (London and New York: Continuum, 2002 [1995]), 33–8.

98. See Greta Kent, *A View from the Bandstand* (London: Sheba, 1983); Carol Neuls-Bates, "Women's Orchestras in the United States, 1925–45," in Jane Bowers and Judith Tick, *Women Making Music: The Western Art Tradition, 1150–1950* (Urbana and Chicago: University of Illinois Press, 1987); and Sherrie Tucker, *Swing Shift: "All Girl" Bands of the 1940s* (Durham, NC: Duke University Press, 2000). All three texts examine the phenomenon of the upsurge of all-women jazz bands during the Second World War.

99. Green, *Music, Gender, Education*, 229.

100. Attali, *Noise*, 29; italics in original.

101. "Letters," *Sounds* (10 July 1976): 42.

5. The Aftermath

1. George Melly, *Revolt into Style* (Oxford: Oxford University Press, 1989), 254.

2. David Muggleton, *Inside Subculture: The Postmodern Meaning of Style* (Oxford and New York: Berg, 2000), 133.

3. Though these bands are officially dubbed "post-punk," essentially the rawness of their sound and the intent behind their music defines them as punk in retrospect.

4. See his comments quoted in Chapter 6.

5. *The End of Music*, pamphlet (Glasgow, 1978), 32–3, in Sadie Plant, *The Most Radical Gesture: The Situationist International in the Postmodern Age* (London and New York: Routledge, 1992), 145–6. The idea of buying into the revolution is explored at length by Joseph Heath and Andrew Potter in *The Rebel Sell: How the Counterculture became Consumer Culture* (Chichester: Capstone, 2006). Melisse Lafrance in her analysis of female pop musicians, *Disruptive Divas*, accepts that there is a complex problem regarding consumption (being exploited by capitalism) and the fact that "we win because these musicians ignite us, educate us and infuse us with a sense of oppositional solidarity." Lori Burns and M. Lafrance, *Disruptive Divas: Feminism, Identity and Popular Music* (New York and London: Routledge, 2002), 18.

6. Interview, 3 March 2006.

7. "[In 1981] the average 1955 baby was aged 26 and large numbers of them were trying to cope with conditions that were entirely new to them. A hitherto unbroken diet of rising expectations easily and quickly gratified suddenly came to a halt. 60 per cent of the men and 75 per cent of the women were by then married, and a majority of those married couples had at least one dependent child. By August 1981, 12.2 per cent of the nation's working population were registered as unemployed, and 50 per cent of the nearly 3 million unemployed had been out of work for over six months. The crock at the end of the rainbow turned out to be full of woodworm." Mark Abrams, "Demo-

graphic Correlates of Values," in Abrams, David Gerard and Noel Timms (eds), *Values and Social Change in Britain* (Basingstoke and London: Macmillan, 1985), 24.

8. Peter York, *Style Wars* (London: Sidgwick and Jackson, 1980), 48.

9. M. Presdee, "Invisible Girls: A Study of Unemployed Working Class Young Women" (Unpublished paper, Tenth World Congress of Sociology, Mexico City, 1982), 13, cited in Michael Brake, *Comparative Youth Culture* (London and New York: Routledge, 1993), 195.

10. Simon Frith, *Sound Effects* (New York: Pantheon, 1981), 225.

11. Mica Nava, "Youth Service Provision, Social Order and the Question of Girls," in Angela McRobbie and Mica Nava (eds), *Gender and Generation* (Basingstoke and London: Macmillan, 1984), 3.

12. Muggleton, *Inside Subculture*, 79. Muggleton says that people can be members of several subcultures either at once or serially; he was a serial subculturalist himself.

13. Paul E. Willis, *Profane Culture* (London and Boston: Routledge and Kegan Paul, 1978), 176.

14. Ibid., 179.

15. Interview, 23 June 2000.

16. Interview with Pauline Murray, 8 February 2011.

17. Interview with June Miles-Kingston, 3 February 2006.

18. This was a second-hand record store in Notting Hill, famous for providing income for hard-up musicians and collectors from their second-hand vinyl. It worked almost like a pawn shop; in better times one could return to replace the recordings sold in hard times.

19. Interview with Gina Birch, 23 June 2000. It is interesting how this mirrors Kate Hayes's remarks about her experience of the hippy subculture prior to punk: "I'd been in this love and peace thing and had got really fucked over by it and was angry and wasn't sure where to place it; feeling that I'd been sold down the river somehow but wasn't sure why or who'd done it or whose fault it was. It was a very confusing period." Interview, 8 June 2002.

20. Interview with Peter Martin in *The Face* 41 (September 1983): 9.

21. Interview, 9 October 2001.

22. Interview, 18 October 2001.

23. Interview, 26 January 2000.

24. Interview, 6 December 2001.

25. Interview, 8 June 2002.

26. The introduction of heroin into the London punk scene by New Yorkers and its destructive influence is detailed in Stephen Colegrave and Chris Sullivan, *Punk: A Life Apart* (London: Cassell, 2001), 182 and elsewhere.

27. At http://www.3ammagazine.com/musicarchives/2003/nov/interview_tessa_pollitt.html (accessed 17 April 2011).

28. Interview, 30 January 2006.

29. From interview with Mike Appelstein, at http://www.nstop.com/paloma/intervw.html (accessed 17 April 2011).

30. Interview with Rhoda Dakar, 3 March 2006.

31. Interview with June Miles-Kingston, 3 February 2006.

32. Interview with Lesley Woods, 30 July 2010.

33. Sian Trehearne, bass guitar, "Scream and Scream Again," Gloucestershire, via questionnaire.

34. Caroline Coon, "The Stranglers," in *1988: The New Wave Punk Rock Explosion* (London and New York: Omnibus, 1982), 97.

35. Questionnaire response from S.L., bass guitar-player, band name unknown, Gateshead.

36. Questionnaire response from G.S., bass-player, Devon.

37. Interview with Jane Munro, 23 April 2010.

38. Rimmer describes the constant arguments between the various members of Culture Club as making it difficult for the band to write songs, for instance. See Dave Rimmer, *Like Punk Never Happened: Culture Club and the New Pop* (London and Boston: Faber and Faber, 1985). Mavis Bayton, in *Frock Rock* (Oxford: Oxford University Press, 1998), 36–8, also discusses the constraints applied by boyfriends and husbands.

39. Interview with Christine Robertson, 9 October 2001.

40. Judith Williamson, "Urban Spaceman," in *Consuming Passions: The Dynamics of Popular Culture* (London and New York: Marion Boyars, 1991), 209.

41. The relationship between Sony and the record industry regarding their "rubber-stamping" of home taping by the introduction of the Walkman will not be discussed here, although it is interesting to note the parallels between this and the more recent MP3 debate.

42. According to a mutual friend of Jamie Reid and Sophie Richmond, McLaren had gone to Paris and attempted to start a paedophile magazine called *Chicken* (the slang term for underage sexual partners). They had told him this was too risky, and I believe Bow Wow Wow to be the more "tame" expression of his sexual curiosity.

43. Unattributed, "Malcolm McLaren/Bow Wow Wow," *The Face* 13 (May 1981): 45.

44. This is a frequent bone of contention in bands and is only rarely dealt with democratically. A common way of working is described here by non-instrumentalist Debbie Harry:

    > Glenn O'Brien: Did you ever write the music for any of your songs?
    > Deborah: Sometimes. I wrote the music for *Little Girl Lies*. Mostly I don't write tunes, but little lines that are expandable. *Little Girl Lies* was a total composition. Chris developed the chord changes and the figure in the beginning. I think it's really necessary to write with an instrument. You really have to play a piano or a guitar. It's virtually impossible even on a bass guitar. You have to play an instrument that you can make chords with. You can only hum one note at a time... It's not easy to envision a sound.

    Glenn O'Brien, "Debbie Harry," *Interview* magazine, vol. ix, no. 6 (June 1979): 145.

45. Unattributed, "Malcolm McLaren/Bow Wow Wow," 40.

46. S. Reynolds and J. Press, *The Sex Revolts: Gender, Rebellion and Rock'n'Roll* (London: Serpent's Tail, 1995), 38.

47. Ibid.

48. Interview, 21 February 2006.

49. Jon Savage, "The Sound of the Crowd," in Karen Kelly and Evelyn McDonnell (eds), *Stars Don't Stand Still in the Sky* (London: Routledge, 1999), 146–7.

50. Ian Cranna, "In Time with the Rhythm and Rhyme," *The Face* 27 (July 1982): 24.

51. It is interesting to note that even the most "bloke-ish" of the music papers, *Sounds*, published an article entitled "Sexism is No Joke" by female journalist Robbi Millar in 1980, which criticized the attitudes, lyrics and artwork of bands such as The Scorpions and Sniff 'n' the Tears; *Sounds* had championed heavy metal and its attendant attitudes for years, and this appeared to be a major change in attitude at the time. See Robbie Millar, "Sexism is No Joke," *Sounds* (20 September 1980): 31–4.

52. Martin Cloonan, *Banned!: Censorship of Popular Music in Britain: 1967–92* (Aldershot and Vermont: Arena, 1996), 140; bold in original.

53. Graham Lock, "Censored! The Au Pairs, the Beeb and the Orgasm," *New Musical Express* (2 February 1980): 13. Later in the same issue (p. 42), Lock says that The Au Pairs, "epitomise the perfect marriage of punk and pop" at the steelworkers' benefit at the Notre Dame Hall.

54. Interview with Lesley Woods, 30 July 2010.

55. Cloonan, *Banned!*, 55.

56. This single was played on Radio 1 in the evening a few times before being dropped "in the wake of a judge's remarks that a rape victim had been guilty of contributory negligence by hitch-hiking alone at night." Cloonan, *Banned!*, 114.

57. Lucy Toothpaste, "Bodysnatchers," *Spare Rib* 100 (November 1980): 13.

58. Judy Parsons expresses her regret that The Belle Stars were so amenable to the fact that their record company would only release covers. See Bayton, *Frock Rock*, 163–5, where there is also a general discussion of the "artistic control" issue.

59. Interview, 3 March 2006.

60. And so is every male rock band, almost by definition.

61. Interview, 19 October 2001.

62. I regularly played gigs on the same bill as The Shillelagh Sisters in the early 1980s and saw the band disintegrate at first hand. The lead singer went on to replace Siobhan Fahey in Bananarama.

63. Sally Potter, "On Shows," in Rozsika Parker and Griselda Pollock (eds), *Framing Feminism: Art and the Women's Movement 1970–85* (London: Pandora, 1987), 30. The author's manager, Claudine Martinet-Riley, was told by A&M Records, "We already have a woman artist" (Joan Armatrading), when approached by her.

64. Paul Rambali, interview with New Order, *The Face* 39 (July 1983): 30.

65. See Lucy Green, *Music, Gender, Education* (Cambridge: Cambridge University Press, 1997), 75.

66. John Street, *Rebel Rock: The Politics of Popular Music* (Oxford: Blackwell, 1986), 181.

67. Ibid.

68. Ibid., 182.

69. Andrew Goodwin, "Rationalization and Democratization in the New Technologies of Popular Music," in James Lull (ed.), *Popular Music and Communication* (London: Sage, 1992), 92.

70. Interview with Viv Albertine, 26 March 2010.

71. Jon Savage, "Androgyny: Confused Chromosomes and Camp Followers," *The Face* 38

(June 1983): 23. Reynolds and Press (*The Sex Revolts*, 67) remark on the chaste lyrics of The Clash, but interestingly, The Au Pairs lyrics dealt specifically with sexuality.

72. I believe also that the experience of their audience, watching with bated breath in case the whole performance fell apart, was completely different to that of the styled artifice of camp acts. See Susan Sontag, "Notes on 'Camp'," in Elizabeth Hardwick (ed.), *A Susan Sontag Reader* (Harmondsworth: Penguin, 1982), 105–19, for definitions of camp. As Adrian Thrills once wrote, "The Slits – in some ways to their credit – could never *fake* a Good Professional Show." Adrian Thrills, "Up Slit Creek," *New Musical Express* (8 September 1979): 28.

73. See John Shepherd, *Music as Social Text* (Cambridge: Polity, 1991), chapter 8, for discussion about vocal timbres and gender implications.

74. Carole Spedding, Review of The Au Pairs' single "Diet"/"It's Obvious," *Spare Rib* 107 (June 1981): 41–2.

75. Greil Marcus, "It's Fab, It's Passionate, It's Wild. It's Intelligent! It's the Hot New Sound of England Today!," in *Ranters and Crowd Pleasers: Punk in Pop Music 1977–92* (New York: Doubleday, 1993), 110.

76. Greil Marcus, "Suspicious Minds, Delta 5," in *Ranters and Crowd Pleasers*, 151, 153.

77. Jon Savage, *England's Dreaming* (London and Boston: Faber and Faber, 1991), 20–21, 23. Wendy Webster describes the campaign song by Ronald Millar which said of Thatcher that there was "not a man around to match her." She continues, "This was the main basis of the cult of Mrs Thatcher. She was celebrated as a gender bender, although not in the most obvious form in which other female stars, from Vesta Tilley to Marlene Dietrich and beyond, had played with notions of gender – by cross dressing. Mrs Thatcher produced a different play which was to do with the contrast between the femininity of her outward appearance and the masculinity of her inner qualities, a synthesis of opposites." Wendy Webster, *Not a Man to Match Her: The Marketing of a Prime Minister* (London: Women's Press, 1990), 73.

78. For instance, Patti Smith, a symbol of powerful female rock guitarists, was frequently mimicked by Wayne County (later, "Jayne County"); one headline, placed on a double-page spread that included a live review of one of her concerts, describes County thus: "Patti Smith impersonator makes good." See *New Musical Express* (6 August 1977): 37. There is a short discussion about the implications of male–female cross-dressing in the film *Some Like It Hot*, in Green, *Music, Gender, Education*, 70–71, remarking on the ability of Tony Curtis and Jack Lemmon to blend in with the plain women instrumentalists, who are "sufficiently like men for the two impostors not to be identified."

79. Williamson, *Consuming Passions*, 47.

80. "...a sobriety that excludes not laughter but romanticism." Marcus, *Ranters and Crowd Pleasers*, 152.

81. Interview with Gina Birch, bass-player and guitarist, The Raincoats, 23 June 2000. Cindy Sherman is a performance artist whose work involves photographing herself in many different guises, both male and female, to reveal how much one's identity is conferred by one's clothing.

82. This comment may be apocryphal; I asked Peel whether he had said this and he admitted he probably had. It "did the rounds" around 1980/81. It is, however, reiterated by John Lydon: "Very ugly girls had a look-in. You didn't have to be beautiful. You could go out of your way to uglify yourself and that would be beautiful in itself, and that

would be interesting and open and free-minded, and that helped women in music no end." In John Robb, *Punk Rock: An Oral History* (London: Ebury Press, 2006).

83. Vicky Aspinall was The Raincoats' violinist/guitarist, whom Gina credits with raising the band's awareness of feminism; she had previously been a member of all-women band Jam Today and had become frustrated by their insistence on playing all-women gigs; see Conclusion.

84. Amy Raphael, *Never Mind the Bollocks* (London: Virago, 1995), 109.

85. As well as The Belle Stars, bands such as The Thompson Twins (originally a collective of various numbers of people), Culture Club (drummer Jon Moss had played with punk band London) and, especially, the newly pantomimic Adam and the Ants all had their roots in punk.

86. Just after its launch, in January–June 1979, *Smash Hits* boasted a circulation of 166,200 as against 202,000 for the *NME*, 120,000 for *Sounds*, 149,600 for *Melody Maker*, and 107,000 for *Record Mirror*. By July–December 1984, *Smash Hits* was selling just over half a million, while the circulation for all its original competitors had plummeted: 123,192 for the *NME*, 89,398 for *Sounds*, 71,485 for *Record Mirror*, and 68,217 for *Melody Maker* (Rimmer, *Like Punk Never Happened*, 163–7). The triumvirate I refer to excludes *Record Mirror*, which during this period was concerned mainly with chart pop and disco.

87. Interview with Enid Williams, bass-player, Girlschool, 30 November 1999; this is all the more ironic since she was involved with such a male-identified genre.

88. For instance, in *New Musical Express* (3 December 1977): 56, there is a bad review of Debbie Harry at the Rainbow by Julie Burchill, noting her lack of movement.

89. E. Ann Kaplan, *Rocking around the Clock: Music Television, Postmodernism, and Consumer Culture* (London and New York: Routledge, 1987), xi.

90. Deena Weinstein, "Art versus Commerce: Deconstructing a (Useful) Romantic Illusion," in Kafen Kelly and Evelyn McDonnell (eds), *Stars Don't Stand Still in the Sky* (London: Routledge, 1999), 61–2.

91. White male artists, 83 per cent of 24-hour flow. Only 11 per cent have central figures who are female. Figures from Kaplan, *Rocking around the Clock*, 115.

92. Ibid., 126.

93. Interview, 21 February 2006.

94. Mimi Schippers, *Rockin' Out of the Box: Gender Maneuvering in Alternative Heavy Rock* (New Brunswick, NJ and London: Rutgers University Press, 2002), 126–7.

95. Robin Roberts, *Ladies First: Women in Music Videos* (Jackson: University of Mississippi Press, 1996), xvi.

96. McRobbie paraphrased by Roberts, *Ladies First*, 14, from Angela McRobbie, *Postmodernism and Popular Culture* (New York: Routledge, 1994). Although Roberts put up an admirable argument for feminist postmodernism, histories of postmodernism are likely to ignore feminism, as current writing shows. See Doreen Massey, *Space, Place and Gender* (London: Polity, 1994), whose chapter "Flexible Sexism" discusses the ignoring of feminism by postmodern theorists Harvey and Soja (p. 212) and the fact that Harvey does not "get" the work of postmodern photographer Cindy Sherman (p. 238).

97. Roberts, *Ladies First*, 14.

98. Interview, 21 February 2006.
99. Jock Scott, in Colegrave and Sullivan, *Punk*, 352.
100. Joan Smith, "Taking up the Slacks," *The Guardian* (5 June 2001).
101. Christine Griffin, *Typical Girls? Young Women from School to the Job Market* (London: Routledge, 1985), 127.

6. The Social Context

1. Stanley Cohen, *Folk Devils and Moral Panics: The Creation of the Mods and Rockers* (Oxford: Martin Robertson, 1993 [1972]), ii.
2. And if we did not have such stringent libel laws, it would have been possible to expose activities verging on the illegal in several cases.
3. See D. Sanjek, "Can Fujiyama Mama be the Female Elvis? The Wild, Wild Women of Rockabilly," in Sheila Whiteley (ed.), *Sexing the Groove: Popular Music and Gender* (London: Routledge, 1997), 137–67, for a discussion on the "disappearance" of female rockabilly performers caused by the lack of, or destruction of, vinyl recordings.
4. Cohen's statement was made in 1993.
5. Angela McRobbie, "Settling Accounts with Subcultures: A Feminist Critique," in Simon Frith and Andrew Goodwin (eds), *On Record* (London and New York: Routledge, 1998 [1990]), 68.
6. Valerie Walkerdine, *Daddy's Girl: Young Girls and Popular Culture* (Basingstoke and London: Macmillan, 1997).
7. Neil Nehring, *Popular Music, Gender and Postmodernism* (Thousand Oaks, CA: Sage, 1997).
8. Sheila Rowbotham, *Woman's Consciousness, Man's World* (Harmondsworth and New York: Penguin, 1981).
9. See, for example, Carol Diethe, *Nietzsche's Women: Beyond the Whip* (Berlin and New York: W. de Gruyter, 1996).
10. It has also been interesting to observe the gradual infiltration of her observations on partiality into studies of young people, to the extent where some later writers, notably Neil Nehring (mentioned above) and David Rowe, acknowledge their gender bias at the beginning of their studies. For instance, Rowe states: "Authors...as historically constituted human subjects, can hardly be exempt from the kind of explanatory framework they seek to impose on their research objects. The tension between writing and being history must be recognised rather than tranquillised." *Popular Cultures: Rock Music, Sport and the Politics of Pleasure* (London, Thousand Oaks and New Delhi: Sage, 1995), 2. Psychologist Valerie Walkerdine takes this even further, incorporating biographical details and empirical observation alongside meticulous sociological research based on young girls' relationship to pop, into a refreshing, if challenging, style of analysis. See Walkerdine, *Daddy's Girl*.
11. Rosalind Miles, *The Woman's History of the World* (London: Paladin, 1990), "Preface," 14.
12. See my section, "Women and Research: A Brief Discussion," in the Introduction, above.
13. Christine Griffin, *Typical Girls? Young Women from School to the Job Market* (London: Routledge, 1985), 5.

14. See Catharine MacKinnon, "Points Against Postmodernism," *Chicago-Kent Law Review* 75.3 (2000): 687–712, for a detailed critique of the tensions between feminism and postmodernism as cultural theories.
15. Barbara Bradby, "Sampling Sexuality: Gender, Technology and the Body in Dance Music," *Popular Music* 12.2 (1993): 155–76, quote on p. 158. The implications of embracing postmodernism as an academic theory will be explored later.
16. Mark Abrams, *The Teenage Consumer* (London: London Press Exchange, 1959). I returned my copy of this to the library, thinking that the section on young women was missing and had accidentally been torn off the laser copy that I'd been given. It was only later that I realized that there had not been a section on young women in the first place.
17. Howard Becker, *Outsiders: Studies in the Sociology of Deviance* (New York: Free Press, 1963), 81.
18. The Mod subculture was regarded as deviant, although it involved a subversion of mainstream style that necessitated a certain amount of conformity (reasonably paid jobs, for instance) in order to finance the purchase of tailor-made suits and imported vinyl recordings; although it started as a middle-class movement, it came to be identified with working-class white males (and, as noted in the Introduction, there was more than one gender that belonged to this subculture). The difference between the "last resort" nature of the punk subculture as a result of feelings of rejection and this manipulation of subcultural styles to draw attention to oneself and capitalize on this will be clarified later.
19. Stuart Hall and Tony Jefferson (eds), *Resistance through Rituals: Youth Subcultures in Post-War Britain* (London: Hutchinson, 1975).
20. Irwin Silber, quoted by Hall and Jefferson, *Resistance through Rituals*, 68.
21. Paul E. Willis, *Profane Culture* (London and Boston: Routledge and Kegan Paul, 1978), 5.
22. Mark Abrams, David Gerard and Noel Timms (eds), *Values and Social Change in Britain* (Basingstoke and London: Macmillan, 1985), 44.
23. Dick Hebdige, *Subculture, the Meaning of Style* (London: Routledge, 1979).
24. Sarah Thornton, *Club Cultures: Music, Media and Subcultural Capital* (Cambridge: Polity, 1995).
25. It would be easy to dismiss girls' involvement in punk rock as the latter. In the summer of 2000 a journalist from *The Independent* newspaper made contact with me, having read one of the appeals for interview participants in his local paper. The resulting article led to a flurry of interest and "Where Are They Now?"-type articles in several newspapers, including the *News of the World*, which wrote a small piece in its "Bizarre" column as well as constructing an article several weeks later from other reports. Almost all of the interest (which included three calls from documentary-makers) centred on what girl punks wore, rather than what they did.
26. David Muggleton, *Inside Subculture: The Postmodern Meaning of Style* (Oxford and New York: Berg, 2000).
27. Hebdige, *Subculture, the Meaning of Style*, 139.
28. Ibid., 94.
29. Thornton, *Club Cultures*, 129.
30. This is indeed what has happened in the dance culture described in her book, and it

falls very much within the category of the "commodity form." However, condemnation of punks came from more sources than just the media: local councils, the police, parents and other relatives, and members of other subcultures.

31. Willis, *Profane Culture*, 113.

32. See Muggleton, *Inside Subculture*, for a full exploration of this concept. While creating a subcultural community has always relied on a visible sense of difference from the mainstream, cultural commentators now expect new subcultures to form regularly, and are ready to pounce on them with their definitions and analyses, which feed straight back into the subcultures themselves. It is now understood that youth subcultures constantly shift in focus and degree of involvement, and that it is almost impossible to create an accurate snapshot of what happens in the world of the subculture.

33. Hebdige, *Subculture, the Meaning of Style* (used with reference to the Teds and Mods), 84.

34. Ibid., 122.

35. Simon Frith, *Sound Effects* (New York: Pantheon, 1981), 219.

36. Ibid., 220.

37. Julien Temple (dir.), *The Filth and the Fury: A Sex Pistols Film* (Filmfour, 1999).

38. Charles Shaar Murray, *Shots from the Hip* (London: Penguin Books, 1991), 212.

39. For instance, by Johnny Rotten (John Lydon, *Rotten: No Irish, No Blacks, No Dogs* [London: Coronet, 1995]); Nils Stevenson, who managed the band Siouxsie and the Banshees (Nils Stevenson and Ray Stevenson, *Vacant: A Diary of the Punk Years 1976–79* [London: Thames and Hudson, 1999]); Chris Sullivan, a Welsh punk who later opened nightclubs in London (Stephen Colegrave and Chris Sullivan, *Punk A Life Apart* [London: Cassell, 2001]); journalist Caroline Coon, *1988: The New Wave Punk Rock Explosion* (London and New York: Omnibus, 1982); and George Gimarc, *Punk Diary: 1970–1979* (London: St Martin's Press, 1994).

40. John Street, *Rebel Rock: The Politics of Popular Music* (Oxford and New York: Blackwell, 1986), 176.

41. Interview, 7 September 2000.

42. Ibid.

43. Jon Savage, "The Great Rock'n'Roll Swindle," in Paul Taylor (ed.), *Impresario: Malcolm McLaren and the British New Wave* (Cambridge, MA and London: MIT Press, 1988), no pagination.

44. Simon Frith and Howard Home (eds), *Art into Pop* (London and New York: Routledge, 1989), 28. Later, they quote the artist Richard Hamilton, who says, "As more people become unemployed, the more of them that become artists the better" (p. 36).

45. Hebdige, *Subculture, the Meaning of Style*, 87. Note, however, that Hebdige never mentions the fact that engagement with production differentiates punk from other subcultures.

46. From *New Musical Express* (9 April 1977): 35.

47. Malcolm Ross discusses the point in their development at which the young person tries to control the world by manufacturing interpretative objects: "By using the stratagem of the holding form it may be possible to keep the affective element alive at the moment that it is most threatened. To become conscious of art is to become conscious – self-conscious – about feeling. Older children are tempted either to run from the expression of feeling altogether (and for ever) as childish (and therefore

contemptible), or to reach for the well tried feeling formulae of the adult world. In either event their work loses authenticity – they fake it and soon become convinced that faking it is what it's all about, which means it's a waste of time." Malcolm Ross (ed.), *The Arts and Personal Growth* (London: Pergamon, 1980), 106–7.

48. Angela McRobbie, *Feminism and Youth Culture* (Basingstoke and London: Macmillan, 2nd edn, 2000), 29.
49. Chambers discusses Robert Christgau's *Any Old Way You Choose It* (Harmondsworth: Penguin, 1973) on Joni Mitchell's self-absorbed lyrics, noting that they are an "act of defiance" in a woman. See Iain Chambers, *Urban Rhythms: Pop Music and Popular Culture* (Basingstoke and London: Macmillan, 1985), 121.
50. Dick Bradley, *Understanding Rock'n'Roll: Popular Music in Britain 1955–1964* (Buckingham and Philadelphia: Open University Press, 1992), 11; since McRobbie's precedent, however, many male writers do acknowledge this fact.
51. Feminist writers discuss this in depth, and these discussions will be examined later.
52. Lawrence Grossberg, *We Gotta Get Out of This Place* (New York and London: Routledge, 1992), 206. Rock is seen here to be described in terms of territory, and indeed in the US has become symbolic as a world-conquering phenomenon. The symbolic relationship between rock activity and violence will be explored later in this work.
53. Jacques Attali, *Noise: The Political Economy of Music* (Minneapolis and London: University of Minnesota Press, 1985), 29 (emphasis in original).
54. Michel Foucault, quoted in Lawrence D. Kritzman, *Michel Foucault: Politics, Philosophy, Culture: Interviews and Other Writings 1977–1984* (New York and London: Routledge, 1988), 316.
55. Frith, *Sound Effects*, 209.
56. See Simon Frith and Angela McRobbie, "Rock and Sexuality," in A. McRobbie (ed.), *Feminism and Youth Culture* (Basingstoke and London: Macmillan, 2000 [1991]), 137–58. Frith gained a considerable amount of "gender-cred" by writing this essay with Angela McRobbie.
57. Frith, *Sound Effects*, 11.
58. Theodor Adorno, "On Popular Music" (1940), in Frith and Goodwin, *On Record* (London: Routledge, 1990), 301.
59. Howard S. Becker, *Art Worlds* (Berkeley, CA: University of California Press, 1982), 131–64.
60. Iain Chambers, "A Strategy for Living: Black Music and White Subcultures," in Hall and Jefferson, *Resistance through Rituals*, 164.
61. Sheila Whiteley, *The Space between the Notes* (London and Boston: Routledge, 1992), 118.
62. Interview, 3 February 2006.
63. Dave Laing, *One Chord Wonders: Power and Meaning in Punk Rock* (Milton Keynes and Philadelphia: Open University Press, 1985), 37.
64. And the implications of this for female instrumentalists are therefore severe.
65. Mimi Schippers, *Rockin' Out of the Box: Gender Maneuvering in Alternative Heavy Rock* (New Brunswick, NJ and London: Rutgers University Press, 2002), 187.
66. I am using Raymond Williams's definitions of social movements, from Raymond Williams, *Keywords: A Vocabulary of Culture and Society* (London: Fontana, 1975).

67. Sara Cohen, *Rock Culture in Liverpool: Popular Music in the Making* (Oxford: Clarendon Press, 1991), 132.

68. Sadie Plant, *The Most Radical Gesture: The Situationist International in the Postmodern Age* (London and New York: Routledge, 1992), 74.

69. Although Richard Branson was running Virgin Records at this time, his activities pre-dated the proliferation of small-label exploitation of punk music, and instead he became involved with The Sex Pistols when Virgin had already become a successful record company.

70. Plant, *The Most Radical Gesture*, 74.

71. Peter York, *Style Wars* (London: Sidgwick and Jackson, 1980), 131; italics in original.

72. Paul Taylor (ed.), *Impresario: Malcolm McLaren and the British New Wave* (Cambridge, MA and London: MIT Press, 1980), 24.

73. Post-materialism here is a reference to the phrase coined by Ronald Inglehart in 1976, in Abrams, Gerard and Timms, *Values and Social Change*, 169.

74. David Phillips, "Participation and Political Values," in Abrams, Gerard and Timms, *Values and Social Change*, 172.

75. Street, *Rebel Rock*, 176.

76. This point is arguable: surely pop fans need their "fix" of music just as much as rock fans need theirs?

77. Simon Frith, *Music for Pleasure* (Cambridge: Polity, 1988), 174.

78. Street, *Rebel Rock*, 176.

79. In fact, the first person I went to interview in Brighton gave "fun" as the only reason she joined a band! This was later contradicted by other musicians I spoke to, but the variety of views of people involved in punk cannot be overestimated.

80. McRobbie, *Feminism and Youth Culture*, "Introduction," 1–8, for her personal memoir that includes the crossover between Kristeva-reading students from Birmingham University and girls from working-class backgrounds in a shared house.

81. In this work, I rely mainly on the *New Musical Express* as a source of information; this is because, among my peers at the time, this paper had the most credibility, and, we believed, the most lively journalists.

82. Information directly from the weekly papers will be referred to during the section on the media, as well as tabloid reports and interview material from *Spare Rib*, whose writers frequently championed music made by women, punk or not. The glossy lifestyle magazines picked up on the tail-end of punk, and *The Face* has provided some interesting material that throws light on the demise of interest in punk music.

83. Helen Davies, "All Rock and Roll is Homosocial: The Representation of Women in the British Rock Music Press," *Popular Music* 20.3 (2001): 295–313.

84. See Abrams, Gerard and Timms, *Values and Social Change*, 212: "Paradoxically, the exclusion of women was as characteristic of the new 'radical' or sceptical theories of deviance as it had been of traditional criminology. The editors of *Critical Criminology* argue that the 'new deviancy theory' often amounted to 'a celebration rather than an analysis of the deviant form with which the deviant theorist could vicariously iden-tify – an identification by powerless intellectuals with deviants who appeared more successful in controlling events' (Taylor, Walton and Young, 1975)."

85. Elizabeth Nelson, *The British Counter-culture 1966–73: A Study of the Underground Press* (Basingstoke and London: Macmillan, 1989), 138–40.

86. For instance, Lesley Ferris's history of theatre in Europe describes a time when women were regular stage performers; one hundred years later, the pope had massacred the Cathars, who had permitted this activity. See Lesley Ferris, *Acting Women: Images of Women in Theatre* (Basingstoke and London: Macmillan, 1990).

87. Rowbotham, *Woman's Consciousness, Man's World*.

88. Elizabeth Wilson, *Bohemians: The Glamorous Outcasts* (London and New York: I. B. Tauris, 2000).

89. Charlotte Greig, *Will You Still Love Me Tomorrow? Girl Groups from the 50s on* (London: Virago, 1989).

90. See Spencer Leigh, *Baby, That is Rock and Roll: American Pop, 1954–1963* (Folkestone: Finbarr International, 2001).

91. See, for example, Donna Gaines, "Girl Groups: A Ballad of Co-dependency," in Barbara O'Dair (ed.), *The Rolling Stone Book of Women in Rock* (New York: Random House, 1997), 103.

92. Spencer Leigh's book contains interview material from singers of this era that throws light on the commodity nature of their personae and vocal skills. Leigh, *Baby, That is Rock and Roll*, 216–27.

93. Ibid.

94. See S. Reynolds and J. Press, *The Sex Revolts: Gender, Rebellion and Rock'n'Roll* (London: Serpent's Tail, 1995).

95. Sue Steward and Sheryl Garratt, *Signed, Sealed and Delivered: The Life Stories of Women in Pop* (London and Sydney: Pluto, 1984).

96. Keith Negus, *Producing Pop: Culture and Conflict in the Popular Music Industry* (London: Edward Arnold, 1992).

97. Steward and Garratt, *Signed, Sealed and Delivered*.

98. For instance, the women at EMI's pressing plant who refused to pack The Sex Pistols' single because of their objections to its cover. Ibid., 63–4.

99. Reynolds and Press, *The Sex Revolts*.

100. Deena Weinstein, *Heavy Metal: The Music and its Culture* (Cambridge, MA: Da Capo, 2000).

101. Robert Walser, *Running with the Devil: Power, Gender and Madness in Heavy Metal Music* (Middletown, CT: Wesleyan University Press, 1993).

102. Mavis Bayton, *Frock Rock* (Oxford: Oxford University Press, 1998).

103. Lucy Green, *Music, Gender, Education* (Cambridge: Cambridge University Press, 1997).

104. Leslie G Roman, "Intimacy, Labor and Class: Ideologies of Feminine Sexuality in the Punk Slam Dance," in L. G. Roman and L. K. Christian-Smith (eds), *Becoming Feminine: The Politics of Popular Culture* (London: Falmer Press, 1988), 143–84.

105. Cressida Miles, "Spatial Politics: A Gendered Sense of Place," in S. Redhead, D. Wynne and J. O'Connor (eds), *The Clubcultures Reader: Readings in Popular Cultural Studies* (Oxford: Blackwell, 1997), 66–78.

106. Lauraine Leblanc, *Pretty in Punk: Girls' Gender Resistance in a Boys' Subculture* (New Brunswick, NJ and London: Rutgers University Press, 2001).

7. Conclusion

1. Interview (uncredited) with Peggy Seeger, "Folk with Feeling," *Spare Rib* 48 (July 1976): 41.
2. Sarah Cooper, interview with Liz Naylor, "Access Some Areas: PR in the Music Industry," in Cooper (ed.), *Girls! Girls! Girls! Essays on Women and Music* (London and New York: Cassell, 1995), 151.
3. Dale Spender, *Man Made Language* (London: Pandora, 1990), 191.
4. Interview, 24 January 2002.
5. There is a constant debate within women's music-making about issues to do with process versus product and innovation versus assimilation. S. Reynolds and J. Press discuss this with regard to Riot Grrrl music for instance; see their *The Sex Revolts: Gender, Rebellion and Rock'n'Roll* (London: Serpent's Tail, 1995). Mavis Bayton in particular (in *Frock Rock* [Oxford: Oxford University Press, 1998]) is concerned by this issue. Frith's discussion of van der Merwe's theories (from *Origins of the Popular Style*, 3) in *Performing Rites* (Oxford and New York: Oxford University Press, 1996) debates the values ascribed to expressive ability versus technical skill. This is an important issue to women learning a "language" for the first time.
6. Greil Marcus, "It's Fab, It's Passionate, It's Wild, It's Intelligent! It's the Hot New Sound of England Today!" in *Ranters and Crowd Pleasers: Punk in Pop Music 1977–92* (New York: Doubleday, 1993), 113.
7. Interview, 27 November 2001. It was interesting that the commercial success of Girlschool reflected their more traditional rock approach.
8. This interview was given prior to Joe Strummer's death in 2002.
9. Interview, 27 November 2001. Christine continues: "People like to know what they're buying: is it a female rock'n'roll band? If it had been a female rock'n'roll band I think they would have been more successful, 'cos people would have known what they were buying (Girlschool). But they are parodies of a male rock band, aren't they, Girlschool, and they fit in neatly."
10. *Tiswas* was an "anarchic" children's television programme broadcast on ITV from 1974 to 1981, which featured, from 1979, a puppet "punk" dog called Spit operated by comedian Bob Carolgees, and which helped to launch Lenny Henry as a comedian. See http://www.tiswasonline.com/.
11. Interview, 9 October 2001.
12. Bayton, *Frock Rock*, 205.
13. Angela McRobbie describes women in rock as "unskilled rock workers" who "are a source of cheap labour," *Feminism and Youth Culture* (Basingstoke and London: Macmillan, 2000 [1991]), 145. No wonder males were threatened when we became skilled! The interest in not promoting skilled women is rooted in the fact that men think they will be squeezed out by the combination of appearance and skill that they cannot compete with; they are therefore not prepared to take the consequences of their emphasis on women's appearance as a selling-point.
14. "Recent feminist debates have used psychoanalytic theory to explore why the 'male gaze' is dominant in mainstream cinema. But there may be a more concrete (if related) explanation: that the masculine point of view is prevalent simply because men control the industry." Comment by Anne Ross Muir, "The Status of Women Working

in Film and Television," in Lorraine Gamman and Margaret Marshment (eds), *The Female Gaze: Women as Viewers of Popular Culture* (London: Women's Press, 1988), 143. She also remarks that Richard Attenborough was moved to tears by racism when filming *Gandhi*, not noticing that women in the film industry are more likely to be cleaners than directors, as witnessed on the set of the film itself.

15. Interview, 24 January 2001. Unfortunately, there is hidden discrimination at grass-roots level even today. Sue Bradley told me: "Interestingly, when I trained as a music teacher we had these things that a well-known session bass-player runs, and I went to the very first one that he had, and since then I've dipped into a couple. And it's, like, 99.9 per cent boys go on this thing. They get sent from school. And I was trying to work out how was it that it was nearly all boys. It seems to be something to do with the word 'rock' and the schools say, 'Oh, it's rock, we'll send all the people that play guitars,' and it's always the boys; it's exactly the same as it was when I was at school. I noticed that there were three girls who had arrived with instruments – one was bass, two were brass-players. They described themselves, 'Oh, I'm a bass-player,' 'I'm a saxophone-player.' About two hours later, the instruments had totally disappeared and the girls were now describing themselves as backing vocalists. It was astonishing, because that was the only way that the boys would accept these girls into the groups they were forming on this rock weekend." Interview, 20 November 2001.

16. Denial of, or "forgetting about," instances of opposition seemed to be a common factor in my research too; often, when the tape recorder was switched off, a flood of revelations would be unleashed, with requests for the information either to be off-record, non-attributed, or, occasionally, not used at all.

17. Linda Dahl, *Stormy Weather: The Music and Lives of a Century of Jazzwomen* (London: Quartet, 1984), 178. For Karen Carpenter, *fronting* The Carpenters had been the "unnatural" act; her skill was playing the drums, but she was "pushed into the spot-light of singing lead to complement her brother's skills." Sue Cummings, "Karen Carpenter," in Barbara O'Dair (ed.), *The Rolling Stone Book of Women in Rock* (New York: Random House, 1997), 240.

18. Lisa Kennedy, "Joni Mitchell," in O'Dair, *Rolling Stone Book of Women in Rock*, 175.

19. Fanny were a four-piece all-female US rock band that was operational between 1969 and 1975. In spite of being described by George Harrison as "the female Beatles," drummer Alice de Buhr remarked in a "Where are they now?" article that "Articles about women in rock still don't mention us, which tends to reaffirm my feelings after I quit," Martin Aston, Q magazine, n.d., p. 60.

20. Barbara Charles, "Jam Today," *Spare Rib* 66 (January 1978): 29.

21. Violinist Vicky Aspinall left Jam Today to join The Raincoats because she felt their atti-tude was too strict. However, even the more relaxed all-female bands had ethical dif-ficulties, articulated here by Georgina Born: "She [Bayton] shows how many feminist rock musicians, in trying to maintain control over the production and dissemination of their music, have found it necessary to work outside the dominant structures of the music industry, and are therefore able to connect with only a limited audience. Here a politicized context of production, whatever the character of the resultant texts, leads unavoidably to confrontation with, and disengagement from, corporate capitalist power." "Afterword: Music Policy, Aesthetic and Social Difference," in Tony

Bennett *et al.* (eds), *Rock and Popular Music: Politics, Policies, Institutions* (London and New York: Routledge, 1993), 274–5.

22. "I feel equal"; this could be an example of narrow horizons, or perhaps misguided optimism! Poly Styrene interviewed by Lucy Toothpaste, *Spare Rib* 60 (July 1977): 51.

23. Interview with Caroline Coon, 24 January 2002.

24. Steve Beresford, session player with The Slits, interview, 4 April 2004.

25. Interview, 21 February 2006.

26. Martha Zaenfell, "Love Sex, Hate Sexism?...," report on Rock Against Sexism gig, *New Musical Express* (1 April 1979): 15. The difficulties of this concept were also articulated in the feminist press: "Many feminists felt the event was out of their control: the Roundhouse ruled, men guarded the doors, put on the records, brought on the bands. I felt that too, but would have been glad that the music wasn't 'ours,' the audience not just 'us' – if only we'd made clear who 'we' were." Jill Nicholls, Review of National Abortion Campaign Benefit at the Roundhouse, Camden, *Spare Rib* 68 (March 1978): 35–6 (gig headlined by X-Ray Spex).

27. Caroline Coon told me that this phenomenon was not purely British: "I interviewed Talking Heads, but David Byrne absolutely would not allow anyone else in the band to be interviewed. So it was very difficult to get to Tina, although I did speak to Tina. Tina Weymouth was one of those women who to enable her to maintain her position there, absolutely did not want to talk about being a feminist." Hynde declined to be interviewed for this work (24 January 2002).

28. Interview by Andrea Juno, in her *Angry Women in Rock*, vol. I (New York: Juno Books, 1996), 193.

29. I was frequently told (as a "compliment") that I was "more like a bloke than a girl." There appears to be a general belief that even a modest level of competence in music is a by-product of maleness, let alone Hynde's "innovators." Christine Battersby writes, "Great artists and scientists have *male* sexual drives, whether or not they are biologically female. Males can *transcend* their sexuality; females are *limited* by theirs – or, if not, must have *male* sexual energy" – the assumptions of her male colleagues. See Battersby, *Gender and Genius: Towards a Feminist Aesthetics* (London: Women's Press, 1989), 18.

30. Holly George-Warren, "Hillbilly Fillies: The Trailblazers of C&W," in O'Dair, *Rolling Stone Book of Women in Rock*, 46. In 1993, *Musician* magazine chose Maybelle Carter as one of the top guitarists of all time. Hynde's views echo those made by Burchill, quoted earlier, in the preface to *Never Mind the Bollocks*.

31. Wendy Webster's book about Thatcher's self-creation as a "special woman" gives an insight into the type of focused professional denial of the influence of feminism that both Hynde and Poly Styrene subscribe to; Webster quotes the famous *Woman's Own* article of 17 October 1981 where Thatcher declared, "There is no such thing as society. There are individual men and women, and there are families" (p. 57), and reports on Thatcher's refusal to acknowledge the need for more women in parliament; it was women's own fault if they didn't "get on" (pp. 66–7). Webster, *Not a Man to Match Her: The Marketing of a Prime Minister* (London: Women's Press, 1990). This individualism struck a chord with some punks: anarchy is arguably the most extreme form of it.

32. This is what she claims Vivienne Westwood once called her.

33. John Lydon, *Rotten: No Irish, No Blacks, No Dogs* (London: Coronet, 1995), 95.
34. "We had a following from day one; there were just so many people. The women's centre in Oxford was quite big. There was a women's cafe, a women's food co-op, and there was a women's centre, it was all on a shoestring... There was an advice centre, there was a big space... What was important was the following...within eight weeks of forming we played outdoors to one-and-a-half thousand people in the open air festival, the annual Mayfly." Interview, 14 July 2000.
35. Interview, 21 February 2006.
36. Interview with Gina Birch, in Amy Raphael, *Never Mind the Bollocks* (London: Virago, 1995), 98.
37. Interview with Gina Birch, bass-player and guitarist, The Raincoats, 23 June 2000.
38. Interview with Liz Naylor, The Gay Animals, 7 September 2000.
39. Ian Penman, "Mod, Mode, Mo-dettes," *New Musical Express* (18 August 1979): 25. This is a perfect example of Sheila Whiteley's "play power," mentioned earlier. See Sheila Whiteley, *The Space between the Notes* (London and Boston: Routledge, 1992), 118.
40. Interview with Hester Smith, Dolly Mixture, 26 January 2000. After the interview, Hester told me how relieved she was when she found that she was ill, and thus unable to continue drumming; she now has a flute, which she delights in carrying around in its small case. Incidentally, Kathleen Hanna's experience (beginning of Chapter 2) gives the lie to Hester's optimistic comments about "now."
41. Sally Potter, "On Shows," in Rozsika Parker and Griselda Pollock, *Framing Feminism: Art and the Women's Movement 1970–85* (London: Pandora, 1987), 30, and this work, Chapter 2.
42. Interview, 23 June 2000.
43. Gillian G. Gaar, *She's a Rebel* (London: Blandford, 1993), 272.
44. Neil Norman, "A Rock Folly," review of Tour De Force (Deirdre and Bernice Cartwright's band), *New Musical Express* (24 November 1979): 70.
45. E. Ann Kaplan, *Rocking around the Clock: Music Television, Postmodernism, and Consumer Culture* (London and New York: Routledge, 1987), 150.
46. Interview, 24 January 2002.
47. Lucy Green, *Music, Gender, Education* (Cambridge: Cambridge University Press, 1997), 57.
48. See Deanne Pearson, "Women in Rock," *New Musical Express* (29 March 1980): 27, for a collection of interviews with "electric girls" The Passion, The Raincoats, The Modettes, Girlschool and The Au Pairs. This article gives a very strong insight into the variety of attitudes of female band personnel at this time.
49. Leslie Gourse, *Madame Jazz: Contemporary Women Instrumentalists* (New York and Oxford: Oxford University Press, 1995), 14.
50. Interview with Dottie Dodgion in Dahl, *Stormy Weather*, 222.
51. Interview, 30 November 1999.
52. Christine Griffin, *Typical Girls? Young Women from School to the Job Market* (London: Routledge, 1985), 155.
53. Julie Burchill, Review of The Adverts with picture of Gaye *without* guitar, *New Musical Express* (2 July 1977): 33.
54. Simon Frith, *Sound Effects* (New York: Pantheon, 1981), 6, 8.

55. Simon Frith and Howard Home, *Art into Pop* (London and New York: Routledge, 1989), 30.

56. Mary Ann Clawson, "When Women Play the Bass: Instrument Specialization and Gender Interpretation in Alternative Rock Music," *Gender and Society* 13.2 (1999): 200. Clawson's study was undertaken in Boston in 1990 and 1991, but has much to offer this study. She writes, "Women respondents in the Rumble sample began to play their rock instruments at the median age of 19, followed by participation in a first band at the median age of 21. This was in marked contrast to male respondents, who began to play at 13 and joined first bands at the median age of 15.3" (pp. 199–200).

57. Conversation with Rachel, Dolly Mixture, 2 February 2000.

58. Michael Fogarty, "British Attitudes to Work," in Mark Abrams, David Gerard and Noel Timms (eds), *Values and Social Change in Britain* (Basingstoke and London: Macmillan, 1985), 196. Fogarty also concludes that women collude in the unsatisfactory work/home situation.

59. Even The Devil's Dykes, a lesbian, separatist band, had to be shown where on their amplifiers to insert their jack-plugs at a gig I attended.

60. Broadcast date 19 July 2000.

61. Chrissie Hynde taught Johnny Rotten to play guitar. For an example from the US (from *NME* [10 June 1978]: 20), Paul Rambali, writing about cult band The Cramps, says only Poison Ivy, their guitarist, could play an instrument at first: "Ivy taught Bryan some chords." Their original drummer was Ivy's sister, then another girl drummer replaced her until Nick Knox joined.

62. Interview, 10 February 2006.

63. "It was purely for fun; I always knew that it would be short-lived. And it was an intense and very enjoyable time. If they can do it, we can, in the sense of one-chord wonders. A lot of people started to do things musically because they could see it was possible." Interview with Julie Blair, keyboards, The Mockingbirds, 7 October 1999.

64. Interview with Liz Naylor, 7 September 2000.

65. Simon Reynolds, *Rip it Up and Start Again: Post-punk 1978–1984* (London: Faber and Faber, 2005), 82.

66. Interview with Viv Albertine, 26 March 2010.

67. Green, *Music, Gender, Education*, 190. Several issues arise from this that are of relevance: first, the "folk" nature of some rock bands, which does not necessarily involve skill – this should be an advantage to women instrumentalists; second, the feeling of female jazz musicians that they need to be ultra-skilled to get on in the male world – perhaps the relative maturity of the jazz scene has taught them something that the female punks did not learn; and, third, Green alludes to punk's scorning the pomposity that had become attached to the world of pop and rock music – ultimately, this factor reasserted itself. Mick Jagger and Rod Stewart have as high a profile as ever; only Chrissie Hynde survives in the rock world of today, and it is arguable that she never identified herself as a punk musician, but owes her longevity to being first and foremost a rock musician, in a similar way to The Clash. Finally, jazz bears a resemblance to classical music in its requirement for measurable skills, knowledge of repertoire, and so on.

68. Interview, 13 July 2000.

69. Charles, "Jam Today," 26.

70. Interview, 26 January 2000.

71. Interview, 3 February 2006.
72. Ibid.
73. Interview, 21 February 2006.
74. See Dick Hebdige, *Subculture, the Meaning of Style* (London: Routledge, 1979), 87.
75. *New Musical Express* (28 April 1979): 17.
76. *New Musical Express* (2 June 1979): 52.
77. *New Musical Express* (12 January 1980): 35. This was a review of their first gig in New York.
78. Susan Rubin Suleiman, *Subversive Intent: Gender, Politics and the Avant-garde* (Cambridge, MA and London: Harvard University Press, 1990), 14.
79. "The conditions of production are just as much determined by social, ideological and broad cultural structures as the conditions of consumption. The artist/cultural producer is confronted with certain materials with which to work – existing aesthetic codes and conventions, techniques and tools of production – and is, moreover, himself or herself formed in ideology and in social context... The political consciousness of, and the possibilities of aesthetic innovation for, the artist are constructed in the social historical process." Janet Wolff, *The Social Production of Art* (London: Macmillan Education, 1981), 94.
80. Clawson, "When Women Play the Bass," 200–203.
81. Ann Phillips and Barbara Taylor, "Sex and Skill: Notes towards a Feminist Economics," *Feminist Review* 4.6 (1980): 82.
82. McRobbie, *Feminism and Youth Culture*, 145.
83. Robbi Millar, "Sexism is No Joke," *Sounds* (20 September 1980): 34.
84. Email interview with Penelope Tobin, 15 May 2006.
85. Particularly, perhaps, because some earlier singer-songwriters such as Carole King and Laura Nyro were also pianists. However, even in New Order and The Fall, the women keyboard-players' voices were rarely heard in interviews.
86. Interview, 6 December 2001.
87. At http://lists.ibiblio.org/mailman/listinfo/typicalgirls (accessed 18 April 2011).
88. At http://www.comnet.ca/~rina/ (accessed 28 March 2007). Rina's site was active for many years but it is no longer accessible.
89. We have in the past been devalued in and excluded from writing (Spender), radical politics (Rowbotham), avant-garde art movements (Suleiman), and Bohemia (Liz Wilson). There have been other false dawns for women performers as far back in history as the thirteenth century, when the Cathars accepted female actors on stage until they were exterminated by the Pope in 1209 – see Lesley Ferris, *Acting Women: Images of Women in Theatre* (Basingstoke and London: Macmillan, 1990).
90. Sara Cohen, for instance, showed that in 1996 rock music was still "actively produced as male" in Liverpool, and in spite of activities by women on the scene, it is still very much a male-dominated arena. See "Men Making a Scene: Rock Music and the Production of Gender," in Sheila Whiteley (ed.), *Sexing the Groove: Popular Music and Gender* (London: Routledge, 1997), 17. See also Matthew Bannister, *White Boys, White Noise: Masculinities and 1980s Guitar Rock* (London: Ashgate, 2006) for a description of the way that Indie "works" and a reclamation of the concept of the enthusiast who learns his (*sic*) craft in a band environment.
91. Interview, 30 November 1999.

Appendix: List of Interviewees

Ari Up, The Slits, London 1976–1982.

Barb Dwyer, The Lillettes, Brighton 1978–1980.

Bethan Peters, The Delta 5, Leeds 1979–1981.

Enid Williams, Painted Lady, London 1975–1978; Girlschool, London 1978–1982.

Gaye Black, The Adverts, London 1976–1979.

Gina Birch, The Raincoats, London 1977–1984.

Heather De Lyon, The Objeks, Brighton 1980–1981.

Hester Smith, Dolly Mixture, Cambridge 1979–1984.

Jane Munro, The Au Pairs, Birmingham 1979–1983.

Jane Woodgate, The Mo-dettes, London 1979–1983.

Julie Blair, The Mockingbirds, Brighton 1979–1980.

June Miles-Kingston, The Mo-dettes, London 1979–1983.

Kate Hayes, The Objeks, Brighton 1979–1981.

Kate Stephenson, The Baddies, Isle of Wight, 1978.

Lesley Woods, The Au Pairs, Birmingham 1979–1983.

Lia Naylor, The Gay Animals, Manchester 1977.

Lora Logic, X-Ray Spex, London 1976–1978; Essential Logic, London 1978–1980.

Lucy O'Brien, The Catholic Girls, Southampton 1979–1980.

Mavis Bayton, The Mistakes, Oxford 1978–1981.

Mel Ritter, The Mo-dettes, London 1982–1983.

Mufti Berridge, No Man's Band, Brighton 1977.

Nora Normal, The Gymslips, London 1981–1984.

Pauline Murray, Penetration, Durham 1976–1980; Pauline Murray and the Invisible Girls, various 1980.

Penny Tobin, London, various (date TBC).

Poly Styrene, X-ray Spex, London 1976–1979.

Rachel Bor, Dolly Mixture, Cambridge 1979–1984.

Rhoda Dakar, The Bodysnatchers, London 1979–1981.

Sara Furse, No Man's Band, Brighton 1977.

Sarah-Jane Owen, The Bodysnatchers, email, 18 January 2006.

Shanne Bradley, The Nips, London 1977–1984; The Men They Couldn't Hang, London 1984–1985.

Stella Clifford, The Objeks, Brighton 1980–1981.

Sue Bradley, The New Objeks, Brighton, 1981–1982.

Tessa Pollitt, The Slits, London 1976–1982.

Viv Albertine, The Slits, London 1976–1982.

Vi Subversa, Poison Girls, Brighton/London 1976–1985.

Zillah Ashworth, Rubella Ballet, London 1979–1991.

Bibliography

Abrams, Mark. *The Teenage Consumer*. London: London Press Exchange, 1959.

—"Demographic Correlates of Values." In M. Abrams, D. Gerard and N. Timms (eds), *Values and Social Change in Britain*. Basingstoke and London: Macmillan, 1985.

Abrams, Mark, David Gerard and Noel Timms (eds). *Values and Social Change in Britain*. Basingstoke and London: Macmillan, 1985.

Adorno, Theodore. "On Popular Music." In S. Frith and A. Goodwin (eds), *On Record*. London and New York: Routledge, 1998 [1990].

Amit-Talai, Vered, and Helena Wulff (eds). *Youth Cultures: A Cross-Cultural Perspective*. London and New York: Routledge, 1995.

Attali, Jacques. *Noise: The Political Economy of Music*. Minneapolis and London: University of Minnesota Press, 1985.

Ball, Stuart, and Anthony Seldon (eds). *The Heath Government 1970–74: A Reappraisal*. London and New York: Longman, 1996.

Ballantyne, Christopher. "Music, Masculinity and Migrancy under Apartheid: Gender and Popular Song in Africa c. 1948–1960." In David Hesmondhalgh and Keith Negus (eds), *Popular Music Studies*. London: Arnold, 2002.

Bannister, Matthew. *White Boys, White Noise: Masculinities and 1980s Guitar Rock*. London: Ashgate, 2006.

Battersby, Christine. *Gender and Genius: Towards a Feminist Aesthetics*. London: Women's Press, 1989.

Bayton, Mavis. "Feminist Musical Practice: Problems and Contradictions." In T. Bennett *et al.* (eds), *Rock and Popular Music: Politics, Policies, Institutions*. London and New York: Routledge, 1993.

—*Frock Rock*. Oxford: Oxford University Press, 1998.

Becker, Howard S. *Outsiders: Studies in the Sociology of Deviance*. New York: Free Press, 1963.

—*Art Worlds*. Berkeley, CA: University of California Press, 1982.

Bennett, Andy. *Popular Music and Youth Culture: Music, Identity and Place*. Basingstoke and London: Macmillan Press, 2000.

Bennett, Tony, Simon Frith, Lawrence Grossberg, John Shepherd and Graeme Turner (eds). *Rock and Popular Music: Politics, Policies, Institutions*. London and New York: Routledge, 1993.

Berger, John. *Ways of Seeing*. London: BBC and Pelican Books, 1972.

Bogdanor, Vernon. "The Fall of Heath and the End of the Postwar Settlement." In S. Ball and A. Seldon (eds), *The Heath Government 1970–1974: A Reappraisal*. London and New York: Longman, 1996.

Born, Georgina. "Afterword: Music Policy, Aesthetic and Social Difference." In T. Bennett *et al.* (eds), *Rock and Popular Music: Politics, Policies, Institutions*. London and New York: Routledge, 1993.

Bourdieu, Pierre. *Masculinities*. Cambridge: Polity, 2001.

GOWER COLLEGE SWANSEA
LEARNING RESOURCE CENTRE
LLWYN-Y-BRYN
77 WALTER ROAD
SWANSEA SA1 4QF

Bowers, Jane, and Judith Tick. *Women Making Music: The Western Art Tradition, 1150–1950*. Urbana and Chicago: University of Illinois Press, 1987.

Bracewell, Michael. *England is Mine: Pop Life in Albion from Wilde to Goldie*. London: Flamingo, 1998.

Bradby, Barbara. "Sampling Sexuality: Gender, Technology and the Body in Dance Music." *Popular Music* 12.2 (1993): 155–76.

Bradley, Dick. *Understanding Rock'n'Roll: Popular Music in Britain 1955–1964*. Buckingham and Philadelphia: Open University Press, 1992.

Brake, Michael. *Comparative Youth Culture*. London and New York: Routledge, 1993 [1985].

Buckingham, David. *The Making of Citizens*. London: Routledge, 2000.

Burchill, Julie, and Tony Parsons. *The Boy Looked at Johnny: The Obituary of Rock'n'Roll*. London: Pluto Press, 1978.

Burns, Lori, and Melisse Lafrance. *Disruptive Divas: Feminism, Identity and Popular Music*. New York and London: Routledge, 2002.

Butler, Judith. "Performative Arts and Gender Constitution: An Essay in Phenomenology and Feminist Theory." *Theatre Journal* 40.4 (December 1985): 519–31.

Caputo, Virginia. "Anthropology's Silent 'Others': A Consideration of Some Conceptual and Methodological Issues for the Study of Youth and Children's Cultures." In V. Amit-Talai and H. Wulff (eds), *Youth Cultures: A Cross-Cultural Perspective*. London and New York: Routledge, 1995.

Carson, Mina, Tisa Lewis and Susan M. Shaw. *Girls Rock! Fifty Years of Women Making Music*. Kentucky: University Press of Kentucky, 2004.

Cartledge, Frank. "Distress to Impress." In R. Sabin (ed.), *Punk Rock: So What?* London and New York: Routledge, 1999.

Chambers, Iain. "A Strategy for Living." In S. Hall and T. Jefferson (eds), *Resistance through Rituals: Youth Subcultures in Post-War Britain*. London: Hutchinson, 1975.

—*Urban Rhythms: Pop Music and Popular Culture*. Basingstoke and London: Macmillan, 1985.

Christgau, Robert. *Any Old Way You Choose It*. Harmondsworth: Penguin, 1973.

Citron, Marcia J. *Gender and the Musical Canon*. Cambridge: Cambridge University Press, 1993.

Clawson, Mary Ann. "When Women Play the Bass: Instrument Specialization and Gender Interpretation in Alternative Rock Music." *Gender and Society* 13.2 (1999): 192–211.

Clement, Catherine. *Opera or the Undoing of Women*. London: Virago, 1989.

Cloonan, Martin. *Banned! Censorship of Popular Music in Britain: 1967–92*. Hampshire and Vermont: Arena, 1996.

Cohen, Sara. *Rock Culture in Liverpool: Popular Music in the Making*. Oxford: Clarendon Press, 1991.

—"Men Making a Scene: Rock Music and the Production of Gender." In S. Whiteley (ed.), *Sexing the Groove: Popular Music and Gender*. London: Routledge, 1997.

Cohen, Stanley. *Folk Devils and Moral Panics: The Creation of the Mods and Rockers*. Oxford: Martin Robertson, 1993 [1972].

Colegrave, Stephen, and Chris Sullivan. *Punk: A Life Apart*. London: Cassell, 2001.

Coon, Caroline. *1988: The New Wave Punk Rock Explosion*. London: Omnibus, 1982.

—"The Stranglers." In C. Coon, *1988: The New Wave Punk Rock Explosion*. London: Omnibus, 1982.

GOWER COLLEGE SWANSEA
LEARNING RESOURCE CENTRE
LLWYN-Y-BRYN
77 WALTER ROAD
SWANSEA SA1 4QF

Cooper, Sarah (ed.). *Girls! Girls! Girls! Essays on Women and Music*. London and New York: Cassell, 1995.

Cummings, Sue. "Karen Carpenter." In B. O'Dair (ed.), *The Rolling Stone Book of Women in Rock*. New York: Random House, 1997.

Dahl, Linda. *Stormy Weather: The Music and Lives of a Century of Jazzwomen*. London: Quartet Books; New York: Pantheon, 1984.

Davies, Helen. "All Rock and Roll is Homosocial: The Representation of Women in the British Rock Music Press." *Popular Music* 20.3 (2001): 295–313.

Dibbell, Carola. "Inside Was Us: Women and Punk." In B. O'Dair (ed.), *The Rolling Stone Book of Women in Rock*. New York: Random House, 1997.

Diethe, Carol. *Nietzsche's Women: Beyond the Whip*. Berlin and New York: W. de Gruyter, 1996.

Echenberg, Erica, and Mark Perry. *And God Created Punk*. London: Virgin, 1996.

Eisenberg, Evan. *The Recording Angel: Music, Records and Culture from Aristotle to Zappa*. London and New York: Picador, 1987.

Engh, Barbara. "Adorno and the Sirens: Tele-phonographic Bodies." In Leslie C. Dunn and Nancy A. Jones (eds), *Embodied Voices: Representing Female Vocality in Western Culture*. Cambridge: Cambridge University Press, 1994.

Ferris, Lesley. *Acting Women: Images of Women in Theatre*. Basingstoke and London: Macmillan, 1990.

Finnegan, Ruth. *The Hidden Musicians: Music-Making in an English Town*. Cambridge: Cambridge University Press, 1989.

Fogarty, Michael. "British Attitudes to Work." In M. Abrams, D. Gerard and N. Timms (eds), *Values and Social Change in Britain*. Basingstoke and London: Macmillan, 1985.

Frith, Simon. *Sound Effects*. New York: Pantheon, 1981.

—*Music for Pleasure*. Cambridge: Polity, 1988.

—"Popular Music and the State." In T. Bennett *et al.* (eds), *Rock and Popular Music: Politics, Policies, Institutions*. London and New York: Routledge, 1993.

—*Performing Rites*. Oxford and New York: Oxford University Press, 1996.

Frith, Simon, and Andrew Goodwin (eds). *On Record*. London and New York: Routledge, 1998 [1990].

Frith, Simon, and Howard Home (eds). *Art into Pop*. London and New York: Routledge, 1989.

Frith, Simon, and Angela McRobbie. "Rock and Sexuality." In A. McRobbie (ed.), *Feminism and Youth Culture*. Basingstoke and London: Macmillan, 2000 [1991].

Gaar, Gillian G. *She's a Rebel*. London: Blandford, 1993.

Gaines, Donna. *Teenage Wasteland: Suburbia's Dead-End Kids*. New York: Pantheon Books, 1990.

—"Girl Groups: A Ballad of Co-dependency." In B. O'Dair (ed.), *The Rolling Stone Book of Women in Rock*. New York: Random House, 1997.

Gamman, Lorraine, and Margaret Marshment (eds), *The Female Gaze: Women as Viewers of Popular Culture*. London: Women's Press, 1988.

Gay, Leslie C., Jr. "Rockin' the Imagined Local: New York Rock in a Reterritorialised World." In Will Straw, Stacey Johnson, Rebecca Sullivan and Paul Friedlander (eds), *Popular Music: Style and Identity*. Montreal: Centre for Research on Canadian Cultural Industries and Institutions, 1993.

George-Warren, Holly. "Hillbilly Fillies: The Trailblazers of C&W." In B. O'Dair (ed.), *The Rolling Stone Book of Women in Rock*. New York: Random House, 1997.

Gimarc, George. *Punk Diary: 1970–1979*. London: St Martin's Press, 1994.

Glyptis, Sue. *Leisure and Unemployment*. Milton Keynes and Philadelphia: Open University Press, 1989.

Goodwin, Andrew. "Rationalization and Democratization in the New Technologies of Popular Music." In J. Lull (ed.), *Popular Music and Communication*. London: Sage, 1992.

Gourse, Leslie. *Madame Jazz: Contemporary Women Instrumentalists*. New York and Oxford: Oxford University Press, 1995.

Green, Lucy, *Music, Gender, Education*. Cambridge: Cambridge University Press, 1997.

Greig, Charlotte. *Will You Still Love Me Tomorrow? Girl Groups from the 50s on*. London: Virago, 1989.

Griffin, Christine. *Typical Girls? Young Women from School to the Job Market*. London: Routledge, 1985.

Grossberg, Lawrence. "Rock & Roll in Search of an Audience." In J. Lull (ed.), *Popular Music and Communication*. London: Sage, 1992.

—*We Gotta Get Out of This Place*. New York and London: Routledge, 1992.

Hall, Stuart, and Tony Jefferson (eds). *Resistance through Rituals: Youth Subcultures in Post-War Britain*. London: Hutchinson, 1975.

Halstead, Jill, *The Woman Composer: Creativity and the Gendered Politics of Music*. Aldershot: Ashgate, 1997.

Harding, Stephen. "Values and the Nature of Psychological Wellbeing." In M. Abrams, D. Gerard and N. Timms (eds), *Values and Social Change in Britain*. Basingstoke and London: Macmillan, 1985.

Heath, Joseph, and Andrew Potter. *The Rebel Sell: How the Counterculture became Consumer Culture*. Chichester: Capstone, 2006.

Hebdige, Dick. *Subculture, the Meaning of Style*. London: Routledge, 1979.

Hollows, Joanne. *Feminism, Femininity and Popular Culture*. Manchester and New York: Manchester University Press, 2000.

Home, Stuart. *Cranked Up Really High: Genre Theory and Punk Rock*. Hove: CodeX, 1995.

Hudson, Barbara. "Femininity and Adolescence." In A. McRobbie and M. Nava (eds), *Gender and Generation*. Basingstoke and London: Macmillan, 1984.

Jones, Steve (ed.). *Pop Music and the Press*. Philadelphia: Temple University Press, 2002.

Juno, Andrea. *Angry Women in Rock*, vol. 1. New York: Juno Books, 1996.

Kaplan, E. Ann. *Rocking around the Clock: Music Television, Postmodernism, and Consumer Culture*. London and New York: Routledge, 1987.

Kelly, Karen, and Evelyn McDonnell. *Stars Don't Stand Still in the Sky*. London: Routledge, 1999.

Kennedy, Lisa. "Joni Mitchell." In B. O'Dair (ed.), *The Rolling Stone Book of Women in Rock*. New York: Random House, 1997.

Kent, Greta. *A View from the Bandstand*. London: Sheba, 1983.

Kritzman, Lawrence D. *Michel Foucault: Politics, Philosophy, Culture. Interviews and Other Writings 1977–1984*. New York and London: Routledge, 1988.

Kruse, Holly. "Abandoning the Absolute: Transcendence and Gender in Popular Music Discourse." In S. Jones (ed.), *Pop Music and the Press*. Philadelphia: Temple University Press, 2002.

Laing, Dave. *One Chord Wonders: Power and Meaning in Punk Rock.* Milton Keynes and Philadelphia: Open University Press, 1985.

Leblanc, Lauraine. *Pretty in Punk: Girls' Gender Resistance in a Boys' Subculture.* New Brunswick, NJ and London: Rutgers University Press, 2001.

Leigh, Spencer. *Baby, That is Rock and Roll: American Pop, 1954–1963.* Folkestone: Finbarr International, 2001.

Lull, James (ed.). *Popular Music and Communication.* London: Sage, 1992.

Lydon, John. *Rotten: No Irish, No Blacks, No Dogs.* London: Coronet, 1995.

MacKinnon, Catharine. "Points Against Postmodernism." *Chicago-Kent Law Review* 75.3 (2000): 687–712.

McClary, Susan, "Afterword." In J. Attali, *Noise: The Political Economy of Music.* Minneapolis and London: University of Minnesota Press, 1985.

—*Feminine Endings: Music, Gender and Sexuality.* Minneapolis and Oxford: University of Minnesota Press, 1991.

McKay, George. "I'm So Bored with the USA." In R. Sabin (ed.), *Punk Rock.* London and New York: Routledge, 1999.

McLeod, Kembrew. "Between a Rock and a Hard Place: Gender and Rock Criticism." In S. Jones (ed.), *Pop Music and the Press.* Philadelphia: Temple University Press, 2002.

McRobbie, Angela. "Second Hand Dresses and the Ragmarket." In A. McRobbie (ed.), *Zoot Suits: An Anthology of Fashion and Music.* London: Macmillan, 1989.

—*Postmodernism and Popular Culture.* New York: Routledge, 1994.

—"Settling Accounts with Subcultures: A Feminist Critique." In S. Frith and A. Goodwin (eds), *On Record.* London and New York: Routledge, 1998 [1990].

McRobbie, Angela (ed.). *Zoot Suits and Secondhand Dresses: An Anthology of Fashion and Music.* London: Macmillan, 1989.

—*Feminism and Youth Culture.* Basingstoke and London: Macmillan, 2000 [1991].

McRobbie, Angela, and Jenny Garber, "Girls and Subcultures." In A. McRobbie (ed.), *Feminism and Youth Culture.* Basingstoke and London: Macmillan, 2000 [1991].

McRobbie, Angela, and Mica Nava (eds). *Gender and Generation.* Basingstoke and London: Macmillan, 1984.

Marcus, Greil. "It's Fab, It's Passionate, It's Wild, It's Intelligent! It's the Hot New Sound of England Today!" In G. Marcus, *Ranters and Crowd-Pleasers: Punk in Pop Music 1977–92.* New York and London: Doubleday, 1993.

—*Ranters and Crowd-Pleasers: Punk in Pop Music 1977–92.* New York and London: Doubleday, 1993.

—"Suspicious Minds, Delta 5." In G. Marcus, *Ranters and Crowd-Pleasers: Punk in Pop Music 1977–92.* New York and London: Doubleday, 1993.

Marshment, Margaret, "Substantial Women." In L. Gamman and M. Marshment (eds), *The Female Gaze: Women as Viewers of Popular Culture.* London: Women's Press, 1988.

Massey, Doreen. *Space, Place and Gender.* London: Polity, 1994.

Melly, George. *Revolt into Style.* Oxford: Oxford University Press, 1989.

Miles, Cressida. "Spatial Politics: A Gendered Sense of Place." In S. Redhead, D. Wynne and J. O'Connor (eds), *The Clubcultures Reader: Readings in Popular Culture Studies.* Oxford: Blackwell, 1997.

Miles, Rosalind. *The Woman's History of the World.* London: Paladin, 1990.

Muggleton, David. *Inside Subculture: The Postmodern Meaning of Style.* Oxford and New York: Berg, 2000.

Muir, Anne Ross. "The Status of Women Working in Film and Television." In L. Gamman and M. Marshment (eds), *The Female Gaze: Women as Viewers of Popular Culture.* London: Women's Press, 1988.

Mulvey, Laura. "Visual Pleasure and Narrative Cinema." *Screen* 16.3 (1975): 6–28.

Nava, Mica. "Youth Service Provision, Social Order and the Question of Girls." In A. McRobbie and M. Nava (eds), *Gender and Generation.* Basingstoke and London: Macmillan, 1984.

Negus, Keith. *Producing Pop: Culture and Conflict in the Popular Music Industry.* London: Edward Arnold, 1992.

Nehring, Neil. *Popular Music, Gender and Postmodernism.* Thousand Oaks, CA: Sage, 1997.

Nelson, Elizabeth. *The British Counter-culture 1966–73: A Study of the Underground Press.* Basingstoke and London: Macmillan, 1989.

Neuls-Bates, Carol. "Women's Orchestras in the United States, 1925–45." In J. Bowers and J. Tick (eds), *Women Making Music: The Western Art Tradition, 1150–1950.* Urbana and Chicago: University of Illinois Press, 1987.

—*Women in Music: An Anthology of Source Readings from the Middle Ages to the Present.* Boston: Northeastern University Press, 1996.

Oakley, Ann, *The Sociology of Housework.* Oxford and Cambridge, MA: Basil Blackwell, 1985 [1974].

O'Brien, Karen. *Hymn to Her: Women Musicians Talk.* London: Virago Press, 1995.

O'Brien, Lucy. *She-Bop: The Definitive History of Women in Rock, Pop and Soul.* London: Penguin, 2002 [1989].

—*She-Bop II: The Definitive History of Women in Rock, Pop and Soul* (London and New York: Continuum, 2002 [1995]).

O'Dair, Barbara (ed.). *The Rolling Stone Book of Women in Rock.* New York: Random House, 1997.

Ogg, Alex. *No More Heroes: A Complete History of UK Punk from 1976 to 1980.* London: Cherry Red Books, 2006.

Opie, Iona, and Peter Opie. *The Lore and Language of Schoolchildren.* St Albans: Paladin, 1977.

Paglia, Camille. *Sex, Art and American Culture: Essays.* New York: Vintage, 1992.

Palmer, Gareth. "Springsteen and Authentic Masculinity." In S. Whiteley (ed.), *Sexing the Groove: Popular Music and Gender.* London: Routledge, 1997.

Perry, Mark. *Sniffin' Glue: The Essential Punk Accessory.* London: Sanctuary, 2000.

Phillips, Ann, and Barbara Taylor. "Sex and Skill: Notes towards a Feminist Economics." *Feminist Review* 4.6 (1980): 79–88.

Phillips, David. "Participation and Political Values." In M. Abrams, D. Gerard and N. Timms (eds), *Values and Social Change in Britain.* Basingstoke and London: Macmillan, 1985.

Pinker, Steven. *The Language Instinct.* London: Penguin, 1995.

Plant, Sadie. *The Most Radical Gesture: The Situationist International in the Postmodern Age.* London and New York: Routledge, 1992.

Potter, Sally. "On Shows." In Rozsika Parker and Griselda Pollock (eds), *Framing Feminism: Art and the Women's Movement 1970–85.* London: Pandora, 1987.

Presdee, M. "Invisible Girls: A Study of Unemployed Working Class Young Women." Unpublished paper, Tenth World Congress of Sociology, Mexico City, 1982.

Press, Joy. "Shouting Out Loud: Women in UK Punk." In B. O'Dair (ed.), *The Rolling Stone Book of Women in Rock*. New York: Random House, 1997.

Raphael, Amy. *Never Mind the Bollocks*. London: Virago, 1995.

—"Chrissie Hynde." In B. O'Dair (ed.), *The Rolling Stone Book of Women in Rock*. New York: Random House, 1997.

Reynolds, Simon. *Rip it Up and Start Again: Post-punk 1978–1984*. London: Faber and Faber, 2005.

Reynolds, Simon, and J. Press. *The Sex Revolts: Gender, Rebellion and Rock'n'Roll*. London: Serpent's Tail, 1995.

Rimmer, Dave. *Like Punk Never Happened: Culture Club and the New Pop*. London and Boston: Faber and Faber, 1985.

Robb, John, *Punk Rock: An Oral History*. London: Ebury Press, 2006.

Roberts, Robin. *Ladies First: Women in Music Videos*. Jackson: University of Mississippi Press, 1996.

Roman, Leslie G. "Intimacy, Labor and Class: Ideologies of Feminine Sexuality in the Punk Slam Dance." In Leslie Roman and L. K. Christian-Smith (eds), *Becoming Feminine: The Politics of Popular Culture*. London: Falmer Press, 1988.

—"Double Exposure: The Politics of Feminist Materialist Ethnography." *Educational Theory* 43.3 (1993): 297–308.

Ross, Malcolm (ed.). *The Arts and Personal Growth*. London: Pergamon, 1980.

Rowbotham, Sheila. *Woman's Consciousness, Man's World*. Harmondsworth and New York: Penguin, 1981 [1973].

Rowe, David. *Popular Cultures: Rock Music, Sport and the Politics of Pleasure*. London, Thousand Oaks and New Delhi: Sage, 1995.

Rumsey, Gina, and Hilary Little. "Women and Pop: A Series of Lost Encounters." In A. McRobbie (ed.), *Zoot Suits: An Anthology of Fashion and Music*. London: Macmillan, 1989.

Sabin, Roger (ed.). *Punk Rock: So What?* London and New York: Routledge, 1999.

Sanjek, David, "Can Fujiyama Mama be the Female Elvis? The Wild, Wild Women of Rockabilly." In S. Whiteley (ed.), *Sexing the Groove: Popular Music and Gender*. London: Routledge, 1997.

Savage, Jon. "The Great Rock'n'Roll Swindle." In P. Taylor (ed.), *Impresario: Malcolm McLaren and the British New Wave*. Cambridge, MA and London: MIT Press, 1988.

—*England's Dreaming*. London and Boston: Faber and Faber, 1991.

—"The Sound of the Crowd." In K. Kelly and E. McDonnell (eds), *Stars Don't Stand Still in the Sky*. London: Routledge, 1999.

Schippers, Mimi. *Rockin' Out of the Box: Gender Maneuvering in Alternative Heavy Rock*. New Brunswick, NJ and London: Rutgers University Press, 2002.

Shaar Murray, Charles. *Shots from the Hip*. London: Penguin Books, 1991.

Shank, Barry. *Dissonant Identities: The Rock'n'Roll Scene in Austin, Texas*. Hanover and London: Wesleyan University Press, 1994.

Shepherd, John. *Music as Social Text*. Cambridge: Polity, 1991.

Sontag, Susan. "Notes on 'Camp'." In Elizabeth Hardwick (ed.), *A Susan Sontag Reader*. Harmondsworth: Penguin, 1982.

Spender, Dale. *Man Made Language*. London: Pandora, 1990.

Stein, Arlene. "Rock Against Romance: Gender, Rock'n'Roll and Resistance." In K. Kelly and E. McDonnell (eds), *Stars Don't Stand Still in the Sky*. London: Routledge, 1999.

Stevenson, Nils, and Ray Stevenson. *Vacant: A Diary of the Punk Years 1976–79*. London: Thames and Hudson, 1999.

Steward, Sue, and Sheryl Garratt. *Signed, Sealed and Delivered: The Life Stories of Women in Pop*. London and Sydney: Pluto, 1984.

Stith Bennett, H. *On Becoming a Rock Musician*. Amherst: University of Massachusetts Press, 1980.

Straw, Will. "Systems of Articulation, Logics of Change: Communities and Scenes in Popular Music." *Cultural Studies* 5.3 (1991): 368–88.

Street, John. *Rebel Rock: The Politics of Popular Music*. Oxford: Blackwell, 1986.

Street-Howe, Zoe. *Typical Girls? The Story of The Slits*. London: Omnibus, 2009.

Suleiman, Susan Rubin. *Subversive Intent: Gender, Politics and the Avant-garde*. Cambridge, MA and London: Harvard University Press, 1990.

Swiss, Thomas, John Sloop and Andrew Herman. *Mapping the Beat*. Oxford and Cambridge, MA: Blackwell, 1998.

Taylor, Paul (ed.). *Impresario: Malcolm McLaren and the British New Wave*. Cambridge, MA and London: MIT Press, 1988.

Thompson, Dave. *Beyond the Velvet Underground*. London and New York: Omnibus, 1989.

Thomson, Liz. *New Women in Rock*. London: Omnibus, 1982.

Thornton, Sarah. *Club Cultures: Music, Media and Subcultural Capital*. Cambridge: Polity, 1995.

Tucker, Sherrie. *Swing Shift: "All Girl" Bands of the 1940s*. Durham, NC: Duke University Press, 2000.

Upton, George. *Woman in Music*. Boston: J. R. Osgood, 1880.

Van der Merwe, Peter. *Origins of the Popular Style: The Antecedents of Twentieth Century Popular Music*. Oxford: Clarendon Press, 1992.

Walkerdine, Valerie. *Daddy's Girl: Young Girls and Popular Culture*. Basingstoke and London: Macmillan, 1997.

—*Counting Girls Out: Girls and Mathematics*. London and Bristol, PA: Falmer Press, 1998.

Walser, Robert. *Running with the Devil: Power, Gender and Madness in Heavy Metal Music*. Middletown, CT: Wesleyan University Press, 1993.

Warner, Marina. *Monuments and Maidens: The Allegory of the Female Form*. London: Weidenfeld and Nicholson, 1985.

Webster, Wendy. *Not a Man to Match Her: The Marketing of a Prime Minister*. London: Women's Press, 1990.

Weinstein, Deena. "Art versus Commerce: Deconstructing a (Useful) Romantic Illusion." In K. Kelly and E. McDonnell (eds), *Stars Don't Stand Still in the Sky*. London: Routledge, 1999.

—*Heavy Metal: The Music and its Culture*. Cambridge, MA: Da Capo, 2000.

Whiteley, Sheila. *The Space between the Notes*. London and Boston: Routledge, 1992.

Whiteley, Sheila (ed.). *Sexing the Groove: Popular Music and Gender*. London: Routledge, 1997.

Williams, Raymond. *Keywords: A Vocabulary of Culture and Society*. London: Fontana, 1975.

Williamson, Judith. *Consuming Passions: The Dynamics of Popular Culture*. London and New York: Marion Boyars, 1991.

Willis, Paul E. *Profane Culture*. London and Boston: Routledge and Kegan Paul, 1978.

Wilson, Elizabeth. *Bohemians: The Glamorous Outcasts*. London and New York: I.B. Tauris, 2000.

Wolff, Janet. *The Social Production of Art*. London: Macmillan Education, 1981.
Wylie, Philip. *Generation of Vipers*. New York: Larlin Corporation, 1979.
York, Peter. *Style Wars*. London: Sidgwick and Jackson, 1980.

Music Paper Articles

New Musical Express

Burchill, Julie. Review of The Adverts (2 July 1977): 33.
Burchill, Julie. "Debbie Harry at the Rainbow" (3 December 1977): 56.
Davis, Kim. Review of The Damned/The Adverts/Fruit-Eating Bears gig (27 August 1977): 40.
Denom, Sue. Review of Lesser Known Tunisians, The Movies, Gags, Babylon (10 September 1977): 46.
du Noyer, Paul. "Essential Logic, The Nashville" (2 June 1979): 52.
Ellen, Mark. Review of Nico (6 May 1978): 51.
Errigo, Angie. "I was a Dull Housewife until I Discovered Sadisto-Rock" (24 September 1977): 7.
Gordon, Stephen. Review of Cherry Vanilla at The F Club, Leeds, "Oh! the Grinding Sleaze of it all..." (27 May 1978): 56.
Grabel, Richard. "The Slits, New York" (12 January 1980): 35.
Hamblett, John. "*Prag Vec*" (16 June 1979): 7–8.
Hill, Geoff. Review of The Passage, Goldsmiths College (27 May 1978): 58.
Lock, Graham. "Censored! The Au Pairs, the Beeb and the Orgasm" (2 February 1980): 13.
McNeill, Phil. "Women are Strange when you're a Strangler" (30 April 1977): 35.
Miles, Review of Talking Heads at CBGBs (2 April 1977): 49.
Morley, Paul, Interview with Pauline Murray (17 December 1977): 14.
Morley, Paul. "Singles of the Week: Exhilarating" (7 April 1979): 17.
Norman, Neil. "A Rock Folly," review of Tour de Force (24 November 1979): 70.
Parsons, Tony. Review of The Slits (9 April 1977): 35.
Parsons, Tony. Interview with Blondie (4 February 1978): 25.
Pearson, Deanne. "Women in Rock" (29 March 1980): 27–30.
Penman, Ian. Review of The Slits at Liverpool "Eric's" (13 January 1979): 35.
Penman, Ian. Review of The Raincoats, Dresden Banks, Vincent Units at the Acklam Hall (27 January 1979): 43.
Penman, Ian. "Mod, Mode, Mo-dettes" (18 August 1979): 25.
Rambali, Paul. Interview with Talking Heads (4 February 1978): 7.
Salewicz, Chris. Review of The Adverts (11 June 1977): 44.
Thrills, Adrian. Interview/Review of The Adverts (18 February 1978): 43.
Thrills, Adrian. "Up Slit Creek" (8 September 1979): 28.
Zaenfell, Martha. "Love Sex, Hate Sexism?..." (7 April 1979): 15.

Sounds

Coon, Caroline. "Groupies Must Become Musicians" (31 December 1977): 6.
Fielder, Hugh. "Prude or Rude?" (24 January 1976): 8.

Ingham, John. "Rock Special" (2 October 1976): 2.

"Letters" (10 July 1976): 42.

Millar, Robbi. "Sexism is No Joke" (20 September 1980): 31–4.

Myers, Barry. "Orgasmic Review Dept. Runaways: Getting Better all the Time" (27 January 1977): 21.

Unattributed. "Krauts in New Album Sleeve Outrage Horror Shock etc." (18 December 1976): 7.

Unattributed. "Hardware" (26 February 1977): 46–7.

Newspaper Articles

Evening Argus

Archer, Peter. "Spin Off: Now Fan Club Play a Four-Way Cut" (31 March 1979): 11.

Archer, Peter. "Spin Off: Back on the Road" (28 April 1979): 11.

Archer, Peter. "Spin Off: What's in a Name?" (21 July 1979): 11.

Buss, John. "Workers See a Dream End" (7 October 1980): 10.

Partington, Andrew. "With this Pin... Punks Wed for a Bet" (23 February 1979): 1.

The Guardian

Smith, Joan. "Taking up the Slacks" (5 June 2001).

Articles from Other Publications

The Face

Cranna, Ian. "In Time with the Rhythm and Rhyme," no. 27 (July 1982): 24.

Fletcher, Tony. "Campaign Strategies," no. 21 (January 1982): 44–5.

Martin, Peter. Interview with Miranda, The Bodysnatchers, no. 41 (September 1983): 9.

Pearson, Deanne. "Twins: How to Tell Them Apart," no. 11 (March 1981): 54–5.

Rambali, Paul. Interview with New Order, no. 39 (July 1983): 30.

Savage, Jon. "Androgyny: Confused Chromosomes and Camp Followers," no. 38 (June 1983): 23.

Unattributed. "Malcolm McLaren/BowWowWow," no. 13 (May 1981): 39–45.

Spare Rib

Charles, Barbara. "Jam Today," no. 66 (January 1978): 29.

Denom, Sue. "Women in Punk," no. 60 (July 1977): 48–9.

Nicholls, Jill. Review of National Abortion Campaign Benefit at the Roundhouse, Camden, no. 68 (March 1978): 35–6.

Nicholls, Jill, and Lucy Toothpaste. "I Play the Vocals," no. 83 (June 1979): 16.

Spedding, Carole. Review of The Au Pairs' single "Diet"/"It's Obvious," no. 107 (June 1981): 41–2.

Toothpaste, Lucy. Interview with Poly Styrene, no. 60 (July 1977): 51.

Toothpaste, Lucy. "Bodysnatchers," no. 100 (November 1980): 13–14.

Unattributed. "Folk with Feeling," no. 48 (July 1976): 41.

Miscellaneous

Frith, Simon. "What Can a Poor Girl Do?" *Let it Rock: Women and Rock, a Special Issue* (July 1975): 20–21.

Goldstein, Toby. "Have You Seen Your Sisters, Baby, Playing in the Shadows?," *Let it Rock: Women and Rock, a Special Issue* (July 1975): 31.

Hamilton-Des Barres, Wendy. "The Big Lie," *Let it Rock: Women and Rock, a Special Issue* (July 1975): 36–7.

O'Brien, Glenn. "Debbie Harry," *Interview Magazine*, vol. ix, no. 6 (June 1979): 145.

Unattributed. "The End of Music," pamphlet, Glasgow (1978): 32–3.

Fanzines

Graffiti, undated. 1977.
Guttersnipe, issue no. 7, undated.
Rapid Eye Movement, Winter 1980.
Spitting Blood, September 1977.

Websites

http://www.punkbrighton.co.uk
http://www.appelstein.com
http://lists.ibiblio.org/mailman/listinfo/typicalgirls
http://www.tiswasonline.com
http://www.3ammagazine.com
http://www.bbc.co.uk/history

Films and TV Programmes

Rock Follies. ITV, 1976–77.
Tiswas. ITV, 1977–81.
The Filth and the Fury. Dir. Julien Temple, Filmfour, 1999.
You and Yours. BBC Radio 4, 19 July 2000.

Index

Entries for illustrations are indicated by (illus.) after the page number, e.g. The Adverts 50 (illus.). Entries for endnotes are indicated by n. between the page number and the endnote number, e.g. Abrams, Mark 206n.28.